THE
LOWELL
OFFERING

THE LOWELL OFFERING

Writings by New England Mill Women

(1840-1845)

Edited
with an Introduction
and Commentary
by

BENITA EISLER

W. W. NORTON & COMPANY
NEW YORK · LONDON

First published as a Norton paperback 1998
Copyright © 1977 by Benita Eisler.
A hardcover edition of this book was originally
published by J. B. Lippincott Company.

ISBN 0-393-31685-8

W.W. Norton & Company, Inc.
500 Fifth Avenue, New York, N.Y. 10110
www.wwnorton.com
W.W. Norton & Company, Ltd.
Castle House, 75/76 Wells Street London WIT 3QT

5 6 7 8 9 0

Contents

List of Illustrations

Acknowledgments

An unexpected bonus of work on the present anthology was the discovery of a "Mill Girl Subculture," my fond designation for the network of scholars, archivists, and museum people who thrive and multiply throughout New England. Especially generous with help of every kind were Helena Wright of the Merrimack Valley Textile Museum; Lewis T. Karabatsos of the Lowell Museum Corporation; and Elizabeth Lessard of the Manchester Historic Association, who shared her knowledge and memories with me. Others aiding my search for the mill girls were David S. Brooke, John Coolidge, Thomas L. Dublin, Francis H. Jarek, Randolph Langenbach, and Martha Mayo. I should like to thank the staffs of the Library of the Boston Athenaeum and of the Prints Division, the Boston Public Library; Elizabeth Roth and Robert Rainwater, Prints Division, the New York Public Library; and, closest to home and heart, the staff of the New York Society Library, for many years my Athenaeum and "Maine Chance" combined.

Equal in dedication to the Mill Girl Subculture is the Daguerreotype Underground. My obsessive conviction that early photographic documentation must exist was cheered on by Suzanne Boorsch, Peter Bunnell, Tom Burnside, Alan Fern, Jon Gray, Richard Rudisill, and Samuel Wagstaff. The reward of persistence was the beautiful "Woman at the Loom"

9

(late 1840s–early 1850s), the earliest known occupational photograph of this subject, reproduced here for the first time by the kind permission of Keith de Lellis.

I am grateful for the erudition, encouragement, or total recall of friends: Halcy Bohen, Dick Brukenfeld, Naomi Goodman, Susana Leval, Alfred Mayor, Charles McLaughlin, Naomi Miller; the shared enthusiasm of Maryanne Colas and Beatrice Rosenfeld, agent and editor, respectively; and for help and distraction, in just the right measure, to Colin and Rachel Eisler.

B. E.

"The Children of New England
between 1820 and 1840
were born with knives in their brains."

Ralph Waldo Emerson

"Power Loom Weaving," *from George White's* Memoir of Samuel Slater, *1836. Merrimack Valley Textile Museum.*

Introduction

Industrial espionage, implemented by a prodigious feat of memory, was the cornerstone of the American textile industry in the early nineteenth century. The genius who performed this conjuring trick was Francis Cabot Lowell, owner of the Boston Manufacturing Company cotton mill in Waltham, Massachusetts, the first total production factory in the United States. Ancestor of a tribe of proper Bostonians, Lowell had not let himself be thwarted by propriety where potential profit was concerned. While a guest of English cotton manufacturers in 1810, the canny merchant-inventor memorized the design of their new machinery, so jealously guarded by its owners that not a single model had been allowed to leave Britain. When Lowell returned home, he supervised the "re-invention"—as one of his partners, Nathan Appleton, euphemistically termed it—of the Cartwright power loom at the Waltham plant.

The technological efficiency and high stockholder dividends of Lowell's total cotton mill, coupled with his untimely death in 1817, decided his partners on the most appropriate memorial: expansion of their flourishing enterprise on a new site, to be named Lowell in his honor. The Boston Associates, as they now christened their holding company, had learned of endless water power at the confluence of the Merrimack and Concord Rivers and the recently dug Pawtucket Canal. Here, in the

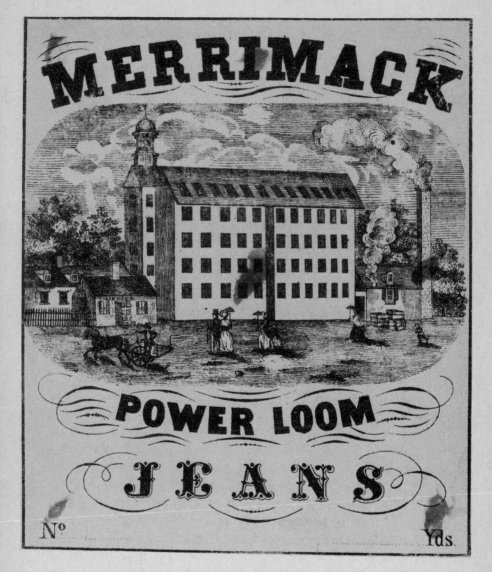

Cloth label for Merrimack power loom jeans, in use probably ca. 1845–1860. Merrimack Valley Textile Museum.

town of East Chelmsford, Massachusetts, they incorporated the Merrimack Manufacturing Corporation in 1822, the first of nineteen five-story mills capitalized and controlled by the same Boston group.

Incorporating more than Francis Lowell's system of total production, the new mills systematized innovations in social engineering that would have far-reaching consequences. The Boston Associates did not want their New Jerusalem tainted by an imported—or newly created—urban proletariat. The European mill wheels had spawned a race of *Untermenschen*—the subject of a rising chorus of reformers' protest—whose lives began with child labor and ended in paupers' graves. Nor did the founders of Lowell see much of an improvement on Old World evils in the existing New England factories, known as "family mills" or the "Rhode Island system" (after Samuel Slater's cotton mill in Pawtucket). The handbills of these factories issued the sinister summons "Men with growing families wanted." These "growing families," with children eight years old and up, were the labor force in the first American textile mills—a system that had to be wrong, since it was rarely profitable. And indeed, these mills failed with alarming regularity, though perhaps more often because of insufficient liquid capital than because of their employment practices.

Instead, the Boston Associates resolved to create a labor force that would be a shining example of those ultimate Yankee ideals: profit and virtue, doing good and doing well. This they accomplished for more than a generation by attracting a special class of temporary help. From the farms of Massachusetts, Vermont, New Hampshire, and Maine came robust young women, lured by the highest wages offered to female employees anywhere in America—from $1.85 to $3.00 a week, depending on skill and speed. This seemingly generous scale represented a considerable saving for the mill owners, since male mill workers were paid twice as much.

Thus, by employing 75 percent women, the Lowell Corporations could certainly claim "low overhead." The average stay in the mills for the female employees was about four years, and the supply of new recruits was endless. They were, as their employers took every opportunity to boast, the "most superior class of factory operative" to be found in any industrialized nation, constituting what mill owner Nathan Appleton called "a fund of labor, well-educated and virtuous." Indeed, in Lowell illiteracy was as rare as child labor. Not only had most mill girls completed "common school," but a considerable number came from the dismally paid ranks of rural schoolteachers, whose work was seasonal. As women were hired to teach school only in summer (the long winter session being reserved for men), on an annual basis mill wages could yield six to seven times more than the average yearly teaching salary for women. Domestic labor, the alternative for daughters of impoverished farmers, might pay fifty cents a week after room and board—if the employers were generous.

In any case, whether they were "hired out" or helping at home, these rural girls were accustomed not only to long hours of unpaid domestic labor on the family farm but also to improving their minds through study. The thrifty magnates of Beacon Hill trumpeted the word that many of these paragons of the Protestant ethic, through hard work at the looms and Yankee self-denial, were helping to pay off the mortgage on the family farm or to send a brother through college or, failing such selfless ends, saving for a dowry or for their own further education! Did not the Lowell Institution for Savings in 1833 report the astonishing sum of $100,000 representing deposits by mill girls? When divided by the thousand-odd depositors, for whom individual amounts might mean the savings of several years, this information, admiringly noted by such distinguished visitors to Lowell as Charles Dickens and Harriet Martineau, is quantitatively less dramatic, but historically even more significant: the Boston Associates had established the existence of women as wage earners, an economic force to be reckoned with and a phenomenon new to American society.

In 1831, Patrick Jackson, one of the Lowell partners, could

"Fales & Jenks's Spinning Frame," from James Geldard, Handbook on the Cotton Manufacture, *1867. Wood engraving. Lowell Museum Corporation.*

boast to a Tariff Lobby Group that "no less than 39,000 females had employment in the cotton manufacture of the United
States, earning wages amounting to upwards of four million
dollars annually." The hard evidence was in: "Daughters are
now emphatically a blessing to the farmer." And not only to
their farmer fathers! Shops, businesses, and suppliers sprang
up in Lowell and other mill centers in the wake of this new
consumer class. But it was Lowell, the "Yankee El Dorado,"
whose idyllic beginnings summoned images of brand-new, glit-
tering promise and profit, and the sense everywhere of youth.
"One would swear," marveled Dickens,

> that every "Bakery," "Grocery" and "Bookbindery" and every
> other kind of store, took its shutters down for the first time, and
> started in business yesterday. The golden pestles and mortars
> fixed as signs upon the sun-blind frames outside the Druggists
> appear to have been just turned out of the United States Mint;
> and when I saw a baby of some week or ten days old in a
> woman's arms at a street corner, I found myself unconsciously
> wondering where it came from: never supposing for an instant
> that it could have been born in such a young town as that.

If the owners did not boast, they readily conceded another advantage to this ever-renewed supply of fresh female labor from
the farms: the girls generally had homes and families to which
they could return. If sickness, exhaustion, or the craving for
vacation overcame any girl after months of dawn-to-dusk labor,
she would not be a charge on company payrolls or occupy a
bed at the one Corporation hospital (where care, in any case,
was at the operative's expense). As Lowell did not have any
charitable institution until the late 1850s, there was no place for
the nonproductive, who went home to the farm. And sisters,
friends, and neighbors swarmed to take the places of those who
did not return.

Unlike their smaller, lower-paying competitors throughout
New England, the Lowell Corporations never had to advertise.
They employed recruiting agents for the farther-flung regions;
these may have lured some by exaggerated tales of idyllic fac-

tory life, but their primary role was providing transportation for the already converted. Glowing firsthand accounts, such as the following report written by one of the girls to her sister back home on the New Hampshire farm, made shills superfluous:

> Since I have wrote you, another pay day has come around. I earned 14 dollars and a half, nine and a half dollars beside my board. The folks think I get along just first-rate, they say. I like it well as ever and Sarah don't I feel independent of everyone! The thought that I am living on no one is a happy one indeed to me.

The young woman home for a visit provided the elegant evidence of new earning power. Rural girls who had rarely seen—let alone owned—paper money could enjoy the fruits of their labor in the Lowell mills: finery, savings bank deposit books, and—inconceivable until this moment in American history—their sense of independence.

From the beginning, the Boston Associates had been aware that high wages alone would not convince God-fearing New England parents that they should permit their daughters to leave home to work in the mills. Yankee ingenuity would, therefore, provide a moral tariff against the evils of the English mill system. Hence, the paternalism that characterized the early mill owners as employers was shaped by two factors: first, the strongly held belief that idle young women were particularly prone to depravity, making their employment itself a contribution to public morality; and second, a social phenomenon beyond public relations or even profit, the shared class and religious origins of labor and management. Both the Boston merchants and the yeoman fathers of the mill girls were descendants of the Puritan settlers of New England; furthermore, some mill owners were less than a generation removed from the same farmlands which now yielded daughters to their corporate paternalism. Management, in turn, could boast of the "wholesome influences" which had produced these "refined and superior young women." How could it be otherwise when these

"James S. Brown's Patent Speeder," from James Geldard, Handbook on the Cotton Manufacture, *1867. Steel engraving. Lowell Museum Corporation.*

Cloth label of the Merrimack Manufacturing Company, Lowell Massachusetts, in use probably ca. 1845–1860. Merrimack Valley Textile Museum.

same influences had produced their own forebears? (The facts of rural life at this time were already quite different; poverty, insanity, and alcoholism seem to have been at least as characteristic as the pastoral virtues.)

Nostalgia has always been good business in America; the Boston industrialists held that the superior daughters of pre-industrial New England produced a superior product. Labels for Lowell cotton goods depicted the neatly coiffed, trim young woman at her loom. This was the first time women employees were used to suggest the quality and refinement of the product—a public relations device the Bell Telephone Company would use so effectively ninety years later.

But it remained for Francis Lowell's most significant innovation to give ultimate moral sanction to the entire enterprise. The Lowell Corporations became generic: they were Boarding-house Mills. From the outset, the Boston Associates could demonstrate reassuringly to fearful fathers, doubtful divines, and radical reformers that their new factory system matched propriety of upbringing with the exemplary milieu their responsible stewardship provided.

The Boston Manufacturing Company in Waltham had added boardinghouses piecemeal to an already converted mill; in Lowell this form of housing for single workers (along with tenements for families) was designed as an integral part of the Corporations; Lowell thus became the first planned industrial community in the United States.

With the first of the Lowell mills, boardinghouses were built on adjoining or nearby streets. As the overseer in the weaving or spinning room was responsible for the working habits and conduct of the girls in his domain, the boardinghouse-keeper—usually a "respectable" widow with a family—was answerable to the Corporation for the moral and physical well-being of the girls in their hours outside the thick mill walls. Residence in the Corporation boardinghouse was mandatory for unmarried female operatives, but it was partially subsidized, a rare form of capitalist benevolence. Though the girls were docked $1.25 of

Mills and Boardinghouses on the Merrimack, 1848. Merrimack Valley Textile Museum.

their weekly wage for board, the Corporation was responsible for paying $.25 a head to the boardinghouse-keeper. Board meant three meals a day, a room with two or three beds, each shared by two—or even three—girls, and some laundry. A typical boardinghouse had from twenty-five to thirty tenants, who adhered to a set of rules established by the Corporations and enforced by the "housemothers." Every aspect of the boarder's life outside working hours was made accountable by these rules, which regulated curfews, candles, and visitors. In addition, compulsory church attendance was part of the contract each girl signed, for the building of churches (and their support by the contributions of the mill girls) had been foreseen as essential to the daughters of Congregationalist and Universalist New England.

Initially, the boardinghouses were well-maintained establishments, whitewashed outside and painted within each spring at Corporation expense. There would even appear to have been lively competition among the "housemothers" to set the best table, since the girls could choose among several houses belonging to a Corporation. Anthony Trollope, on a trip to America, visited the boardinghouses and was impressed by the substantial meals: not only was meat served twice a day, but "hot meat." He went on to observe, however, that for the curiously carnivorous Americans "to live a day without meat would be as great a privation as to pass a night without a bed." Descriptions of menus by the girls themselves, moreover, bear witness to the heartiness of the meals, as well as to the appetites of the consumers:

> . . . for dinner, meat and potatoes, with vegetables, tomatoes and pickles, pudding or pie, with bread butter coffee or tea.

Criticism of the houses focused on poor ventilation, exacerbated by overcrowding. Harriet Martineau, that most acute of English observers, was appalled—and mystified—by the lack of privacy. This was the understandable lot of the poor in a small country like England, but

REGULATIONS

TO BE OBSERVED BY ALL PERSONS EMPLOYED IN THE FACTORIES OF THE

APPLETON COMPANY.

THE Overseers are to be punctually in their rooms at the starting of the mill, and not to be absent unnecessarily during working hours. They are to see that all those employed in their rooms are in their places in due season. They may grant leave of absence to those employed under them, when there are spare hands in the room to supply their places ; otherwise they are not to grant leave of absence, except in cases of absolute necessity.

ALL persons in the employ of the APPLETON COMPANY are required to observe the regulations of the overseer of the room where they are employed. They are not to be absent from their work, without his consent, except in case of sickness, and then they are to send him word of the cause of their absence.

THEY are to board in one of the boarding houses belonging to the Company, and conform to the regulations of the house where they board.

A regular attendance on public worship on the Sabbath is necessary for the preservation of good order. The Company will not employ any person who is habitually absent.

ALL persons entering into the employment of the Company are considered as engaging to work twelve months, and those who leave sooner will not receive a discharge unless they had sufficient experience when they commenced, to enable them to do full work.

ALL persons intending to leave the employment of the Company, are to give two weeks' notice of their intention to their overseer ; and their engagement with the Company is not considered as fulfilled, unless they comply with this regulation.

PAYMENTS will be made monthly, including board and wages, which will be made up to the last Saturday in every month, and paid in the course of the following week.

THESE regulations are considered part of the contract with all persons entering into the employment of the APPLETON COMPANY.

G. W. LYMAN, Agent.

Tompe d Press, Gorham-Street.

Regulations for the Appleton Company, Lowell. Signed and dated on reverse: "Hannah Thompson W.R. No. 2 29 November 1833." Merrimack Valley Textile Museum.

. . . in America, where space is of far less consequence, where the houses are large, where the factory girls can build churches and buy libraries, and educate brothers for learned professions, these same girls have no private apartments and sometimes sleep six or eight in a room, and even three in a bed!

Other critics went further, noting dirt and "vermin" in the bedrooms—not surprising since bathing facilities were minimal. It is unlikely, however, that large families in backcountry farms at home offered the girls more, or even as much, in the way of privacy and amenities. One Manchester mill girl was overcome by the unfamiliar luxury of her "very pleasant front room," reflecting that "it seems funny enough to be boarding. I don't even have my bed to make. Quite a lady, to be sure. . . ."

The function of the boardinghouse as an instrument for surveillance and "moral policing" was clear in terms of intent. Less clear was how well the system worked to these ends. One housemother, whose daughter, Harriet Hanson, later was a contributor to the *Offering*, was turned out of her boardinghouse, along with her family, because the eleven-year-old Harriet, then a "bobbin girl," had followed the older workers out of the mill during a "turnout"! If Mrs. Hanson could not control her boarders, the company agent explained, she must at least bear responsibility for the behavior of her own child. Obviously, the political role of the boardinghouse system—identifying organizers of the strikes or turnouts of the 1830s or proponents of the Ten Hour Movement in the 1840s—depended on the loyalties of the housekeeper—but not on her alone. The Corporations could never have foreseen the role of the boardinghouse as incubator of peer group pressure: the closely knit community of female workers living together created new values, solidarity, and political activism.

The growth of the Ten Hour Movement within the mills and the proliferation of questions directed to the issue of operatives' health all pointed to one fact: conditions in both the mills and

REGULATIONS

FOR THE

BOARDING HOUSES

OF THE

MIDDLESEX COMPANY

THE tenants of the Boarding Houses are not to board, or permit any part of their houses to be occupied by any person except those in the employ of the Company.

They will be considered answerable for any improper conduct in their houses, and are not to permit their boarders to have company at unseasonable hours.

The doors must be closed at ten o'clock in the evening, and no one admitted after that time without some reasonable excuse.

The keepers of the Boarding Houses must give an account of the number, names, and employment of their boarders, when required; and report the names of such as are guilty of any improper conduct, or are not in the regular habit of attending public worship.

The buildings and yards about them must be kept clean and in good order, and if they are injured otherwise than from ordinary use, all necessary repairs will be made, and charged to the occupant.

It is indispensable that all persons in the employ of the Middlesex Company should be vaccinated who have not been, as also the families with whom they board; which will be done at the expense of the Company.

SAMUEL LAWRENCE, Agent.

JOEL TAYLOR, PRINTER, Daily Courier Office.

Boarding-House Regulations of the Middlesex Company, ca. 1850. Merrimack Valley Textile Museum.

the boardinghouses were steadily deteriorating. The Lowell working day had gradually been extended from an average of eleven hours (as shown on the time table reproduced on page 30) to more than thirteen hours a day. However poor the ventilation might have been in the boardinghouse, it was much worse in the mills, where the air was polluted with flying lint and fumes from whale-oil lamps that hung on pegs from each loom. Moreover, to maintain the humidity required to keep threads from breaking, the air had to be sprayed regularly with water and the windows nailed shut. Such an atmosphere undoubtedly aggravated the vulnerability of lungs exposed everywhere to tuberculosis, the "white death" that ravaged urban and rural America alike throughout the nineteenth century. What percentage of the high turnover rate—as high as 40 percent in some mills—was attributable to girls "going home to die," as reformers regularly asserted, will never be known. In vaccinating the operatives against smallpox at company expense, the Boston magnates passed for enlightened philanthropists. Such corporate concern for the health of employees was unheard of beyond the borders of Massachusetts. But defensiveness increased: answers to questionnaires devised by Corporation apologists, both medical and pastoral, for the boardinghouse-keepers in 1841 and 1845 "proved," not astonishingly, that the health of the operatives was statistically "no worse" for having worked four years in the mills. Like most statistical studies today, the same data were promptly cited by adversaries of the factory system to prove the reverse. The most vocal defender of the salubrious nature of mill work not only protested too much, but went further, blaming such ill-health as might exist on the girls themselves. The Reverend Henry Miles noted:

> Some come with the seeds of disease already growing within them, and they find that their constitutions would soon break down by continued labor. Others, freed from the guardianship of parental care, are greatly imprudent in their diet, or dress or exposure to cold and damp air . . . others still, will feel that

devotion to fashion which is characteristic of the sex, and will contract a serious, perhaps fatal cold, through neglect to provide themselves with a warm shawl, or a pair of stout shoes. More— there is something in the monotony of mill life which seems to beget a morbid hankering for little artificial stimulants of the appetite, and the tone of the stomach is frequently deranged by a foolish and expensive patronage of the confectioner.

Whether they left the mills for health or husbands, in protest, or with the certainty of better jobs elsewhere, by the beginning of the Civil War the presence of the Yankee farm girls was mere memory. Of 7,000 women operatives in 1836, less than 4 percent had been foreign-born. By 1860, 61.8 percent of Lowell's work force were immigrants, almost half of whom were Irish. The first generation of Lowell mill girls was also the last WASP labor force in America.

The lure of Lowell had promised more than wider social horizons, higher wages, bustling streets, and shop displays of imported finery. The mill girls and their employers shared another basic New England article of faith: self-improvement. Besides attending evening schools, which featured courses based on the high-school curriculum, girls with energies to spare after the long work day would pool pennies to engage a teacher of German, music, or even botany. Such exceptional systematic study was notable, and the Lowell mill girls as avid readers were mentioned by visitor and resident chronicler alike. Sabbath School libraries paved the way, for the American Sunday School Movement propagated the faith with a heavy emphasis on literacy and edifying literature. And by 1844 most of the Sabbath School teachers in Lowell's twenty-two churches were drawn from the ranks of the mill operatives.

Although the famous library of the Middlesex Mechanics Institute did not open its doors to women until 1884, Lowell's Mechanics and Laborers Reading Room admitted them as early as 1825. The Lowell City School Library was founded in 1844, along with the Merrimack Corporation Reading Room for Fe-

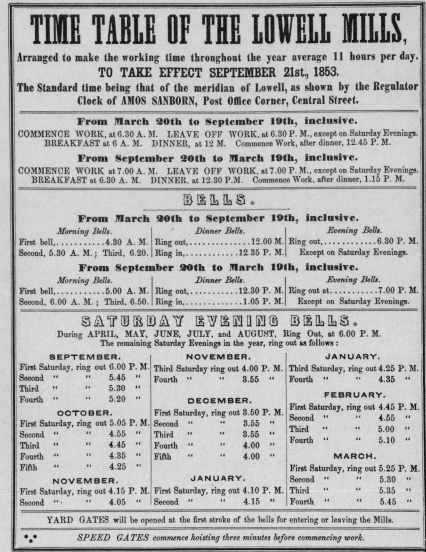

TIME TABLE OF THE LOWELL MILLS,

Arranged to make the working time throughout the year average 11 hours per day.

TO TAKE EFFECT SEPTEMBER 21st., 1853,

The Standard time being that of the meridian of Lowell, as shown by the Regulator Clock of AMOS SANBORN, Post Office Corner, Central Street.

From March 20th to September 19th, inclusive.

COMMENCE WORK, at 6.30 A. M.   LEAVE OFF WORK, at 6.30 P. M., except on Saturday Evenings.
BREAKFAST at 6 A. M.   DINNER, at 12 M.   Commence Work, after dinner, 12.45 P. M.

From September 20th to March 19th, inclusive.

COMMENCE WORK at 7.00 A. M.   LEAVE OFF WORK, at 7.00 P. M., except on Saturday Evenings.
BREAKFAST at 6.30 A. M.   DINNER, at 12.30 P.M.   Commence Work, after dinner, 1.15 P. M.

BELLS.

From March 20th to September 19th, inclusive.

Morning Bells.	Dinner Bells.	Evening Bells.
First bell,...........4.30 A. M.	Ring out,............12.00 M.	Ring out,............6.30 P. M.
Second, 5.30 A. M. ; Third, 6.20.	Ring in,............12.35 P. M.	Except on Saturday Evenings.

From September 20th to March 19th, inclusive.

Morning Bells.	Dinner Bells.	Evening Bells.
First bell,...........5.00 A. M.	Ring out,...........12.30 P. M.	Ring out at...........7.00 P. M.
Second, 6.00 A. M. ; Third, 6.50.	Ring in,.............1.05 P. M.	Except on Saturday Evenings.

SATURDAY EVENING BELLS.

During APRIL, MAY, JUNE, JULY, and AUGUST, Ring Out, at 6.00 P. M.
The remaining Saturday Evenings in the year, ring out as follows :

SEPTEMBER.
First Saturday, ring out 6.00 P. M.
Second   "   "   5.45   "
Third   "   "   5.30   "
Fourth   "   "   5.20   "

OCTOBER.
First Saturday, ring out 5.05 P. M.
Second   "   "   4.55   "
Third   "   "   4.45   "
Fourth   "   "   4.35   "
Fifth   "   "   4.25   "

NOVEMBER.
First Saturday, ring out 4.15 P. M.
Second   " ·   "   4.05   "

NOVEMBER.
Third Saturday ring out 4.00 P. M.
Fourth   "   "   3.55   "

DECEMBER.
First Saturday, ring out 3.50 P. M.
Second   "   "   3.55   "
Third   "   "   3.55   "
Fourth   "   "   4.00   "
Fifth   "   "   4.00   "

JANUARY.
First Saturday, ring out 4.10 P. M.
Second   "   "   4.15   "

JANUARY.
Third Saturday, ring out 4.25 P. M.
Fourth   "   "   4.35   "

FEBRUARY.
First Saturday, ring out 4.45 P. M.
Second   "   "   4.55   "
Third   "   "   5.00   "
Fourth   "   "   5.10   "

MARCH.
First Saturday, ring out 5.25 P. M.
Second   "   "   5.30   "
Third   "   "   5.35   "
Fourth   "   "   5.45   "

YARD GATES will be opened at the first stroke of the bells for entering or leaving the Mills.

. *SPEED GATES commence hoisting three minutes before commencing work.*

Penhallow, Printer, Wyman's Exchange, 28 Merrimack St.

1853 Time Table for the Lowell Mills (probably Lowell Manufacturing Company, makers of worsted yarns and carpets). Merrimack Valley Textile Museum.

male Operatives. Well-attended as these officially patronized sources for literature undoubtedly were, the real magnet for the bookish farm girl was Lowell's circulating libraries. Disdained by clergymen and ignored by historians of the city, this attractive nineteenth-century invention trafficked in that dubious commodity, the novel, held to be especially detrimental to the morals of young women. Harriet Hanson Robinson, whose mother had lost her job as housekeeper of a boardinghouse when she was eleven years old, is unequivocal on its siren call to the rural girls:

> . . . the fame of the circulating libraries, that were soon opened drew them and kept them there, when no other inducement would have been sufficient.

Indeed, one of Harriet Robinson's first memories of Lowell as a child is of one of her mother's boarders, a

> farmer's daughter from the "State of Maine" who had come to Lowell to work, for the express purpose of getting books, usually novels to read, that she could not find in her native place. She read from two to four volumes a week and we children used to get them from the circulating library and return them for her. In exchange for this, she allowed us to read her books, while she was at work in the mill, and what a scurrying there used to be home from school, to get the first chance at the new book!

The usual subscription rate was six and one-quarter cents a week (more, if brand-new novels were included). Business was so brisk in works by Bulwer-Lytton and Walter Scott, and romances with such titles as *Evelina* and *Abellino, the Bravo of Venice*, that in the mid-1830s an enterprising Mr. Stephens moved his circulating library of 2,000 volumes to Lowell from Dover, New Hampshire.

Whether the texts were sacred or profane, reading was so rife among the mill girls that a factory injunction appeared specifying "No Reading in the Mills." One overseer reportedly had a drawerful of confiscated Bibles: even Holy Writ could not corrupt the Yankee sense of duty—and profit. But these uncommon readers were not to be deterred. Lucy Larcom, a poet who later achieved a modest regional renown, recalled co-workers pasting up pages from books in window alcoves and on the wooden loom frames:

> No one objects to papering bare walls. . . .
> As well forbid us Yankee girls to breathe
> As read; we cannot help it.

By the 1830s Lowell could boast another potent cultural attraction: lectures that made the newly built city the second Athens, after Boston, of the Lyceum Movement. Throughout the winter season, the Lyceum lectures (alternating with concerts) embraced topics moral, literary, and scientific.

The role of the Lyceum lecture in popular education has been well documented. It was the road-show version of *The Flowering of New England*, but with all the original stars: Horace Greeley, John Quincy Adams, Edward Everett, Horace Mann, Robert Owen, and Ralph Waldo Emerson. There was the Lowell Institute and the Lyceum itself (sponsored by the Society for the Diffusion of Useful Knowledge) where, for fifty cents in the season of 1839, you could have heard Emerson speak on "Ethical English Literature," a lecture on "The Use of Wine," and an evening devoted to "Palestine and Egypt."

Martha Woolson, a mill worker who had left Lowell after a breakdown of physical, and possibly mental, health, enjoined her sister, gone to replace her at the mill, to make better use of "precious privileges" such as the lectures that "I once enjoyed there and notwithstanding the poor improvement I made of them." The topic of many of the lectures would seem to indicate that relevance was not the primary concern of the so-called lyceum trippers, but apparently their audiences were eager for any knowledge, useful or otherwise. Professor A. P. Peabody of Harvard later recalled:

> I used every winter to lecture for the Lowell Lyceum. Not amusement, but instruction was then the lecturer's aim . . . the

Lowell Hall was always crowded and four-fifths of the audience were factory girls. When the lecturer entered, almost every girl had a book in her hand and was intent upon it. When he rose, the book was laid aside and paper and pencil taken instead. . . . I have never seen anywhere so assiduous note-taking. No, not even in a college class, as in that assembly of young women, laboring for their subsistence.

Other members of the audience, if equally assiduous, were also more skeptical. "We often heard the Brook Farm Community talked of," Lucy Larcom remembered, "and were curious about it as an experiment at air castle building by people who had time to indulge their tastes." Girls who were working in the mills because their families could not survive on the hard-rock New England farms must have found a lecture on "The Neglect of Agriculture" still more mystifying than the bucolic visions of Brook Farmers from Harvard.

In addition to attending evening classes and lyceum lectures, some mill girls went on to explore a less passive intellectual activity: literary composition. By the early 1840s there were no less than seven Mutual Self-Improvement Clubs in Lowell, whose members met to read their writings to one another. Thus, the membership of the first women's literary clubs in America consisted entirely of factory workers. Two of these groups were sponsored by the Universalist and Congregationalist churches. Both groups were encouraged to submit their best sketches, poems, stories, and essays in view of a proposed regional annual, to be called *The Garland of the Mills*. The response so delighted the enthusiastic young Universalist minister, the Reverend Abel C. Thomas, that he could not wait for the annual; he began publishing the *Lowell Offering* irregularly throughout 1840, its success causing plans for the *Garland* to be abandoned. In 1841, the *Offering* was seeking subscriptions as a monthly magazine, thirty pages long, priced at six and one-quarter cents an issue. Its cover bore the banner line that would inspire adulation abroad and pride at home:

A Repository of Original Articles, Written Exclusively by Females Actively Employed in the Mills.

Meanwhile, the *Operatives' Magazine*, published in 1841 by William Schouler, editor and publisher of the *Lowell Courier*, the "Corporation" newspaper, began life more daringly with two mill girls, Abba A. Goddard and Lydia S. Hall, as editors. In 1842, when the Reverend Mr. Thomas's ministry called him from Lowell, he sold the *Offering* to Schouler, who, merging the two magazines, retained the title of the more successful publication. Harriet F. Farley and Harriott Curtis, the new editors, had each worked in the mills for nearly a decade. The bleakly impoverished beginnings of both these young women further validated their editorial claim: unlike other factory magazines, edited and written *for* the operatives by male entrepreneurs, the new *Offering* was reborn female and grass roots. An editorial of 1843, in fact, looked back, noting the degree to which both their consciousness and confidence had been raised by the experience of success the magazine had provided. The editors recalled Mr. Thomas's original proposal that the girls should edit the magazine themselves. They had unanimously rejected his suggestion in terror—"We—the editor!—the idea was very awful." And now the *Offering* was not only edited and written by factory operatives: the Misses Farley and Curtis had recently purchased the magazine from Schouler, who remained, somewhat ambiguously, as publisher.

No one would question the grass-roots origins of the *Lowell Offering:* the growing issue was the extent to which these roots were watered by the Corporations.

The question of patronage by the Boston Associates would not have arisen if the *Offering* had not achieved instant fame: panegyrics to its editors and contributors embraced, both specifically and by implication, the enlightened "philanthropists" who treated their workers so well that they had the leisure and energy to become literary celebrities in their spare time. So intense was Harriet Martineau's admiration for the *Offering* that she persuaded Charles Knight, publisher to the English Society for the Diffusion of Useful Knowledge, to edit an anthology of the magazine. Appearing in 1844 as *Mind Among the Spindles*, and enhanced by a Martineau preface, it spread further word of the intelligence and virtue of the American mill girls (Knight having taken care to choose those *Offering* articles heaviest on moral uplift) and the benevolence of their employers.

In France, Republican adulation was extravagant while Republican ideals were being increasingly betrayed. Adolphe Thiers, who as president of the republic would in 1871 give the order to fire on the Commune, had, nearly three decades earlier, brought a volume of the *Offering* into the Chamber of Deputies to show what the laboring daughters of Democracy could do. George Sand expressed great enthusiasm for its contents, although a compatriot's comparison of Lowell to a Spanish convent town, with the mill girls as resident nuns, cannot have aroused in her much sense of elective affinity. And President Cornelius Felton of Harvard, flushed with regional pride, could report back that Philarète Chasles, professor of comparative literature at the Collège de France, had devoted an entire lecture to the *Lowell Offering*.

Admiration was the more intense, the farther the admirer lived from Lowell. Not that the *Offering* lacked American patronage: its admirers included William Ellery Channing, Horace Greeley, Emma Willard, Elizabeth Peabody, and John Greenleaf Whittier, a sometime resident of Lowell during this period, who occasionally attended editorial meetings and became a lifelong friend of its best-known contributor, poet Lucy Larcom. New Englanders, however, were not surprised to find intellectual aspiration, or even achievement, on the part of factory operatives. There were too many middle-class women, readers of the *Offering* among them, who, for reasons of geography, domesticity, or both, had never enjoyed the independence or "cultural advantages" of its mill girl contributors. Whittier was quick, moreover, to attack the patronizing tone of many of the testimonials: to the democratic Quaker poet, the sense of wonder which greeted "what factory girls had power to do" was distasteful. And such attitudes did not bode well for the hardening of class lines. Low expectations of labor as a race apart, Whittier pointed out, were implicit in many of these effusions,

> . . . as if the compatibility of mental cultivation with bodily labor were still open questions, depending for their decision very much on the production of positive proof that essays may be written and carpets woven by the same set of fingers!

The *Offering* was not born a house organ, nor did it ever actually become one. As such, its value to the Boston Associates would have been negligible. As Lowell was a showcase mill town and its women workers were the "most superior operatives," so their magazine would be a traveling mirror to reflect an ideal system. During the period when Lowell could still claim with some credibility to be the "industrial Utopia" Trollope had observed, it all worked. The *Offering*, uncensored and independent, provided a fortuitous medium for those two expressions of distinctly American genius: public relations and packaging.

From the first, its editorial policy concerning working conditions had tried to set certain limits: "with wages, board etc. we have nothing to do." The literary nature of their enterprise was supposed to seal it off from the turmoil of "issues." Sustaining that position—and surviving as a factory operatives' magazine—became a balancing act that was doomed to fail.

The turnouts of 1834 and 1836, quasi-spontaneous and poorly planned, were not repeated during the *Offering*'s lifetime. But the conditions which had triggered them did not improve; in fact, they worsened. By the 1840s, the degraded British textile workers had won a sixty-nine-hour week, with six annual holidays; the Lowell factory week had been extended to seventy-five hours, with four holidays, while wages for piecework kept dropping. Girls were now forced to tend three and four machines. Those who could not keep pace with the

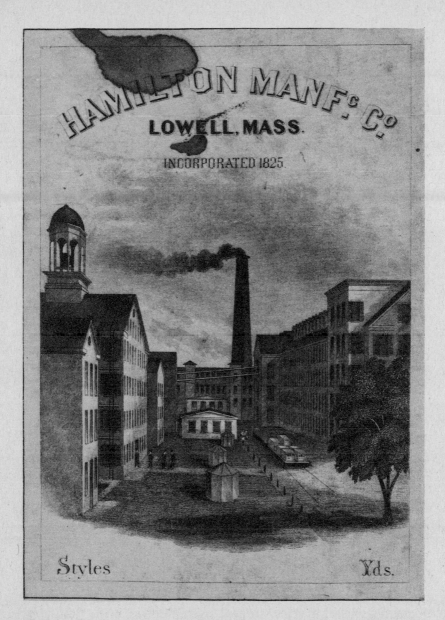

Cloth label for Hamilton Manufacturing Company, Lowell, Massachusetts, ca. 1860. Merrimack Valley Textile Museum.

speedup found wages drastically reduced, while overseers, who now received production premiums, were encouraged to harass the slower workers.

The Ten Hour Movement rallied growing numbers of signatures to its petitions (the majority always from Lowell), despite the fact that women known to be activists, or even those caught reading "radical" newspapers, were subject to instant dismissal and subsequent blacklisting throughout New England. The demise of the *Offering* is clearly reflected in the number of signatures on two of these petitions: in 1845, the last year of the magazine, there were 2,000 signatures from the Lowell mills, and 5,000 in the following year. Apparently the magazine had less to say to more and more of its original constituency. Finally, this constituency itself was leaving the mills—the only effective protest—to be replaced in ever greater numbers by Irish immigrant labor. Only five years separated the end of the *Lowell Offering* from the end of native labor in New England mills.

The issue of editorial independence is still cloudy. With the assumption of editorial duties in 1842, Harriet Farley moved with her coeditor from a corporation boardinghouse to a "rose-covered cottage" on the edge of town. Evidence also suggests that her straitened family received occasional, if discreet, assistance from one of the mill owners, Abbot Lawrence.

There were still more serious accusations directed at the *Offering:* overseers collected subscriptions and supervised deliveries. Agents allegedly purchased a thousand dollars' worth of back issues, thereby "laundering" Corporation subsidy, without which the magazine would not have limped through its final year.

The author of an ongoing *"J'Accuse"* directed against the *Offering* and its editor, Harriet Farley, was Sarah Bagley, one of its most gifted contributors. Bagley began by accusing Farley of rejecting several articles she had submitted, as being "too controversial." This was denied. The issue remained unsolved, but enlivened the pages of two Lowell newspapers, the *Courier* and

Title page of the Lowell Offering, *December, 1845. Merrimack Valley Textile Museum.*

the *Advertiser*, for several weeks. The two disputed pieces appeared as *Factory Tracts*, published by the Lowell Female Labor Reform Association, with Sarah Bagley as its founder and president. The dynamic organizer/journalist now joined the *Voice of Industry*, a newspaper dedicated to the support of the Ten Hour Movement.

In one of her less acrimonious moments—when the enemy was safely dead and buried—Miss Bagley diagnosed the *Offering*'s terminal disease:

> Led on by the fatal error of neutrality, it has neglected the operative as a working being. . . . the very position of the *Offering* as a factory girls' magazine, precludes the possibilities of neutrality.

In fact, a careful reading of *Offering* editorials reveals that they did not ignore deteriorating conditions in the mills and boardinghouses: besides the abundant evidence furnished by the articles themselves, editorials point to the impossibly short time for meals (thirty-five minutes, including travel to and from the mills), greater overcrowding and worse ventilation in the houses (as their once-spacious yards were occupied by other buildings), the abuses of the overseer's premiums. One of the last such editorials was Farley's report on the testimony of the Ten Hour Delegation before a Labor Committee of the Massachusetts Legislature, expressing pride in the witnesses and criticism of the disrespect which greeted them. It was just too late.

Harriet Farley was not a toady; she was what Sartre once described as a "*passéiste*." Accepting the watered-down Fourierism of the day, Farley truly believed that with goodwill, and recognition by labor and management of their mutual interest, Lowell's Golden Age would return. But there could be no turning back. The end of Lowell was the beginning of a large-scale industrial economy, and an ever-widening chasm between two classes new to America: the all-powerful corporate titans and the urban proletariat. The "idyll of work" had ended and the *Offering* with it.

Other factory magazines, some hard-hitting reformist ones among them, waxed and waned through the mid-forties. They rarely contain an article, an editorial, or a story that conveys, as do the pages of the *Lowell Offering*, the sense of immediacy, personal observation, and dailiness that are the stuff of life. Such publications as the *Factory Girls' Garland* and *Factory Girls' Album* were very short lived, changing place and merging names with dizzying inconstancy—and insolvency. They had in common a strange form of schizophrenia. The editorials were essentially agitprop: impersonal, hortatory prose inhabited by the fleeting personification of an Oppressed and Exploited Worker. But when these magazines shifted from the Editorial Imperative, they printed only the popular trash of the day, written by such genteel practitioners of the art as Mrs. Ann S. Stephens and Mrs. Lydia Maria Child. Most of these stories were overtly pirated, moreover, from middle-class women's magazines like *Godey's Lady's Book* and *The Ladies Wreath* and bore titles like "Strabismus, or the Broken Heart," and "Love in a Printing Office." Dickens immediately perceived how relatively free the *Offering* was of the gentility and materialistic fairy tales that characterized most of the popular women's literature of the time, whether written for mill girls or duchesses. Not only were "many of its tales . . . of the Mills and those who work in them," but, even more impressive, he found that there was "scant allusion to fine clothes, fine marriages, fine house or fine life."

Whatever the overblown claims of patrons or admirers, or the rage of radicalized mill women against the magazine for what it could have been, the *Offering* itself is, finally, as modest as its title suggests. It represents the first heady efforts of young women in the process of discovering what they had power to do. Before leaving the mills, "our bright, breezy wide-awake girls" left the first writings by and about American blue-collar women, along with many still unanswered questions about the relationship of work to class, sex, ethnicity, and aspiration in America.

Dutton Street housing of Merrimack Manufacturing Company, Lowell, imme-diately prior to demolition in 1966. Photograph by Richard Graber for the Merrimack Valley Textile Museum.

1
MILL AND BOARDINGHOUSE:
The New Community

Thinly disguised reportage, "Letters from Susan" and "Tales of Factory Life" illustrate the ways in which the boardinghouse served as a "mediating structure" in the transformation of farm girl into factory operative.

"Boarding on the Corporation" usually meant choosing a house where a friend or relative from home had paved the way. Thus began a socialization process which changed the homesick rustic, through pressure to conform, into the trim Lowell mill girl. The shawl pinned under the chin was abandoned for the "scooter" bonnet then in style. The "unintelligible twang" soon gave way through "severe discipline and ridicule" to the "city way of speaking."

More important still, the boardinghouse served as the point of entry for work in the mills. The new arrival would be "sponsored," presented to the overseer by the boardinghouse-keeper or fellow boarder. Once in the mill, newcomers were assigned work as spare hands. In this apprentice capacity, they were paid a daily wage, independent of quantity, until they were skilled enough in the operation of two looms to receive wages based on the usual piecework. The new employees were assigned a more experienced partner for the few months usually needed to master the skills of those jobs allotted to women: spinning, weaving, drawing-in (the stretching and knotting of thousands of threads on the frame), and dressing (a sizing process). When a regular hand left, in the anticipated turnover cycle, the spare hand was ready to take her place.

In case of sickness, girls regularly covered the looms of the absent fellow worker, so that she would not lose pay.

Segregated from male workers by division of labor and removed from patriarchal family structure, the mill women had very little interaction with men in their daily lives. And, indeed, the male figures appearing in the Offering *seem romantically remote heroes from the circulating library. Present reality—as reflected in these stories—was a women's world of fellow workers and roommates.*

"The Pleasures of Factory Life" are rendered brighter by what has been left behind—family tragedies or the horrors of domestic service. But every writer manages to convey the full shock of that first day in the mill: the noise, fear, headache, and swollen feet. Nor do the Offering *contributors gloss over boardinghouse discomforts: downstairs, the noisy, gobbled meals and the aggressive intrusions of tradesmen; upstairs, no place to hide.*

Despite a classically Victorian "surprise" ending, "The Sister" is a chilling illustration of the ugly face of peer pressure: an unhappy vindication of the Reverend Mr. Miles's assurance that "moral policing" began with the girls themselves, who normally ostracize any one of their number suspected of "light conduct." Sisterly compassion toward such offenders (and pleas to guard against calumny of the innocent) are urged in "A Woman's Voice to Woman." Besides providing a spectrum of personalities—the grave and the frivolous, the melancholy and the high-spirited, "Leisure Hours of the Mill Girls" gives affecting evidence of the support, comfort, and love with which a close-knit community of young women could sustain one another.

Letters from Susan

LETTER FIRST

March —, ——.

Dear Mary: When I left home I told you that I would write in a week, and let you have my first impressions of Lowell. I will keep my promise; though, if I should defer my letter a while longer, I think I could make it much more interesting. But you know I promised to be

Woman drawing in warp ends, ca. 1855, from A History of Wonderful Inventions. *Merrimack Valley Textile Museum.*

very minute, and there is always sufficient minutiæ to fill up a letter.

I arrived here safe and sound, after being well jolted over the rocks and hills of New Hampshire; and when (it was then evening) a gentleman in the stage first pointed out Lowell to me, with its lights twinkling through the gloom, I could think of nothing but Passampscot swamp, when brilliantly illuminated by "lightning-bugs." You, I know, will excuse all my "up-country" phrases, for I have not yet got the rust off; and to you, and all my old-fashioned friends, I shall always be *rusty*. My egotism I will not apologize for—it is what you request.

To return to my adventures—for it all appears very romantic to me. The driver carried me to the "corporation," as it is called; and which, so far as I now can describe it, is a number of short parallel streets with high brick blocks on either side. There are some blocks with blinds to them, and some are destitute. Some of the doors have bells, others have not. Contiguous to these *boarding-houses* are the *mills*, of which I will tell you more by and by.

I told the driver to carry me to N. —, and there he left me; where there was not a soul that I knew, if cousin Sarah was gone. I inquired, of an Irish girl who came to the door, if Sarah G. Pollard boarded there. She said that she had gone to Manchester, to work with an overseer who was an old acquaintance. The girl did not invite me in, and there I stood like "a statter," as Aunt Hitty says. I did not feel disposed to make inquiries of the girl, I was so unaccustomed to her brogue. Just then—that is, just as my heart was sinking ten fathoms below zero—a pleasant-looking woman came into the entry; and, in a very motherly way, invited me into her own room; took off my things, ordered away my trunk and bandbox, brought camphor for my head, for it ached with my ride, and told me all about cousin Sarah. She said that I had better not think of following her to Manchester, and promised to do all for me that she could. This was Mrs. C., "the boarding woman"—a widow, with several children, whom she keeps at school, and maintains well, by her own industry and good management.

I had expected coldness, or at least entire indifference, in this city, and the cordiality of the good landlady filled my heart with gratitude. I have since inquired if she were not unusually kind; but, though she is a very good woman, the girls here say that she is not more so to me than to any other new boarder; and that the boarding-women are always "dreadful good" to a new boarder. Every girl, let her be ever so rusty, or rather rustic, fills one of the many niches prepared here for so many, and some, you know, are like nest-eggs, and bring many more. But we will not be so uncharitable as to suppose there is nothing but policy in all this, for there is surely something to excite a woman's sympathies in the sight, which is not uncommon here, of a lonely friendless helpless stranger.

You can hardly think how my heart beat when I heard the bells ring for the girls to come to supper, and then the doors began to slam, and then Mrs. C. took me into the dining-room, where there were three common-sized dining tables, and she seated me at one of them, and then the girls thickened around me, until I was almost dizzy.

At the table where I sat they were very still, for the presence of a stranger is usually "a damper" upon them. But there was quite noise enough at the other tables, and what was wanted in wit was made up in merriment. After a while one or two of my boon companions "opened their mouths and spoke," and I have already found that those who make themselves most conspicuous in the presence of strangers, and would soonest attract their attention, are those who do themselves, and those with whom they are connected, the least credit.

I remember that I must be very minute—so I will inform you that we had tea, flapjacks, and plum-cake for supper. There was also bread, butter, and crackers, upon the table; but I saw no one touch them.

After supper the tables were cleared in a trice. Some of the girls came in with their sewing, some went to their own rooms, and some went "out upon the street"—that is, they went to some meeting, or evening school, or they were shopping, or visiting upon some other corporation, all of which is "going upon the street," in factory parlance.

I retained my seat with the girls in the great keeping-room, for Mrs. C. had company in her own sanctum, and I did not know where else to go. Some book-pedlers, shoe-pedlers, essence-pedlers, and candy-boys came in, and made very strenuous exertions to attract our attention. By most of the girls they were treated with cool civility, but there were some little noisy self-conceited misses, who detained them, under the pretence of examining goods for purchase, but who were slily joking at the expense of the pedler, and collecting material for future merriment. Sometimes the joke was turned upon themselves, and it was seldom that both parties separated in good humor.

At ten o'clock Mrs. C. came in, and told us that it was time for us all to go to bed. Some begged for time to "read this story out;" others just for "a few minutes to finish this seam." She refused them good-naturedly, but those were most cunning who wanted to warm their feet, and detained her by telling queer stories, of what they had seen and heard upon "the street"—and she unconsciously gave them the few minutes she had at first refused.

I was shown up three flight of stairs, into what is called "the long attic"—where they put all poor stranger girls—the most objectionable places being always left for new comers. There were three beds in it, only two of which were occupied, for this is always the room for vacancies. My baggage had already been carried up by "the boys," as the boarders call Mrs. C's. sons; and I looked wofully at the strange girl who was to be my "*chum.*" She took no notice of me, and went to sleep as composedly as if I had been still among the White mountains; but the two girls in the further bed kept whispering together something about "the old man." I was very nervous, and almost wished "the old boy" had them both; but, when the house was still, a strange fear came over me, such as is created in children by telling them about *the old man.*

I heard the bells strike the midnight hour long before I went to sleep, and then I dreamed about "the old man."

As soon as day broke I was awakened by one of the girls jumping out of bed, and beginning to crow. That awakened the others, and they bestirred themselves. One sung

> Morning bells I hate to hear,
> Ringing dolefully, loud, and drear, &c.

Then the other struck up, with a loud voice,

> Now isn't it a pity,
> Such a pretty girl as I,
> Should be sent to the factory
> To pine away and die.

I dressed myself, and followed them down stairs, where I found my place at the table, and our early breakfast was all ready for us. It consisted of hot cakes, and coffee—there was also "hash" upon the table, for those who wanted it.

When the girls had all gone to work I asked Mrs. C. what I should do. She replied that she would go herself and see if I could have a place, for she was well acquainted with many of the overseers, and thought she could "get me in."

She went in for me, but no overseer would take me, even upon her recommendation, until they had seen me themselves. One promised, however, to give me work if he liked the looks of me, and she considers this place as if already engaged, for she says she knows he will like me when he sees me.

You may ask how Mrs. C. could recommend me. She was so well acquainted with cousin Sarah that she had often heard her speak of me, and she says that she is never deceived, either, in her estimate of a good honest country girl.

The overseer said he should not want me until next week, and I felt rather unpleasant at the thought of paying my board while earning nothing. But Mrs. C. said she had some quilts to make, and if I would assist her a little she would give me my board. So I can run round, and see all the lions and lionesses, and get quite an idea of my location, before I go into the mill. O, how I dread to be cooped up there, day after day.

You will ask what I have already seen. I have been out upon a long street, called Central street, and another long street, at right angles with it, called Merrimack street. There are stores filled with beautiful goods upon either side, and some handsome public buildings. There is a great hotel called the Merrimack House, which is much larger than any that I ever saw before, and near it is the Railroad Depot. I waited, one day, to see the cars come in from Boston. They moved, as you know, very swiftly, but not so much like "a streak of lightning" as I had anticipated. If all country girls are like me their first impressions of a city are far below their previous conceptions, and they think there is more difference than there really is. Little as I know of it now I see that the difference is more apparent than real. There are the same passions at work beneath another surface.

When I went out with Mrs. C. she made me put on one of her girls' bonnets, because mine did not turn up behind, and out at the ears, and she said it was O. S., instead of O. K. Well, as I walked along, and saw all the beautifully dressed ladies, I thought, within myself, that, with bonnets and dresses of an old style, they too would not be passable.

You must know that they dress very much here—at least, it so appears to us, who have just come off of the hills, and been accustomed to put on our woollen gowns in the morning, and our better woollen gowns in the "arternoon." Here they wear velvets, and furs, and plumes, and bugles, and *all*. I should wish to know a great deal to be dressed so, for I should think there was a great deal to be expected of one who made such pretensions.

I told Mrs. C. that the city ladies were not so pale as I expected. She said that many of them were painted, and that *rouge* was becoming more fashionable every year. She says that even some of the factory girls use it, and pointed out several highly dressed girls whose cheeks were truly of "a carmine tint."

I have attended meeting the only sabbath I have been here. It seems as though every one went to meeting, the streets are so full on Sundays, but it is not so. Yet Lowell is a church-going place, and they say that they have good meetings and ministers.

I went to the Congregational meeting, for that, you know, is the one I have always been accustomed to attend. The meeting-house is one of the oldest in the city, and not beautiful, though a good respectable looking building. The congregation was very tastefully dressed. I thought, as I looked at some of the ladies, that old Parson Trevor would preach to them from Matthew xxvi. 18. "Top not come down."

In the afternoon I went to the Methodist meeting. This, you are aware, is, with us, "the ragged meeting;" but here—my paper is full, and I can only say ribbons, bows, plumes, ruffles, fringes, wimples, and crimples, "ruffs, puffs, and farthingales." Yet the preaching was of a higher order than I had anticipated.

Next Sunday I shall go to *see* the Episcopalians, and Catholics, of whom we have always heard so little that is good. Yet there was a strange, and not unhallowed sensation excited in my breast when I first saw a church with a spire surmounted by a cross, that symbol of our holy religion; and the dark stone church which was first built here, revived the impressions which were created by our juvenile literature, which you know a few years since was wholly English.

Yours affectionately,

Susan

(Harriet Farley, Vol. IV, 1844, pp. 145–148)

Letters from Susan

LETTER SECOND

Lowell, April —, ——.

Dear Mary: In my last I told you I would write again, and say more of my life here; and this I will now attempt to do.

I went into the mill to work a few days after I wrote to you. It looked very pleasant at first, the rooms were so light, spacious, and clean, the girls so pretty and neatly dressed, and the machinery so brightly polished or nicely painted. The plants in the windows, or on the overseer's bench or desk, gave a pleasant aspect to things. You will wish to know what work I am doing. I will tell you of the different kinds of work.

There is, first, the carding-room, where the cotton flies most, and the girls get the dirtiest. But this is easy, and the females are allowed time to go out at night before the bell rings—on Saturday night at least, if not on all other nights. Then there is the spinning-room, which is very neat and pretty. In this room are the spinners and dof-fers. The spinners watch the frames; keep them clean, and the threads mended if they break. The doffers take off the full bobbins, and put on the empty ones. They have nothing to do in the long intervals when the frames are in motion, and can go out to their boarding-houses, or do any thing else that they like. In some of the factories the spinners do their own doffing, and when this is the case they work no harder than the weavers. These last have the hardest time of all—or can have, if they choose to take charge of three or four looms, instead of the one pair which is the allotment. And they are the most con-stantly confined. The spinners and dressers have but the weavers to keep supplied, and then their work can stop. The dressers never work before breakfast, and they stay out a great deal in the afternoons. The drawers-in, or girls who draw the threads through the harnesses, also work in the dressing-room, and they all have very good wages—bet-ter than the weavers who have but the usual work. The dressing-rooms are very neat, and the frames move with a gentle undulating motion which is really graceful. But these rooms are kept very warm, and are disagreeably scented with the "sizing," or starch, which stiff-ens the "beams," or unwoven webs. There are many plants in these rooms, and it is really a good green-house for them. The dressers are generally quite tall girls, and must have pretty tall minds too, as their work requires much care and attention.

I could have had work in the dressing-room, but chose to be a weaver; and I will tell you why. I disliked the closer air of the dressing-room, though I might have become accustomed to that. I could not learn to dress so quickly as I could to weave, nor have work of my own so soon, and should have had to stay with Mrs. C. two or three weeks before I could go in at all, and I did not like to be "lying upon my oars" so long. And, more than this, when I get well learned I can have extra work, and make double wages, which you know is quite an inducement with some.

Well, I went into the mill, and was put to learn with a very patient girl—a clever old maid. I should be willing to be one myself if I could be as good as she is. You cannot think how odd every thing seemed to me. I wanted to laugh at every thing, but did not know what to make sport of first. They set me to threading shuttles, and tying weaver's knots, and such things, and now I have improved so that I can take care of one loom. I could take care of two if I only had eyes in the back part of my head, but I have not got used to "looking two ways of a Sunday" yet.

At first the hours seemed very long, but I was so interested in learning that I endured it very well; and when I went out at night the sound of the mill was in my ears, as of crickets, frogs, and jewsharps, all mingled together in strange discord. After that it seemed as though cotton-wool was in my ears, but now I do not mind at all. You know that people learn to sleep with the thunder of Niagara in their ears, and a cotton mill is no worse, though you wonder that we do not have to hold our breath in such a noise.

It makes my feet ache and swell to stand so much, but I suppose I shall get accustomed to that too. The girls generally wear old shoes about their work, and you know nothing is easier; but they almost all say that when they have worked here a year or two they have to procure shoes a size or two larger than before they came. The right hand, which is the one used in stopping and starting the loom, becomes larger than the left; but in other respects the factory is not detrimental to a young girl's appearance. Here they look delicate, but not sickly; they laugh at those who are much exposed, and get pretty brown; but I, for one, had rather be brown than pure white. I never saw so many pretty looking girls as there are here. Though the number of men is small in proportion there are many marriages here, and a great deal of courting. I will tell you of this last sometime.

You wish to know minutely of our hours of labor. We go in at five o'clock; at seven we come out to breakfast; at half-past seven we return to our work, and stay until half-past twelve. At one, or quarter-past one four months in the year, we return to our work, and stay until seven at night. Then the evening is all our own, which is more than some laboring girls can say, who think nothing is more tedious than a factory life.

When I first came here, which was the last of February, the girls ate their breakfast before they went to their work. The first of March they came out at the present breakfast hour, and the twentieth of March they ceased to "light up" the rooms, and come out between six and seven o'clock.

You ask if the girls are contented here: I ask you, if you know of *any one* who is perfectly contented. Do you remember the old story of the philosopher, who offered a field to the person who was contented with his lot; and, when one claimed it, he asked him why, if he was so perfectly satisfied, he wanted his field. The girls here are not contented; and there is no disadvantage in their situation which they do not perceive as quickly, and lament as loudly, as the sternest opponents of the factory system do. They would scorn to say they were contented, if asked the question; for it would compromise their Yankee spirit—their pride, penetration, independence, and love of "freedom and equality" to say that they were *contented* with such a life as this. Yet, withal, they are cheerful. I never saw a happier set of beings. They appear blithe in the mill, and out of it. If you see one of them, with a very long face, you may be sure that it is because she has heard bad news from home, or because her beau has vexed her. But, if it is a Lowell trouble, it is because she has failed in getting off as many "sets" or "pieces" as she intended to have done; or because she had a sad "break-out," or "break-down," in her work, or something of that sort.

You ask if the work is not disagreeable. Not when one is accustomed to it. It tried my patience sadly at first, and does now when it does not run well; but, in general, I like it very much. It is easy to do, and does not require very violent exertion, as much of our farm work does.

You also ask how I get along with the girls here. Very well indeed;

only we came near having a little flurry once. You know I told you I
lodged in the "long attic." Well, a little while ago, there was a place
vacated in a pleasant lower chamber. Mrs. C. said that it was my
"chum's" turn to go down stairs to lodge, unless she would waive her
claim in favor of me. You must know that here they get up in the
world by getting down, which is what the boys in our debating society used to call a paradox. Clara, that is the girl's name, was not at all
disposed to give up her rights, but maintained them staunchly. I had
nothing to do about it—the girls in the lower room liked me, and
disliked Clara, and were determined that it should not be at all pleasant weather there if she did come. Mrs. C. was in a dilemma. Clara's
turn came first. The other two girls in the chamber were sisters, and
would not separate, so they were out of the question. I wanted to go,
and knew Clara would not be happy with them. But I thought what
was my duty to do. She was not happy now, and would not be if
deprived of her privilege. She had looked black at me for several days,
and slept with her face to the wall as many nights. I went up to her
and said, "Clara, take your things down into the lower chamber, and
tell the girls that *I will not come.* It is your turn now, and mine will
come in good time."

Clara was mollified in an instant. "No," said she; "I will not go
now. They do not wish me to come, and I had rather stay here."
After this we had quite a contest—I trying to persuade Clara to go,
and she trying to persuade me, and I *"got beat."* So now I have a
pleasanter room, and am quite a favorite with all the girls. They have
given me some pretty plants, and they go out with me whenever I
wish it, so that I feel quite happy.

You think we must live very nice here to have plum-cake, &c. The
plum-cake, and crackers, and such things as the bakers bring upon the
corporations, are not as nice as we have in the country, and I presume
are much cheaper. I seldom eat any thing that is not cooked in the
family. I should not like to tell you the stories they circulate here
about the bakers, unless I *knew* that they were true. Their brown
bread is the best thing that I have tasted of their baking.

You see that I have been quite *minute* in this letter, though I hardly
liked your showing the former to old Deacon Gale, and 'Squire
Smith, and those old men. It makes me feel afraid to write you all I
should like to, when I think so many eyes are to pore over my humble

sheet. But if their motives are good, and they can excuse all defects, why I will not forbid.

'Squire Smith wishes to know what sort of men our superintendents are. I know very well what he thinks of them, and what their reputation is up our way. I am not personally acquainted with any of them; but, from what I hear, I have a good opinion of them. I suppose they are not faultless, neither are those whom they superintend; but they are not the over-bearing tyrants which many suppose them to be. The abuse of them, which I hear, is so very low that I think it must be unjust and untrue; and I do frequently hear them spoken of as *men*—whole-hearted full-souled men. Tell 'Squire Smith they are not what he would be in their places—that they treat their operatives better than he does his "hired girls," and associate with them on terms of as much equality. But I will tell you who are almost universally unpopular: the "runners," as they are called, or counting-room boys. I suppose they are little whipper-snappers who will grow better as they grow older.

My paper is filling up, and I must close by begging your pardon for speaking of the Methodists as having lost their simplicity of attire. It was true, nevertheless, for I have not seen one of the old "Simon Pure" Methodist bonnets since I have been here. But they may be as consistent as other denominations. Had few of us follow in the steps of the primitive Christians.

Yours as ever,
Susan
(*Harriet Farley, Vol. IV, June 1844, pp. 169–172*)

Letters from Susan

LETTER THIRD

Lowell, July—,——.

Dear Mary: You complain that I do not keep my promise of being a good correspondent, but if you could know how sultry it is here, and how fatigued I am by my work this warm weather, you would not blame me. It is now that I begin to dislike these hot brick pavements, and glaring buildings. I want to be at home—to go down to the brook

over which the wild grapes have made a natural arbor, and to sit by
the cool spring around which the fresh soft brakes cluster so lovingly.
I think of the time when, with my little bare feet, I used to follow in
aunt Nabby's footsteps through the fields of corn—stepping high and
long till we came to the bleaching ground; and I remember—but I
must stop, for I know you wish me to write of what I am now doing,
as you already know of what I have done.

Well; I go to work every day— not earlier than I should at home,
nor do I work later, but I mind the confinement more than I should in
a more unpleasant season of the year. I have extra work now—I take
care of three looms; and when I wrote you before I could not well take
care of two. But help is very scarce now, and they let us do as much
work as we please; and I am highly complimented upon my "powers
of execution." Many of the girls go to their country homes in the summer. The majority of the operatives are country girls. These have
always the preference, because, in the fluctuations to which manufac-
tures are liable, there would be much less distress among a population
who could resort to other homes, than if their entire interest was in
the city. And in the summer these girls go to rest, and recruit themselves for another "yearly campaign"—not a bad idea in them either. I
shall come home next summer; I have been here too short a time to
make it worth while now. I wish they would have a *vacation* in "dog
days"—stop the mills, and *make* all the girls rest; and let their "men-
folks" do up their "ditching," or whatever else it is they now do Sundays.

But these mills are not such dreadful places as you imagine them to
be. You think them dark damp holes; as close and black as—as the
Black Hole at Calcutta. Now, dear M., it is no such thing. They are
high spacious well-built edifices, with neat paths around them, and
beautiful plots of greensward. These are kept fresh by the "force-
pumps" belonging to every corporation. And some of the corporations
have beautiful flower gardens connected with the factories. One of the
overseers, with whom I am acquainted, gave me a beautiful boquet
the other morning, which was radiant with all the colors of the rainbow, and fragrant with the sweet perfume of many kinds of mints and
roses. He has a succession of beautiful blossoms from spring till "cold
weather." He told me that he could raise enough to bring him fifty
dollars if he chose to sell them; and this from a little bit of sand not
larger than our front yard, which you know is small for a country

house. But it is so full—here a few dollars have brought on a fresh soil, and "patience has done its perfect work." What might not be accomplished in the country with a little industry and taste.

But I have said enough of the outside of our mills—now for the inside. The rooms are high, very light, kept nicely whitewashed, and extremely neat; with many plants in the window seats, and white cotton curtains to the windows. The machinery is very handsomely made and painted, and is placed in regular rows; thus, in a large mill, presenting a beautiful and uniform appearance. I have sometimes stood at one end of a row of green looms, when the girls were gone from between them, and seen the lathes moving back and forth, the harnesses up and down, the white cloth winding over the rollers, through the long perspective; and I have thought it beautiful.

Then the girls dress so neatly, and are so pretty. The mill girls are the prettiest in the city. You wonder how they can keep neat. Why not? There are no restrictions as to the number of pieces to be washed in the boarding-house. And, as there is plenty of water in the mill, the girls can wash their laces and muslins and other nice things themselves, and no boarding woman ever refuses the conveniences for starching and ironing. You say too that you do not see how we can have so many conveniences and comforts at the price we pay for board. You must remember that the boarding-houses belong to the companies, and are let to the tenants far below the usual city rent— sometimes the rent is remitted. Then there are large families, so that there are the profits of many individuals. The country farmers are quite in the habit of bringing their produce to the boarding-houses for sale, thus reducing the price by the omission of the market-man's profit. So you see there are many ways by which we get along so well.

You ask me how the girls behave in the mill, and what are the punishments. They behave very well while about their work, and I have never heard of punishments, or scoldings, or anything of that sort. Sometimes an overseer finds fault, and sometimes offends a girl by refusing to let her stay out of the mill, or some deprivation like that; and then, perhaps, there are tears and pouts on her part, but, in general, the tone of intercourse between the girls and overseers is very good—pleasant, yet respectful. When the latter are fatherly sort of men the girls frequently resort to them for advice and assistance about other affairs than their work. Very seldom is this confidence abused;

but, among the thousands of overseers who have lived in Lowell, and the tens of thousands of girls who have in time been here, there are legends still told of wrong suffered and committed. "To err is human," and when the frailties of humanity are exhibited by a factory girl it is thought of for worse than are the errors of any other persons.

The only punishment among the girls is dismission from their places. They do not, as many think, withhold their wages; and as for corporal punishment—mercy on me! To strike a female would cost any overseer his place. If the superintendents did not take the affair into consideration the girls would turn out, as they did at the Temperance celebration, "Independent day;" and if they didn't look as pretty, I am sure they would produce as deep an impression.

By the way, I almost forgot to tell you that we had a "Fourth of July" in Lowell, and a nice one it was too. The Temperance celebration was the chief dish in the entertainment. The chief, did I say? It was almost the whole. It was the great turkey that Scroggs sent for Bob Cratchet's Christmas dinner. But, perhaps you don't read Dickens, so I will make no more "classical allusions." In the evening we had the Hutchinsons, from our own Granite State, who discoursed sweet music *so sweetly*. They have become great favorites with the public. It is not on account of their fine voices only, but their pleasant modest manners—the perfect sense of propriety which they exhibit in all their demeanor; and I think they are not less popular *here* because they sing the wrongs of the slave, and the praises of cold water.

But, dear Mary, I fear I have tired you with this long letter, and yet I have not answered half your questions. Do you wish to hear anything more about the overseers? Once for all, then, there are many very likely intelligent public-spirited men among them. They are interested in the good movements of the day; teachers in the Sabbath schools; and some have represented the city in the State Legislature. They usually marry among the factory girls, and do not connect themselves with their inferiors either. Indeed, in almost all the matches here the female is superior in education and manner, if not in intellect, to her partner.

The overseers have good salaries, and their families live very prettily. I observe that in almost all cases the mill girls make excellent wives. They are good managers, orderly in their households, and "neat as waxwork." It seems as though they were so delighted to have houses of their own to take care of, that they would never weary of the labor and the care.

The boarding women you ask about. They are usually widows or single women from the country; and many questions are always asked, and references required, before a house is given to a new applicant. It is true that mistakes are sometimes made, and *the wrong person gets into the pew*, but

> "Things like this you know must be,"
> Where'er there is a factory.

I see I have given you rhyme; it is not all quotation, nor *entirely original*.

I think it requires quite a complication of good qualities to make up a good boarding woman. "She looks well to the ways of her household," and must be even more than all that King Solomon describes in the last chapter of Proverbs. She not only in winter "riseth while it is yet night, and giveth meat to her household, a portion to her maidens," but she sitteth up far into the night, and seeth that her maidens are asleep, and that their lamps are gone out. Perhaps she doth not "consider a field to buy it," but she considereth every piece of meat, and bushel of potatoes, and barrel of flour, and load of wood, and box of soap, and every little thing, whether its quantity, quality, and price are what discretion would recommend her to purchase. "She is not afraid of the snow for her household," for she maketh them wear rubber overshoes, and thick cloaks and hoods, and seeth that the paths are broken out. "Her clothing is silk and purple," and she looketh neat and comely. It may be that her husband sitteth *not* "in the gates," for it is too often the case that he hath abandoned her, or loafeth in the streets. "She openeth her mouth with wisdom, and in her tongue is the law of kindness." Her maidens go to her for counsel and sympathy, if a decayed tooth begins to jump, or a lover proves faithless; and to keep twoscore young maidens in peace with themselves, each other, and her own self, is no slight task. The price of such a woman is, indeed, *above rubies*. "Give her of the fruit of her hands, and let her own works praise her."

I have now told you of mill girls, overseers and their wives, and boarding-housekeepers, and I feel that I have won forgiveness for neglecting you so long. You think that I have too high an opinion of our superintendents. I hope not. I do think that many of them are chosen as combining, in their characters, many excellent qualities. Some of them may be as selfish as you suppose. But we must remember that they owe a duty to their employers, as well as to those they employ. They are agents of the companies, as well as superintendents of us. Where those duties conflict I hope the sympathies of the man will always be with the more dependent party.

Country people are very suspicious. I do not think them perfect. A poet will look at a wood-cutter, and say "there is an honest man;" and as likely as not the middle of his load is rotten punk, and crooked sticks make many interstices, while all looks well without. A rustic butcher slays an animal that is dying of disease, and carries his meat to the market. The butcher and the woodman meet, and say all manner of harsh things against the "*grandees*" of the city, and quote such poetry as,

"GOD made the country—
Man made the town," &c.

It is true that with the same disposition for villany the man of influence must do the most harm. But, where there is most light, may there not be most true knowledge? And, even if there is no more principle, may there not be, with more cultivation of mind, a feeling of honor and of self-respect which may be of some benefit in its stead.

But I have written till I am fairly wearied. Good by.

Yours always,
Susan

(*Harriet Farley, Vol. IV, 1844, pp. 237–240*)

Letters from Susan

LETTER FOURTH

Dear Mary: You say that you wish to come to Lowell, and that some others of my old acquaintance wish to come, if I think it advisable; and, as I have but a few moments to write, I will devote all my letter to this subject.

There are girls here for every reason, and for no reason at all. I will speak to you of my acquaintances in the family here. One, who sits at my right hand at table, is in the factory because she hates her mother-in-law. She has a kind father, and an otherwise excellent home, but, as she and her mama agree about as well as cat and mouse, she has come to the factory. The one next her has a wealthy father, but, like many of our country farmers, he is very penurious, and he wishes his daughters to maintain themselves. The next is here because there is no better place for her, unless it is a Shaker settlement. The next has a "well-off" mother, but she is a very pious woman, and will not buy her daughter so many pretty gowns and collars and ribbons and other etceteras of "Vanity Fair" as she likes; so she concluded to "help herself." The next is here because her parents and family are wicked infidels, and she cannot be allowed to enjoy the privileges of religion at home. The next is here because she must labor somewhere, and she has been ill treated in so many families that she has a horror of domestic service. The next has left a good home because her lover, who has gone on a whaling voyage, wishes to be married when he returns, and she would like more money than her father will give her. The next is here because her home is in a lonesome country village, and she cannot bear to remain where it is so dull. The next is here because her parents are poor, and she wishes to acquire the means to educate herself. The next is here because her beau came, and she did not like to trust him alone among so many pretty girls. And so I might go on and give you the variety of reasons, but this is enough for the present.

I cannot advise you to come. You must act according to your own judgment. Your only reasons are a desire to see a new place, a city, and to be with me. You have now an excellent home, but, dear M., it may not seem the same to you after you have been here a year or two—for it is not advisable to come and learn a new occupation unless you can stay as long as that. The reasons are that you may become unaccustomed to your present routine of home duties, and lose your relish for them, and also for the very quiet pleasures of our little village. Many, who are dissatisfied here, have also acquired a dissatisfaction for their homes, so that they cannot be contented any where, and wish they had never seen Lowell.

But tell Hester that I advise her to come. She has always lived among relatives who have treated her as a slave, and yet they would not allow her to go away and be a slave in any other family. I think I can make her happier here, and I see no better way for her to do than to break all those ties at once, by leaving her cheerless drudgery and entering the mill.

I don't know what to say to Miriam, so many pleasant and unpleasant things are mingled in her lot now. There she lives with Widow Farrar, and every thing about them looks so nice and comfortable that people think she must be happy. The work is light, but every thing must be just as the old lady says, and she has strange vagaries at times. Miriam has to devote a great deal of time to her whims and fancies which is not spent in labor. Yet she would find it unpleasant to leave her nice large chamber, with its bureau and strip carpet and large closets, for the narrow accommodations of a factory boarding-house. And the fine great garden, in which she now takes so much pleasure, would be parted from with much sadness. But then her wages are so low that she says she can lay aside nothing and still dress herself suitably, for she is always expected to receive and help entertain the old lady's company. When the widow dies, Miriam will have nothing, unless she leaves her a legacy, which, on account of the many needy relatives, is not to be expected. So you had better tell her to make all arrangements for coming here, and then if the old lady will retain her by "raising her salary," tell her to stay with her.

As for Lydia I think she had better not come. I know how disagreeable her home is in many respects, but it is her home after all. She has to be up at four o'clock in the morning, and to be "on her feet," as she says, till nine o'clock at night, unless she sits down for an hour to patch the boys' clothes or keep her father's accounts. She has to be every body's waiter, and says that all seem to think she was born for that occupation. Then she has no accommodations but a little crowded attic, which she shares with old Jenny and three or four little ones, and she has told me that she never knew what it was to have a dollar of her own to spend as she might like. Yet there she is an important personage in the family, while here it would be quite different. She enjoys excellent health, and her varied employment appears to suit her. It might be very different here in that respect also. She has nothing of her own now, but she is sure of care and comforts in case of sickness, and necessaries always. When her father dies, or when she marries, she will probably have something of *her own*. "But," you will reply, "her father may live as long as she will, and she may never marry." True; but tell her to consider all things, and, before she decides to leave home, to request her father to pay her a stated sum as wages. If he will give her a dollar a week I should advise her to stay with him and her mother. Here she would have as many of the comforts and accommodations of life as there, but perhaps no more. She could dress better here, but not better compared with others. That is something to consider.

Nancy wishes also to come, because her trade does not suit her. If she is losing her health by a sedentary employment, I certainly advise her to change it. I think she could do well here, and then she has a voice like a nightingale. It would gain for her notice and perhaps emolument.

But I have hardly room to say good-by.

Yours, as ever,
Susan
(*Harriet Farley, Vol. IV, 1844, pp. 257–259*)

Pleasures of Factory Life

Pleasures, did you say? What! pleasures in *factory* life? From many scenes with which I have become acquainted, I should judge that the pleasures of factory life were like "Angels visits, few and far between"—said a lady whom fortune had placed above labor. [Indolence, or idleness, is not *above* labor, but *below* it.—EDS.] I could not endure such a constant clatter of machinery, that I could neither speak to be heard, nor think to be understood, even by myself. And then you have so little leisure—I could not bear such a life of fatigue. Call it by any other name rather than pleasure.

But stop, friend, we have some few things to offer here, and we are quite sure our views of the matter are just,—having been engaged as an operative the last four years. Pleasures there are, even in factory life; and we have many, known only to those of like employment. To be sure it is not so convenient to converse in the mills with those unaccustomed to them; yet we suffer no inconvenience among ourselves. But, aside from the talking, where can you find a more pleasant place for contemplation? There all the powers of the mind are made active by our animating exercise; and having but one kind of labor to perform, we need not give all our thoughts to that, but leave them measurably free for reflection on other matters.

The subjects for pleasurable contemplation, while attending to our work, are numerous and various. Many of them are immediately around us. For example: In the mill we see displays of the wonderful power of the mind. Who can closely examine all the movements of the complicated, curious machinery, and not be led to the reflection, that the mind is boundless, and is destined to rise higher and still higher; and that it can accomplish almost any thing on which it fixes its attention!

In the mills, we are not so far from God and nature, as many persons might suppose. We cultivate and enjoy much pleasure in cultivating flowers and plants. A large and beautiful variety of plants is placed around the walls of the rooms, giving them more the appearance of a flower garden than a workshop. It is there we inhale the sweet perfume of the rose, the lily, and geranium; and, with them, send the sweet incense of sincere gratitude to the bountiful Giver of these rich blessings. And who can live with such a rich and pleasant source of instruction opened to him, and not be wiser and better, and consequently more happy.

Another great source of pleasure is, that by becoming operatives, we are often enabled to assist aged parents who have become too infirm to provide for themselves; or perhaps to educate some orphan brother or sister, and fit them for future usefulness. And is there no pleasure in all this? no pleasure in relieving the distressed and removing their heavy burdens? And is there no pleasure in rendering ourselves by such acts worthy the confidence and respect of those with whom we are associated?

Another source is found in the fact of our being acquainted with some person or persons that reside in almost every part of the country. And through these we become familiar with some incidents that interest and amuse us wherever we journey; and cause us to feel a greater interest in the scenery, inasmuch as there are gathered pleasant associations about every town, and almost every house and tree that may meet our view.

Let no one suppose that the "factory girls" are without guardian. We are placed in the care of overseers who feel under moral obligations to look after our interests; and, if we are sick, to acquaint themselves with our situation and wants; and, if need be, to remove us to the Hospital, where we are sure to have the best attendance, provided by the benevolence of our Agents and Superintendents.

In Lowell, we enjoy abundant means of information, especially in the way of public lectures. The time of lecturing is appointed to suit the convenience of the operatives; and sad indeed would be the picture of our Lyceums, Institutes, and scientific Lecture rooms, if all the operatives should absent themselves.

And last, though not least, is the pleasure of being associated with the institutions of religion, and thereby availing ourselves of the Library, Bible Class, Sabbath School, and all other means of religious instruction. Most of us, when at home, live in the country, and therefore cannot enjoy these privileges to the same extent; and many of us not at all. And surely we ought to regard these as sources of pleasure.

S. G. B.

(Sarah G. Bagley, Series I, 1840, pp. 25–26)

We have taken the liberty to change several sentences in the preceding article, and to transpose two of the paragraphs. The hints of the writer might be amplified in a series of illustrations. Who will undertake it? Eds.

Plants and Flowers in the Mills

In the article entitled "Pleasures of Factory Life," mention is made of the cultivation of Flowers in the Mills.

We have been greatly pleased with the taste and care displayed in the introduction and culture of plants and flowers, on all the Corporations. These children of nature, whether growing wild or receiving the fostering attention of man, are "apt to teach;" and the lessons they inculcate are of the purest and most pleasing character. And it is highly gratifying to see them exalted to companionship in the sitting-room and parlor, when they most need shelter from the blighting frost. It is especially gratifying to behold them thriving beneath the kindly care of the female operatives in our factories. In the dressing-room of No. 3 on the Boott Corporation, we counted over 200 pots of plants and flowers! This is probably the largest number congregated in any apartment in the city; and some rooms, in consequence of an entirely northern exposure, or inconvenience in other respects, are without any: nevertheless a larger or smaller collection may be found in the apartments generally.

The Superintendents manifest a lively interest in this matter; and some of them have furnished large numbers of plants and flowers, with instructions to the Overseers to furnish every facility to the girls for the cultivation thereof; and several proprietors have displayed commendable liberality in sending floral contributions, in rich variety, to ornament the mills.

A few suggestions may not be considered out of place. We design them for every manufacturing district.

1. Proprietors, owners of stock, and others, would confer a favor on the factory population, and indirectly benefit themselves, by sending a few pots of plants and flowers to the mills. Let every room be generously supplied. The expense and trouble would be trifling.

2. Persons employed in the mills usually visit their kindred at least once in a year. On these occasions, let them select a few fine cuttings or roots; and when they return to their stations, mention the fact to an Overseer. Pots or boxes would, without doubt, be furnished to any reasonable extent at the expense of the Corporation.

3. Let the flowers and plants be carefully attended to. Lessons of wisdom, purity, and holy trust, will thence be derived. And when you look on such as you brought from "home," remember the love of your kindred and the joys of your childhood; and haply your thoughts will be in harmony with the teachings of flowers as "the alphabet of angels."

(From the Editorial Corner in Series I, No. 2, 1840, p. 32)

Tales of Factory Life, No. 1

Sarah T. was scarcely twelve years old, when her parents removed to New England. Her education had been neglected, not on account of her inability to learn, but because her parents had been unfortunate, and had not means to educate their large family. Her mother had given her the first rudiments of learning, and many valuable lessons of domestic economy. Her father's health had far declined, and his days were soon numbered, leaving a widow and seven orphan children. Mrs. T.'s grief was nearly overwhelming. The reflection that she was left among strangers, without the means of returning to her friends, to her was truly gloomy. After a short period, she found it was necessary to adopt some plan for the support of her children. She solicited advice from some of the few who had interested themselves in her behalf, and it was soon decided that Sarah and a brother still younger should "live out." Accordingly, a place was provided for Sarah with a Mrs. J., who kept what is termed a genteel boarding house in the city, about five miles distant.

Mrs. J. was much pleased with Sarah's activity and readiness to obey, and used every means (except the right ones) to retain her services. She was often treated with much severity, and sometimes cruelty. She had a proud spirit, and could not well endure the mortification of hearing the daughter of Mrs. J. inquire why she was so meanly clad, and did not attend school to study French and Music. She determined to leave the service of Mrs. J., and find employment where she could procure the means of educating and clothing herself.

She had been in the service of Mrs. J. about two years, when the daughter of Mrs. J. commenced an attack upon Sarah about her being so ignorant; and Sarah very frankly told her, that she possessed the means of educating herself, and would employ them very soon to that end. Mrs. J. overheard the conversation, and was highly displeased with the resolution Sarah had formed, and gave her many harsh words, calling her a poor little beggar, &c. The proud spirit of Sarah could endure such treatment no longer. She determined to leave, and that night made preparation to depart.

Early next morning, Sarah took leave, without stopping to bid the family "good bye." When the sun arose, she was about three miles from the affectionate Mrs. J. She arrived at home in season to breakfast with her mother and other friends. After breakfast, her mother made inquires, about her unexpected appearance. She very frankly replied, "I have run away from Mrs. J., and I will tell you all"— which she did. Mrs. J. soon made her appearance, and wished Sarah to return with her. Sarah wept bitterly, and told her mother she would not stay with her, she was so unkind, and made her work so hard, and would not send her to school, nor give her clothes suitable for attending church.

As they were returning, Mrs. J. inquired, "What would have become of you, if I had not had the kindness to take you home with me?" Sarah replied, with great simplicity, "I had determined to go to Lowell, and work in the factory." "Well, if you are mean enough in your own opinion, to be a factory girl, I may as well despair of thinking to make any thing of you, first as last—for it will be of no use to try." "But," said Sarah, "I know of more than one girl who has worked in the factory, who is much better than I ever expect to be, if I stay with you as long as I live—if I should judge by the past."

The first business of Mrs. J. after their return, was to employ the usual remedies for the removal of the "Lowell fever" as she termed it, with which Sarah had been attacked. The preventives were cheap, and at hand: for every one possessed them who had read the news of the day. She did not tire in the application, and often gave them effect by a box on the ear. Notwithstanding all her caution, the fever raged within, and fears were entertained that it would *take her off;* and their fears were not groundless.

One morning, Mrs. J. arose at her usual time, thinking all was well; and the fire was not kindled, nor any one to be seen about the kitchen. She was in a great rage, and opened the door at the back stairs, and, with her usual emphasis on such occasions, exclaimed, "Sarah, come down here this minute. I thought the coffee was boiling before this time; but instead of this, not even a fire is kindled. I would not give a fig for such help; it is just no help at all"—(closing the door with a vengeance, and talking to herself). "There is no dependence to be put in any one. I thought if I took her when she was so young, I could prevent her being crazy to get into the factory; but there is no such thing now-a-days. I wish from my heart there was not a factory this side of France. I'll see if you won't come down." She entered the chamber at full speed, and behold! Sarah was among the missing. We will leave the old lady to make her own coffee, and enquire after Sarah's sudden disappearance.

She prepared her bundle the night previously, and at dawn of day commenced a journey of thirty miles, on foot, without a cent in her purse. She walked with rapid haste the first three miles, and began to feel somewhat weary. As she was ascending a hill, she discovered a stage-coach behind her, and wept that she had not money to procure her passage. Well, she knew that she could not walk so great a distance in one day; and she could not imagine where she might be obliged to stay through the night—for, thought she, "no one would keep such a looking child as I am."

The stage-man, with a kindness peculiar to those of like calling, interrogated Sarah, with "Good morning, my little friend: how far are you walking?" She looked up with the big tears fast falling, and replied, "As far as Lowell, sir." "To Lowell! walk to Lowell! it is near thirty miles. It will take you a week. You may ride with me if you will." "But I have no money," said Sarah. "I want none," replied her kind friend; "I will carry you without pay; for I contend, with the old maxim, that 'we should not kill those that try to live,' and surely you are making a strong effort."

He stepped down to open the stage door, and Sarah told him she was afraid the passengers would object to riding with her, on account of her singular appearance. She was not a lady, with the usual paraphrenalia of travelling; but only a bare-footed girl, with a small bundle.

The passengers were interested in her behalf, and took the trouble to enquire the cause of her unusual appearance. She gave them a full and satisfactory history of herself and family, and the woman whose service she had left. They made a collection for her benefit, and one of the passengers, a factory girl, took the trouble to purchase a pair of shoes, hose and other necessary articles, at their first stopping-place. When she arrived at Lowell, they enquired where she would stop. She told them, at any good boarding-house—as she had no acquaintance. Her friend, the factory girl, invited her to stay with her; which invitation she unhesitatingly accepted.

The next day, she went into the mill with her friend, who procured a place for her, much to her satisfaction. She commenced work the day following, and felt a new motive to action; for, thought she, "I shall be paid for what I do now."

Nothing worthy of notice occurred during the first six months. She worked every day, and spent her evenings in reading and writing. She wrote to her mother to send her younger sister; and they are still seen going to and from work together.

Sarah has studied and faithfully learned the lessons of usefulness and practical benevolence. In my last interview with her, she expressed a sort of pride in saying, that although she had been a runaway beggar, she had been more fortunate than many within the circle of her acquaintance; and though there may be difficulties, yet a little perseverance will overcome them. I went, by her invitation, to the Savings Bank, and learned that she had deposited four hundred dollars, since the commencement of 1838.

S.G.B.

(Sarah G. Bagley, Vol. I, 1841, pp. 65–68)

Tales of Factory Life, No. 2

THE ORPHAN SISTERS

Catherine B. was the eldest of three sisters. Actual misfortune placed her parents in such an embarrassed state of affairs, as to make it necessary for Catherine and a younger sister to support themselves at an early age. They had learned the pecuniary advantages of factory life, from some of their young friends who had returned from a neighboring village, where they had been employed in a cotton mill. They earnestly requested the leave of their parents to go to Lowell to seek their fortune, as they termed such an adventure. After some deliberation, they gave their consent, but not without much solicitude for their safety.

The evening previously to their departure, the family met around the altar of devotion, where, with the faltering voice of emotion, the benediction of Heaven was invoked in behalf of the sisters, who were about to leave the paternal home for a residence among strangers.

The next morning, the sisters left their much-loved home, to obtain a livelihood—and as they cast a wishful eye upon the friends they had left, a sadness stole unconsciously over their buoyant spirits, unknown to them before.

They arrived at their place of destination, and were successful in finding employment. But what a great contrast from the quiet country-home in the neighborhood of the White Mountains, was the City of Spindles, to the sisters! They had been accustomed to listen only to

"Nature's wild, unconscious song,
O'er thousand hills that floats along."—

But here was confusion in all its forms; and truly, said Catherine, "I should like to find myself alone for a brief space, that I might hold communion with my own heart undisturbed."

Time soon rendered these scenes less annoying; and soon were our young friends able to fix their attention upon any subject within their range of thought, with the multitude around them.

Nothing of much importance occurred during their first year's stay in Lowell; only they wrote often to their friends, and received letters from them often in return, abounding in such advice as their friends thought might be useful to them, under the circumstances in which they were placed. They were requested to return in one year from the time they left, and visit their friends, and had made their arrangements to be absent a few weeks, when a message was received from their mother for them to return as soon as possible, as their father was dangerously ill.

Next morning they started, and arrived the day following. Their mother met them at the door, with the sad intelligence that their father could survive but a few hours at most. He was very weak, and could only give them a few words of advice; and then bade them a long farewell.

Their mother was nearly exhausted with fatigue; and constant watching had rendered her health very low. She was attacked by a like disease, and survived their father but a few weeks. The same grave opened to receive her, that had been prepared for their father, and these sisters were truly orphans.

Could this sad tale of suffering end here, the deep feelings of sympathy might be spared the reader, in a good measure; but there are other scenes too interesting to leave without notice.—A little brother and sister are here, and what shall be done with *them?* Catherine was to take charge of them, by special request from her mother, in her last moments. But how to provide for them a home, was what most troubled her. The advice of friends was cheap: every one would bestow it gratuitously—and there were as many opinions as persons. Some gave it as their opinion, that it might be proper to throw them on the public charity; but to this, Catherine replied, with her usual decision—"Give them into the care of strangers! No. I will work till I die, before I will consent to such a course. If any one must suffer privation, let it fall on me, and not on these children, who have not yet learned that the cup of human existence is mixed with bitterness and sorrow."

After having heard various opinions, they thought proper to ask advice of one who had manifested much kindness in their time of trouble—and he gave it as his opinion, that it would be well to board their little brother in a good family in the neighborhood, and take their sister with them to Lowell—to which they consented. The little furniture, and what else that remained, was disposed of, to settle some trifling debts that would unavoidably be contracted under the circumstances in which they were placed; and only a few things were reserved by them as a memorial of the past. And as they gave the last fond farewell to the home of their earliest years, how sad and dejected were the once buoyant spirits of the sisters!

A kind neighbor bade them welcome to his house as their home during their short stay, and assisted them in arranging their affairs, by procuring a boarding-place for their brother, and rendering them such other assistance as they needed. The evening previously to their departure, Catherine went to the place sacred to memory, where lay the slumbering dust of all that we claim as friends, under all circumstances. It was a lone, dreary spot. Nought but the plaintive notes of the whippoorwill, and the waving branches of the willow, were heard to break the silence of evening. She sat down upon a stone, near the quiet resting place of those loved friends, and gave full vent to the sorrowful emotions of her heart. She felt that there is a power to soothe in holding communion with the dead; and most fervently did she pray, that she might be strengthened to fulfil the duties of a mother to those little ones, who had been left in her care by the death of her parents.

Next day, the sisters started again for Lowell; but not with the same thoughts and feelings as when they left before. They left now with the gloomy reflection that they had no home—no friends on whom they could rely, if sick or unfortunate; and in their care was a little sister; and a brother still younger, whose board they were under obligation to pay, they had left behind.

They arrived safely in Lowell, and with heavy hearts; for they thought it would be difficult for them to procure board for a child so young. They consulted a lady of their acquaintance, who very kindly offered to board her; and look after her, during their absence in the mill. And if he that giveth a cup of cold water shall in no wise lose his reward, how abundant is the satisfaction of that kind-hearted woman, in having contributed so much to relieve the heavy burdens of those orphan sisters!

Heaven smiled upon their efforts, and good health and prosperity have attended them; but no one can suppose, for a moment, that they have not possessed a self-sacrificing spirit.

The little sister was kept at school, until she was old enough to earn her living, with a little assistance; and then she was sent into the country, to reside with a friend, and go to school a part of the time. The little brother is able to earn his living six months in the year, and the sisters furnish means to keep him at school the remainder.

But let no one suppose that the care of these children has diminished the real happiness of the sisters—for they assured me it was a rich source of pleasure to review the past, and call to mind the many times when they were obliged to spend all but a few shillings, in providing for those little ones. "And," said Catherine, "it has taught me lessons of practical benevolence; for I have seen the time when it would cost an effort to give half a dollar, be its object ever so praiseworthy."

The sisters have of late been able to lay by a small sum for themselves—thereby evincing the utility of perseverance in well-doing; and though it may seem to many that their lot has been a hard one, still they are blest with sunshine and flowers; and when next you see Catherine's name, it shall be in the list of marriages.   S.G.B.

(Sarah G. Bagley, Vol. I, 1841, pp. 263–266)

Editorial

HOME IN A BOARDING-HOUSE

Home in a boarding-house is always different from home anywhere else; and home in a factory boarding-house, differs materially from home in any other. This difference is perceptible at the first entrance. There is a peculiarity "all its own," in the great domicil, which usually shelters us. One might readily see by its accommodations, or rather its "fixings," (we beg pardon of Dickens) for they are not always acknowledged as accommodations, by the party most directly concerned, that it cannot be exactly a home, but only a place to eat and lodge in, a sort of rendezvous, after the real home, the daily habitation, is abandoned. This is tacitly acknowledged, by the cognomen of the room, which is the only one common to all the boarders. This is the dining-room—or, more properly, the eating-room, for breakfast and supper, as well as dinner, are demolished in its precincts. This is always amply furnished with chairs and tables, though but little of anything else, for, amidst all our deprivations, we have never been deprived of the privilege of sitting at our meals. Chairs, chairs—one, two, three, four, and so on to forty. It is really refreshing, sometimes, to go where there is only now and then a chair. This pleasure we can usually enjoy, by leaving the dining-room for our chambers, where there is not often a surplus of this article of furniture; but then there are always plenty of trunks, boxes, &c., which will answer for seats, and the bed is easily persuaded to stand proxy for a sofa.

But these are all trifles, compared with the perplexities to which we are subjected in other ways; and some of these might be remedied by the girls themselves. We now allude to the importunities of evening visitors, such as pedlers, candy and newspaper boys, shoe-dealers, book-sellers, &c., &c., breaking in upon the only hours of leisure we can call our own, and proffering their articles with a pertinacity which will admit of no denial. That these evening salesmen are always unwelcome, we will not assert, but they are too often inclined to remain where they know they are considered a nuisance. And then they often forget, if they ever knew, the rules of politeness which should regulate all transient visitors. They deal about their hints, inuendoes, and low cunning, as though a factory boarding-house was what no boarding-house should ever be.

The remedy is entirely with the girls. Treat all of these comers with a politeness truly lady-like, when they appear as gentlemen, but let your manners change to stern formality when they forget that they are in the company of respectable females.

Never encourage evening traders, unless you see some very good reason for so doing. The reason usually given is, that they can trade cheaper with these men, than with the storekeepers of Lowell. There is competition enough among the shopkeepers to keep things at a reasonable price, and *good* articles are seldom purchased cheaper of a pedler. "But," say others, "it is much more convenient for us, if we can be suited at home, to have our things brought us, than to go out for them." Even where this is true, it should be remembered that each buyer is interrupting the occupations of one, two, or three dozen girls.

But it is not wholly by traders that we are imposed upon. Sometimes an impudent charlatan, calling himelf a practical phrenologist, intrudes upon us with the assurance that he can tell us what we are, even better than we know ourselves. And as far as they have any actual knowledge, or a tolerable Yankee faculty of guessing, they abuse it, to pander to the vanity of those who are ready to believe they are possessed of every virtue and talent under the sun, because the *phrenologist* tells them so. . . .

(Author unknown, Vol. III, 1842, pp. 69–70)

A Week in the Mill

Much has been said of the factory girl and her employment. By some she has been represented as dwelling in a sort of brick-and-mortar paradise, having little to occupy thought save the weaving of gay and romantic fancies, while the spindle or the wheel flies obediently beneath her glance. Others have deemed her a mere servile drudge, chained to her labor by almost as strong a power as that which holds a bondman in his fetters; and, indeed, some have already given her the title of *"the white slave of the North."* Her real situation approaches neither one nor the other of these extremes. Her occupation is as laborious as that of almost any female who earns her own living, while it has also its sunny spots and its cheerful intervals, which make her hard labor seem comparatively pleasant and easy.

Look at her as she commences her weekly task. The rest of the sabbath has made her heart and her step light, and she is early at her accustomed place, awaiting the starting of the machinery. Every thing having been cleaned and neatly arranged on the Saturday night, she has less to occupy her on Monday than on other days; and you may see her leaning from the window to watch the glitter of the sunrise on the water, or looking away at the distant forests and fields, while memory wanders to her beloved country home; or, it may be that she is conversing with a sister-laborer near; returning at regular intervals to see that her work is in order.

Soon the breakfast bell rings; in a moment the whirling wheels are stopped, and she hastens to join the throng which is pouring through the open gate. At the table she mingles with a various group. Each despatches the meal hurriedly, though not often in silence; and if, as is sometimes the case, the rules of politeness are not punctiliously observed by all, the excuse of some lively country girl would be, "They don't give us time for *manners.*"

The short half-hour is soon over; the bell rings again; and now our factory girl feels that she has commenced her day's work in earnest. The time is often apt to drag heavily till the dinner hour arrives. Perhaps some part of the work becomes deranged and stops; the constant friction causes a belt of leather to burst into a flame; a stranger visits the room, and scans the features and dress of its inmates inquiringly; and there is little else to break the monotony. The afternoon passes in much the same manner. Now and then she mingles with a knot of busy talkers who have collected to discuss some new occurrence, or holds pleasant converse with some intelligent and agreeable friend, whose acquaintance she has formed since her factory life commenced; but much of the time she is left to her own thoughts. While at her work, the clattering and rumbling around her prevent any other noise from attracting her attention, and she *must think*, or her life would be dull indeed.

Thus the day passes on, and evening comes; the time which she feels to be exclusively her own. How much is done in the three short hours from seven to ten o'clock. She has a new dress to finish; a call to make on some distant corporation; a meeting to attend; there is a lecture or a concert at some one of the public halls, and the attendance will be thin if she and her associates are not present; or, if nothing more imperative demands her time, she takes a stroll through the street or to the river with some of her mates, or sits down at home to peruse a new book. At ten o'clock all is still for the night.

The clang of the early bell awakes her to another day, very nearly the counterpart of the one which preceded it. And so the week rolls on, in the same routine, till Saturday comes. Saturday! the welcome sound! She busies herself to remove every particle of cotton and dust from her frame or looms, cheering herself meanwhile with sweet thoughts of the coming sabbath; and when, at an earlier hour than usual, the mill is stopped, it looks almost beautiful in its neatness.

Then approaches the sabbath—the day of rest! If the factory girl keeps it well, it must be at church; for there are some in every boarding-house who find an excuse for staying at home half the day at least. One of her room-mates is indisposed; another says she *must* write a letter to her friends; another has to work so hard during the week that she thinks she *ought* to make this *literally* a "day of rest," so that retirement and meditation are out of the question. But in the sabbath school and sanctuary her time is well spent. No one is more constant at church, or earlier in her seat, than the operative who has been trained to know the value of the institution of the gospel. The instructions which she receives sink deep into her heart, giving her a fund of thought for the coming week. Her pastor and her sabbath school teacher are felt to be her best friends; and their kindness is a strong allurement to her spirit, often keeping her long from her less-favored home. If it is said that many a one has here found a grave, shall it not also be said that many a one has here found the path to Heaven?

The writer is aware that this sketch is an imperfect one. Yet there is very little variety in an operative's life, and little difference between it and any other life of labor. It lies

"half in sunlight—half in shade."

Few would wish to spend a whole life in a factory, and few are discontented who do thus seek a subsistence for a term of months or years.

(Author unknown, Vol. V, 1845, pp. 217–218)

A Second Peep at Factory Life

There is an old saying, that "When we are with the Romans, we must do as the Romans do." And now, kind friend, as we are about to renew our walk, I beg that you will give heed to it, and do as factory girls do. After this preliminary, we will proceed to the factory.

There is the "counting-room," a long, low, brick building, and opposite is the "store-house," built of the same material, after the same model. Between them, swings the ponderous gate that shuts the mills in from the world without. But, stop; we must get "a pass," ere we go through, or "the watchman will be after us." Having obtained this, we will stop on the slight elevation by the gate, and view the mills. The one to the left rears high its huge sides of brick and mortar, and the belfry, towering far above the rest, stands out in bold relief against the rosy sky. The almost innumerable windows glitter, like gems, in the morning sunlight. It is six and a half stories high, and, like the fabled monster of old, who guarded the sacred waters of Mars, it seems to guard its less aspiring sister to the right; that is five and a half stories high, and to it is attached the repair-shop. If you please, we will pass to the larger factory,—but be careful, or you will get lost in the mud, for this yard is not laid out in such beautiful order, as some of the factory yards are, nor can it be.

We will just look into the first room. It is used for cleaning cloth. You see the scrubbing and scouring machines are in full operation, and gigging and fulling are going on in full perfection. As it is very damp, and the labor is performed by the other half of creation, we will pass on, for fear of incurring their jealousy. But the very appearance might indicate that there are, occasionally, *fogs* and *clouds;* and not only fogs and clouds, but sometimes plentiful showers. In the second room the cloth is "*finished,*" going through the various operations of burling, shearing, brushing, inking, fine-drawing, pressing, and packing for market. This is the pleasantest room on the corporation, and consequently they are never in want of help. The shearing, brushing, pressing and packing is done by males, while the burling, inking, marking and fine-drawing is performed by females. We will pass to the third room, called the "cassimere weaving-room," where all kinds of cloths are woven, from plain to the most exquisite fancy. There are between eighty and ninety looms, and part of the dressing is also done here. The fourth is the "broad weaving-room," and contains between thirty and forty looms; and broad sure enough they are. Just see how lazily the lathe drags backward and forward, and the shuttle—how spitefully it hops from one end of it to the other. But we must not stop longer, or perchance it will hop at us. You look weary; but, never mind! there was an end to Jacob's ladder, and *so* there is a termination to these stairs. Now if you please we will go up to the next room, where the spinning is done. Here we have spinning jacks or jennies that dance merrily along whizzing and singing, as they spin out their "long yarns," and it seems but pleasure to watch their movements; but it is hard work, and requires good health and much strength. Do not go too near, as we shall find that they do not understand the established rules of *etiquette,* and might unceremoniously knock us over. We must not stop here longer, for it is twelve o'clock, and we have the "carding-room" to visit before dinner. There are between twenty and thirty set of cards located closely together, and I beg of you to be careful as we go amongst them, or you will get caught in the machinery. You walk as though you were afraid of getting blue. Please excuse me, if I ask you not to be afraid. 'Tis a wholesome color, and soap and water will wash it off. The girls, you see, are partially guarded against it, by over-skirts and sleeves; but as it is not *fashionable* to wear masks, they cannot keep it from their faces. You appear surprised at the hurry and bustle now going on in the room, but your attention has been so engaged that you have forgotten the hour. Just look at the clock, and you will find that it wants but

Woman winding shuttle bobbins, after a drawing by Winslow Homer in W. C. Bryant's Song of the Sower, *1871. Merrimack Valley Textile Museum.*

five minutes to "bell time." We will go to the door, and be ready to start when the others do; and now, while we are waiting, just cast your eyes to the stair-way, and you will see another flight of stairs, leading to another spinning-room; a picker is located somewhere in that region, but I cannot give you a description of it, as I have never had the courage to ascend more than five flight of stairs at a time. And—but the bell rings.

Now look out—not for the engine—but for the rush to the stair-way. O mercy! what a crowd. I do not wonder you gasp for breath; but, keep up courage; we shall soon be on terra firma again. Now, safely landed, I hope to be excused for taking you into such a crowd. Really, it would not be fair to let you see the factory girls and machinery for nothing. I shall be obliged to hurry you, as it is some way to the boarding-house, and we have but thirty minutes from the time the bell begins to ring till it is done ringing again; and then all are required to be at their work. There is a group of girls yonder, going our way; let us overtake them, and hear what they are talking about. Something unpleasant I dare say, from their earnest gestures and clouded brows.

"Well, I do think it is too bad," exclaims one.

"So do I," says another. "This cutting down wages *is not* what they cry it up to be. I wonder how they'd like to work as hard as we do, digging and drudging day after day, from morning till night, and then, every two or three years, have their wages reduced. I rather guess it wouldn't set very well."

"And, besides this, who ever heard, of such a thing as their being raised again," says the first speaker. "I confess that I never did, so long as I've worked in the mill, and that's been these ten years."

"Well, it is real provoking any how," returned the other, "for my part I should think they had made a clean sweep this time. I wonder what they'll do next."

"Listeners never hear any good of themselves" is a trite saying, and, for fear it may prove true in our case, we will leave this busy group, and get some dinner. There is an open door inviting us to enter. We will do so. You can hang your bonnet and shawl on one of those hooks, that extend the length of the entry for that purpose, or you can lay them on the banisters, as some do. Please to walk into the dining-room. Here are two large square tables, covered with checked clothes and loaded down with smoking viands, the odor of which is very inviting. But we will not stop here; there is the long table in the front room, at which ten or fifteen can be comfortably seated. You may place yourself at the head. Now do not be bashful or wait to be helped, but comply with the oft-made request, "help yourself" to whatever you like best; for you have but a few minutes allotted you to spend at the table. The reason why, is because you are a rational, intelligent, thinking being, and ought to know enough to swallow your food whole; whereas a horse or an ox, or any other dumb beast knows no better than to spend an hour in the *useless* process of mastication. The bell rings again, and the girls are hurrying to the mills; you, I suppose, have seen enough of them for one day, so we will walk up stairs and have a *tete-a-tete*.

You ask, if there are so many things objectionable, why we work in the mill. Well, simply for this reason,—every situation in life, has its trials which must be borne, and factory life has no more than any other. There are many things we do not like; many occurrences that send the warm blood mantling to the cheek when they must be borne in silence, and many harsh words and acts that are not called for. There are objections also to the number of hours we work, to the length of time allotted to our meals, and to the low wages allowed for labor; objections that must and will be answered; for the time has come when something, besides the clothing and feeding of the body is to be thought of; when the mind is to be clothed and fed; and this cannot be as it should be, with the present system of labor. Who, let me ask, can find that pleasure in life which they should, when it is spent in this way. Without time for the laborer's own work, and the improvement of the mind, save the few evening hours; and even then if the mind is enriched and stored with useful knowledge, it must be at the expense of health. And the feeling too, that comes over us (there is no use in denying it) when we hear the bell calling us away from repose that tired nature loudly claims—the feeling, that we are *obliged to go*. And these few hours, of which we have spoken, are far too short, three at the most at the close of day. Surely, methinks, every heart that lays claim to humanity will feel 'tis not enough. But this, we hope will, ere long, be done away with, and labor made what it should be; pleasant and inviting to every son and daughter of the human family.

There is a brighter side to this picture, over which we would not willingly pass without notice, and an answer to the question, why we work here? The time we *do* have is our own. The money we earn comes promptly; more so than in any other situation; and our work, though laborious is the same from day to day; we know what it is, and when finished we feel perfectly free, till it is time to commence it again.

Besides this, there are many pleasant associations connected with factory life, that are not to be found elsewhere.

There are lectures, evening schools and libraries, to which all may have access. The one thing needful here, is the time to improve them as we ought.

There is a class, of whom I would speak, that work in the mills, and will while they continue in operation. Namely, the many who have no home, and who come here to seek, in this busy, bustling "City of Spindles," a competency that shall enable them in after life, to live without being a burden to society,—the many who toil on, without a murmur, for the support of an aged mother or orphaned brother and sister. For the sake of them, we earnestly hope labor may be reformed; that the miserable, selfish spirit of competition, now in our midst, may be thrust from us and consigned to eternal oblivion.

There is one other thing that must be mentioned ere we part, that is the practice of sending agents through the country to decoy girls away from their homes with the promise of high wages, when the market is already stocked to overflowing. This is certainly wrong, for it lessens the value of labor, which should be ever held in high estimation, as the path marked out by the right hand of GOD, in which man should walk with dignity.

And now, kind friend, we must part. I beg pardon for intruding so long upon your time and patience, and also for not introducing you to Dorcas Hardscrabble. I feared I should weary you, and besides, many hardscrabbling Dorcases may be found among the factory girls.

One word for what has been said. It has been uttered for *truth's* sake, and because called for. If it does not answer your expectations, a companion must be sought, that will please the fancy better.

J. L. B.
(*Josephine L. Baker, Vol. V, 1845, pp. 97–100*)

The Affections Illustrated in Factory Life

NO. I—THE SISTER

One pleasant summer evening, the girls at No. 20 were grouped in the doorway, to view a beautiful sunset sky. There are few evenings in the year when their hours of labor permit them this privilege, excepting upon the Sabbath, and those evenings are not always favorable to a glorious exhibition of the exit of the King of Day. They gazed upon him now, sinking lower and lower, "trailing clouds of glory," and, when he was gone, they turned away with the feeling, that this had been a happier and *longer* day than they had known for weeks. "The days and nights are as long as ever," is a common saying; but is it always true? Is not the brilliant summer day, which gives the laborer time to enjoy a rising sun before commencing his daily task, and to look upon its setting glories, as a brilliant closing scene to a wearisome drama, and which is followed by a long pleasant dreamy twilight—is not a day like this longer than that of a dark dull dreary desolate winter month, eked out at either end by the yellow stifling light of lamps, and demanding for the body a longer time for repose?

The girls in that doorway would have answered *yes*, and they turned away with the feeling that one pleasant incident is more of a day than hours of monotonous toil. Two of them still lingered, and throwing on a couple of bonnets and shawls, which hung near the door, they prepared for a walk by the river, in whose roseate depths the shadows of clouds and rocks and trees were transfixed, as if it were all one brilliant specimen of mosaic. Ere they left the house the stage stopped, and, leaving one female passenger and her trunk, wheeled rapidly away.

The new comer was a slight delicate-looking girl, apparently about sixteen years of age. With a faltering voice she inquired for the mistress of the house, and the girls kindly shew her into the sitting-room, and called Mrs. Matthews. Mrs. Matthews soon made her appearance, and the girls went out to the river.

"Can I be accommodated here with board, if I succeed in obtaining a place to work?" said the stranger, with a redder cheek and glistening eye.

"Why, let me see!" said Mrs. M., giving the plate, which she held in her hand, an extra wipe, with a coarse brown towel; "let me see, child: there's Hitty and Angeline, and their two cousins, in the lower front; and the four Graves girls in the upper front; and the bed-rooms are full; and the lower back is stuffed with down-easters, and so are the attics; but there is one place in the upper back, if you will sleep with a Scotch girl in the trundle-bed. May be you wouldn't like to do that, though it's as good a bed, and as good a girl, as any in the house."

"I have no objections to my bed-fellow being a Scotch girl, or to my bed being a trundle-bed, if those are the only difficulties," replied the new boarder; who then gave her name as Hannah Felton, and requested to be shown to her room.

"If this is your trunk, in the entry, wont you just take hold of one end of it, and I will help you take it up stairs; and then it will be out of the way," said Mrs. Matthews.

Hannah took hold of one handle, but she was weary and dispirited, and let it drop before she reached the stairs. Mrs. Matthews took hold of both, and carried the trunk up two flights of stairs.

"The Stillman girls are gone to meeting, but here is Ellen Campbell; may be you can talk with her; and I will get you some tea in less than five minutes;" and she left Hannah with Ellen, who shew her where to put her trunk, and made a place in the closet for her bonnet and shawl.

Hannah could easily understand Ellen, though her accent was strongly Scotch; and there was nothing in her looks to distinguish her from a Yankee girl. In less than five minutes a little bell tinkled in the passage, and Ellen told her that her supper was ready. Hannah soon found her way into the dining room, and sat down to take some much-needed refreshment. Mrs. Matthews had not troubled herself to replace the table-cloth, but, upon the usual oil-cloth cover, were huddled together the remnants of some hot cakes and custards, butter and cheese, a bowl of preserves, and some cold tea, with milk, but no sugar. The traveller's hunger was soon appeased, and Hannah felt no disposition to prolong her visit to the tea-table.

"You can sit here by the window, and I will get you the rocking-chair," said Mrs. M., who had been waiting to clear the table.

"She is a kind woman, after all," said Hannah to herself, as she sat down in the nicely cushioned chair; and she was correct.

There was a deep vein of the kindest feeling in Mrs. Matthews's heart; though, above it, there was a slight crust of asperity, which was misconstrued by those who did not consider how much of it was the effects of vexation and toil. With a large family of boarders to take care of, and no one to assist her, but a lame and stupid sister-in-law, it was not strange that she often fretted, and, at times, seemed harsh and unreasonable.

There is much in our condition to affect our tempers for better or worse; and those, whose lines have always been in pleasant places, should have much charity for the less-favored ones, who have been always exposed to neglect, disappointment, contempt, and never-ending toil.

The room grew darker and darker, and the girls retired to their chambers, but Mrs. Matthews brought no lamp to Hannah, for she was too weary to stir, unless compelled by necessity, and she thought she could rest herself in the dark. The eyes of the stranger were strained at every passer-by; with a look of hope, as they approached, and disappointment as they went their way. At length she caught a glimpse of a tall robust form, whose lifted eyes scanned the numbers over the doors, and, exclaiming "It is Orville!" she sprang to the door, and welcomed the gentleman ere he had time to inquire for her.

Mrs. Matthews heard a bass voice in the room, and she brought them a lamp, and closed the doors. Hannah did not introduce her visitor; and when, after a short though earnest interview, he left her, she retired to her room.

She did not awake the next morning till Phebe Matthews hobbled into the room to make her bed, and then she found that her room-mates had all been at work more than an hour. She immediately arose, and was dressed in season to join the gay and loud-talking company at the breakfast-table. There was enough to eat, and that which was very good, but the girls had all given the stranger a scrutinizing stare and finished their meal, ere she had got through with her first cup of coffee.

"We always make room-mates take care of each other," said Mrs. M., entering the room with another plate of hot cakes, "and Martha Stillman must take the new boarder with her, when she goes into the mill, and show her the overseers, and counting-room folks, and help get her a place."

Martha hung her head, and looked sheepish; but, at length mustered courage to say that they must go then, or the gate would be shut.

The pretty face of Hannah Felton was a passport wherever she applied, and she had no difficulty in securing a situation; especially as no letters of recommendation were ever required: a custom which she thought very favorable for her, though she did not know whether it was best or not for all.

We will pass over the first months, and even the first year, of Hannah's novitiate in the mill; for, to herself, it passed much as the first year of such labor does to all. But there was trouble thickening around her. Her innocent looks and quiet manners had ingratiated all in her favor, with whom she had much personal intercourse; and, but for one circumstance, her situation would have been made as pleasant as possible, and that was the mystery that hung around her. Of her past life she had revealed nothing. Ellen Campbell felt too grateful and flattered by her invariable kindness to seek a confidence which was not voluntary. The Stillman girls were at meeting all day, on the Sabbath, and nearly every evening in the week, and with them there was but little opportunity for communications; and for a long time it was not observed, in the large family, how little they knew of the history of the stranger. To those who have any thing to conceal, or who feel unwilling that their affairs should be subject to general remark and investigation, there is a decided advantage in living where the observations of those about them are distributed among so many. Hannah was so gentle, so quiet, and pleasant, that she would have got along very well had it not been for the visits of the unknown gentleman. It was remarked that he never came till after dark, as though he wished to escape all observation that he could avoid, and that they never conversed freely before any of the family, appearing to feel much constraint in the presence of others; and that they often walked together till it was quite late. There was a general desire in the family to know who he was, but it was considered one ascertained fact that he belonged to the city, for some of the boarders had passed him in the streets, and Martha Stillman knew that he attended Mr. B's. meeting.

"I will ask her who he is," said Phebe Matthews, one day, to her sister. "She sha'n't receive company here, that she is ashamed of, or who is ashamed of her, and of the house he visits."

"No, no, Phebe," replied Mrs. Matthews; "let her alone—it would make her feel bad to be asked now, she has kept it to herself so long; and you know we have never seen any hurt in either of them."

Phebe made no answer, for she felt that Hannah could be accused of no other impropriety than the mere reception of the gentleman's visits. It also required some bravery to ask, bluntly, a question which had always been so carefully evaded. But she was resolved to "screw her courage to the sticking point."

"Pray, who is that gentleman, who has just left the house?" said she to Hannah, one Sabbath evening, just as her visitor left her. "What is his name?"

Poor Hannah turned red and white, and then red and white again, and stammered out, "He is a friend, Phebe—a dear friend—indeed we are related; we bear the same name—his is Orville Felton. You know I always call him Orville." And she had fled to her chamber ere Phebe could resume her questioning.

"I don't believe any thing about his being a relative," said Phebe to herself; "and, with all her pretty looks and innocent ways, I believe she is a dreadful hypocrite; and may be something worse." She put on one of her blandest smiles, and went to Hannah's chamber, to get the lamp. "Isn't he your lover?" said she, endeavoring to look very cunning.

"We have loved each other, ever since we have known each other," replied Hannah, quietly.

"But don't you feel a particular regard for him?"

"Perhaps so."

"And hav'n't you ever thought of him as a lover?"

"*Never.*"

"But don't you think he loves you?"

"I hope so."

"Well, I should think if he had any proper respect and regard for you, that he would not visit you in the manner he does; and that he might show you some attention publicly; and go with you to meeting, and to the lyceum, and to concerts; or, if he is ashamed to be seen with you anywhere else, I should think he might take you to the museum. You know it isn't so much matter there who a gentleman is seen with."

Poor Hannah reddened more furiously than ever, and hid her blushing face in the pillow. Phebe stood watching her, with the lamp in her hand, and did not leave her till she saw, by the heavings of the counterpane, that her frame was convulsed with suppressed sobbings.

"I don't know what to make of the girl," said she to her sister, when she related the occurrence. "She does not appear to be a wicked girl;

and you know she does not dress up, nor any thing of that sort. There is not a girl in the house who spends so little money. If it was not for that man I should think her one of the best boarders that we have."

The next time the stranger came the girls all left the room, that his usual short interview might not be constrained by their presence. Phebe Matthews went into the room, and, under pretence of taking her knitting-work from the window-sill, she drew the curtain slightly awry. After she had left them together long enough to suppose they might have forgotten every thing, and every body, but themselves, she went out, and peeped through the window. Horror of horrors! the unknown had his arm around Hannah's neck, and she was looking into his face with a very sad and earnest expression. She held in her hand a small ivory miniature.

"I must go now," said Orville, for this was really his name; and, taking from her the miniature, he gallantly touched it to his lips, and then placed it in his bosom.

"Will you not come again soon?" said Hannah imploringly. "I sometimes feel as though I should die if you did not visit me, and I don't know but they will kill me if you do."

"I cannot come often, but whenever I can you shall certainly see me."

"And when will you be married, Orville? O, will it not be soon? It seems as though I should die to stay here much longer. I am sick now, mind and body both. I shall be really sick I know."

"Cheer up, my dear, for a little while. Better days are certainly coming for us both;" and he kissed her cheek, as she burst into tears.

Phebe turned from the window when she saw him take his hat, and she was soon sitting beside her sister.

"I do believe the Old Harry is in the girl," said she, at length, "and we must tell her to find another boarding place. The Stillman girls say that they shall go away if she stays here longer."

"Well," replied Mrs. Matthews, "Ellen Campbell says that she will go, if Hannah is turned away, so that would make it even; and I cannot turn Hannah away until I see something myself. I should not feel as though it was right."

"Well, I don't want to see any thing more than I have seen to-night," replied Phebe, with a very mysterious look. "I am convinced now, and you know I have had my thoughts this long while." She then related what she had seen, coloring all the circumstances from her own suspicious imagination, and justifying herself for her mode of obtaining the information.

"Tell her," said Mrs. Matthews, "that she must promise to see the gentleman no more, or leave my house at the close of the week."

"I will never make such a promise," said Hannah, decidedly, to Phebe, when the message was given.

The whole family were in a state of high excitement. All were arrayed against Hannah but Ellen Campbell, and Mrs. Matthews, who endeavored to remain neutral. Martha Stillman was sister to the overseer's wife, and went over to his house to tell him about it, and advise him to discharge Hannah from his room. She thought it was high time that such girls should see that they could not come to a factory, to do whatever they pleased. The overseer had a room full of help, and one of his old favorites, who had just returned from a visit to her relatives, was waiting for frames. Martha carried back word to Hannah that she must leave her work in a fortnight. The poor girl made no reply, but her lips were pale and compressed, and her eyes were bloodshot. The next morning she was not at work in the mill; and, when the girls met at the breakfast-table, her place was vacant. Ellen Campbell went to her room, and found her in a high fever. She called Mrs. Matthews, who looked conscience-stricken, as she witnessed the effect of mental excitement and trouble on the slight and over-tasked frame of Hannah.

A physician was sent for, who shook his head, and looked very dubious. "She may recover; and she may not," said he, feeling of her pulse.

"I know that," replied Mrs. Matthews, "but which do you think is most probable?"

"The chances are equal," was his reply. "Is there a good girl to take care of her?"

"I will do it," said Ellen Campbell; "for that purpose I can obtain leave of absence from the mill."

The doctor soon left them, and Ellen took her station, as nurse, beside the sick bed. For several days she did all in her power to keep her charge as quiet as possible, and for that reason did not allow her to converse, especially upon the exciting subject which was on her lips and heart.

As the fever approached its crisis Ellen felt alarmed. "If she should die," thought she to herself, "what other friend has she to grieve for her loss? There is *that one* certainly; and I, at least, may know more about him."

"Hannah!" said she, approaching the bed-side, and speaking in a low, but apparently cheerful, voice.

"Dear Ellen," replied Hannah, faintly.

"Have you no friends whom you wish to have informed of your sickness?"

"Tell me truly, Ellen, do you think I shall die? I am prepared for any answer."

"The doctor said, this morning, that your recovery was very doubtful."

Hannah turned away her face with an expression of agony, and large tears stole down her fevered cheeks.

She then directed Ellen to go to a house in the city, naming the street and number, and inquire for Olivia Ainsworth. If she was there, to request her to visit her immediately.

Ellen called Mrs. Matthews to her place by the sick bed, and complied with the wish of her friend. She soon found the house, and the young lady promptly made her appearance. She drew up haughtily as Ellen delivered her message, without giving the name of the sick girl.

"I am not acquainted upon the corporations," she replied, with an air of offended dignity.

"My friend did not say that she was an acquaintance of yours; but she is dying, and would like to see you once."

"Are you sure that I am the person?"

"If your name is Olivia Ainsworth, you are the one whom my friend wishes to see."

Miss Ainsworth's curiosity was excited, and she consented to accompany Ellen to the sick bed of her friend. She said nothing till they reached the house, and then merely uttered the exclamation, "How disagreeable!" as she ascended the first flight of stairs. She put her handkerchief to her nostrils, as she entered the sick-room; but, when she had cast one glance at the dying girl, her haughtiness vanished, in an instant, and she stood, a sympathizing woman, by the unknown female.

"Is there any thing that I can do for you?" she gently inquired.

"Tell me," asked Hannah, exerting herself for the interview, "if you are engaged to be married to Orville Felton."

"*I am*," replied Miss Ainsworth; and she turned pale as the idea of a lowly and much-wronged rival entered her mind.

"But you are wealthy, and he is poor."

"I have wealth enough for us both."

"But his connexions are not among the wealthy and fashionable."

"He has talents which, in time, will shed a lustre upon them."

"But would you marry him if you knew that his only sister was *a factory girl?*"

A new light seemed to flash upon Miss Ainsworth, as she scanned more earnestly the features and complexion of the sufferer.

"I would *never* marry a man who could deceive me."

At that moment the door opened, and Phebe Matthews limped into the room, followed by Orville Felton.

"My dear sister!" he exclaimed, springing towards the bed.

Hannah faintly returned his embrace, and there was, upon her features, a transient smile of mingled bitterness and joy.

He started as he first observed Miss Ainsworth, but offered her his hand, though he crimsoned to the roots of his hair.

She coldly declined the proffered salute, which Hannah observed, and, starting from her pillow, she exclaimed, "For my sake, be friends now! This is no time for reproaches, even if we have any right to rebuke each other. But we have all done wrong, though Orville may have been the most to blame."

Miss Ainsworth arose to go, and Felton followed, promising to return immediately. She pressed the hand of the patient tenderly in her own, ere she departed, and said she would call upon her soon.

She rejected the arm of Felton, and he felt that he was a discarded suitor; but he was resolved she should hear something in his defence.

He told her of his admiration upon their first acquaintance; and that, though he was much struck with her beauty, her talents, and accomplishments, he was equally aware of her extreme pride. But he considered that her only fault, and did not expect to find a woman faultless. And, when he had resolved to win her for his bride, he knew that it must be by concealing all in his own situation which would offend her sense of dignity. He had sent for his sister to work in the mill, that the small pittance, she received from the remains of their father's fortune, might be appropriated for his expenses, which were much increased by his connection with her. He had intended to repay her quadruple, when his approaching marriage should bestow upon him the means of being generous; and it was in accordance with his earnest desire that she had faithfully kept the secret of their relationship. He did not tell all; for he did not inform her that part of Hannah's earnings had been willingly given to him, and that he had lavished them upon love-tokens for her. He said enough, however, to make her feel that she had been wronged, insulted, and basely deceived, and she told him, plainly, that she was disgusted. Requesting that his visits might thenceforth cease, she bade him adieu, and retired to her room.

And did there come to Olivia Ainsworth no thought that she had done wrong? that in her pride, and foolish contempt of the factory operative, so often and vehemently expressed to her lover, had been the origin of all this sorrow, and vexation, and perhaps of *death?* No, not then; for it was no time for calm reflection; but, in her visits to the sick girl, she learned many a sad and much-needed lesson.

And if the deepest contrition, the firmest resolves of amendment, be any expiation, then was the sin of Orville Felton forgiven as he watched by the bed of his lovely affectionate self-sacrificing sister. In her love, and her sweet silent influence, he felt that he was a regenerated being. She did more than this, she reconciled him to her who still loved him, and whom he yet loved; for who could resist the sweet pleadings of the gentle girl? or the humbling influences of that sickroom? When they sat with her during her long convalescence, for she did recover, she told them gently, but truly, how much they had erred—how they had cherished the opinions and prejudices of the vain and fashionable, in spite of their own better judgment, and their own kinder feelings.

They could listen to these gentle reproaches from her, and acknowledge their justice; and when, one day, they sat each with a hand of hers in theirs, she pressed them together, and prayed that what she had joined might not be put asunder.

The hand of Olivia trembled in that of Orville, and he looked at her with a troubled, yet hopeful, expression.

"For the sake of calling this sweet girl my sister, I will be your wife," replied Olivia, blushing. "Her love has saved us all."

O, beautiful is the love of a sister! It is a love as pure as deep and tender, as the human heart can feel. A mother's love is all this, but it is also too often a blind love. She too seldom sees the imperfections of her son, or looks at them with an eye which turns the dark spots to brightness. And there is another love in woman's heart. "I love him with his faults; nay, I love him faults and all," is the language of passion. It may do well for a bride, but too *true* for this should be a sister's love. She should love with an eye open to every fault, but watching to correct it. This is her hardest task, and how is it to be accomplished? One thing she should ever remember, and that is, that man's proud spirit will not brook reproach or rebuke from a sister. Remonstrance, gentle kind warning and advice, are all that she can utter with her lips, but if she wish to preach it must be by her actions. Let the brother see her steadfast in duty, firm in principle, and unchanging in affection, and an influence, silent, sweet and sure, is shed around him. But for this she must really love; she must be ready and willing to sacrifice her pleasures, comforts, and, if need be, her interests, for his sake. I have seen those who, from what I thought mistaken ideas of duty, were continually lecturing their brothers. But it did no good. "That is women's talk," would be the only reply. And harm was done, for the sweet intercourse of brother and sister was rudely broken, and passions aroused which had better have slept for ever. In some cases silence may be a sister's most effectual remonstrance, and in others, a single expression of wounded feeling will work far more of cure than hours spent in reproof. But when the sister does reprove, it should be with this concession, that not her better knowledge of right and wrong, but her superior advantages for perceiving them have given her the power. When the brother embarks upon the busy sea of life, the sister is often left an idle spectator on the strand. She can mark the tide as it ebbs and flows; she can see the vessels as they rush along upon the billows; she can watch the gathering clouds, and catch the first glimpses of the coming storm. Then can she warn him of his danger, firmly and truly, but without arrogance or conceit, for this has been unheeded by him, not from less strength of vision, but because his eyes were fixed upon far other objects. Happy is the sister who has not this task; she who looks upon a brother's sunny career, and there beholds no cloud or shadow.

The brother may leave a lowly home with the determination that riches and honors shall be his; down in the humble vale the sister may stand, and view, with a heart that leaps at every joyful throb of his, the upward path he treads; and if he ascends where the sun of fame and fortune glitters brightly upon him, and his dazzled eye sees not the snares and pitfalls which surround his steps, then should she raise the voice of love, and kindly tell him of his danger. If he heed her not, but stumble and fall, she should come with a soothing voice and ready hand, to bind his wounds and cheer his heart.

When men are in affliction, to our sex they turn for sympathy and consolation; and if they find it not, they are but too ready to accuse all mankind of selfishness, obduracy, and hardness of heart. When a brother finds himself sunk in misfortune and infamy, to whom should he turn but to a sister? And she should be ever ready to receive him to her heart, for she alone (unless he has a mother) can do this without a sacrifice of principle or delicacy. Wretched and degraded he may be, but she should think of early days spent happily together, and of those who were alike the parents of both. But if, far above her, the brother keeps his onward way, and the world set a broad line between them, and treat him with much distinction, but pass her unheeded by, still she should heed it not. Ever should she retain her self-respect, for by this means, and this alone, can she preserve his. Never should she forget that kindred blood fills the veins of each, and that the same fond bosom pillowed both their infant heads. To him should she be still the same—calm and dignified, though kind and affectionate. If she continues to influence him, it will be by the steady love she cherishes, and the respect which virtue and affection inspire in all men. A sister can, in one respect, exert an influence which the mother cannot: she can enter more warmly into his plans and pursuits—can feel and talk more with him about them, for the young often slight the counsels of the aged and wise, because they think them dictated by unsympathizing hearts.

If the brother go far from his friends, and seek among strangers a home and a name, even there should he feel that a sister's changeless love has followed him; that she prays for his weal, and sorrows in his wo; that she cherishes his remembrance at the fireside he has left, and often reminds his acquaintance of the one they might otherwise forget. And never by neglect should she allow his love for her and the dear ones at home to lessen or decay. It is a hallowed flame, which should be fed by a constant interchange of thought and feeling. Though his duties to God and his fellow-man, are not affected by her conduct towards him, yet the fear of giving a pang to those who still love and watch him, may be a safeguard in the hour of trial and temptation.

And when the brother seeks to replace, by other ties, those which have been severed, the sister should not be troubled. She may never more hold her wonted place in his heart, but she should rejoice that the place is not vacant. It should be enough for her that he is more happy; and never, for frivolous causes, should she indulge in feelings of dislike, or distrust, towards the new sister with which he presents her. She may be disappointed at his choice—she may grieve if he was infatuated or deceived, but never should pride, anger, or jealousy, make wide a breach which should never have been opened. Seldom should she interfere in his matrimonial choice, unless she receive that greatest proof of confidence which a brother can give, the right to assist and guide him in his selection, and then readily, cheerfully and conscientiously should she render her aid. And in every period and situation of life, should the brother feel, that in a sister's love he possesses a treasure greater than Golconda's mines or Peruvian mountains can bestow.

I know that it is easier to theorize than to practice, but she who cannot act well and truly the sister's part, should beware how she take upon herself other ties, and other obligations.

The first time that Hannah Felton left the house it was to attend the bridal fete of her happy brother, and the beautiful Miss Ainsworth; and as Orville looked upon his blushing wife, and then turned to his pale and lovely sister, he knew not which was dearest to him, the full-blown rose, or budding lily.—

"I declare," said Mrs. Matthews, as she divided a slice of the wedding cake with her sister, "I always knew they looked alike. Strange that we never thought of their being brother and sister."

"Well, I could never bring my mind to believe that there was any thing *bad* about her," replied Phebe.

"Not even when you saw her brother put his arm around her neck, and kiss her," said Ellen Campbell, archly.

Phebe limped away, for she knew that her version of that story was now known to be incorrect. And there was not one of the family but wished they had been as kind and forbearing with the gentle stranger as Ellen Campbell.

Adelia

(*Harriet Farley, Vol. IV, 1843, pp. 14–23*)

A Woman's Voice to Woman

It was remarked in one of our most widely circulated newspapers, in reference to a trial recently before the supreme court, that among the ladies there was a most lamentable want of charity toward the prisoner, an injured and unprotected woman, upon whose character all the efforts of the government instituting the trial, have failed to cast the shadow of guilt. In conclusion, the editor remarks, "Different indeed would have been the verdict, we fear, had the *ladies* been allowed to sit in judgment on her case."

And has it come to this? that the sorrows of an injured woman appeal in vain for sympathy to female hearts! Nay, still worse—Has woman so fallen, that the wrongs, which have called forth universal interest from the sterner sex, have left all untouched the chords of kindness in her soul, which should ever vibrate to tones of sorrow wrung from a sister's misfortunes!—And need we the eloquence of *man* to enlist our charity in the cause of a wronged and suffering sister? Has the angel of mercy assumed the form of woman only in poetry and romance, that we are thus reproachfully told, these virtues find no response in *our* hearts?

I confess that, in reading the article from which I have quoted, my spirit swelled with proud indignation, at what I deemed a base slander, a foul libel upon the virtues of my sex. But the tide of resentment was checked, by a voice whispering, "Look back upon what has come within thine own observation, even in the last year which has gone by, and see if there is no truth in this fearful charge." Then rolled back the wheels of time, and many a sad picture passed in review before me; on which I gazed until, wearied and sick of the weakness and folly of human nature, I would fain have stayed their course,— but my gentle monitor again whispered, "Shrink not from beholding the melancholy truths which are unveiled before thee, for by it thou shalt be profited."

I turned to gaze again upon the sombre picture,—when the loud tones of voices in earnest conversation arrested my attention; and by listening, I discovered they spoke of the woman to whom I have alluded, and many were the severe expressions of condemnation they uttered. So uncharitable were they, I looked whence the sound proceeded, expecting to see a group of reckless and hard-hearted men;

but instead, I saw a party of women, *gentle, compassionate* and *forgiving* WOMEN! talking of their sister's follies, or faults perchance. Yes, they may have been faults—but if so, she is still no less our sister; neither are the duties of charity and kindness less binding upon us. Yet even this supposition we have no right to make. This unfortunate woman has been arraigned at the bar of human justice and wisdom; and there fully and honorably acquitted, even of the suspicion of guilt; therefore justice forbids that *we* condemn, and all the better feelings of our hearts respond to its decrees. If she is *innocent*, all the kindness we can bestow will be but a poor compensation for the wrong she has received. If she is *guilty*, enough of thorns, heaven knows, already lie within her pathway; and far from *us* be the wish to add to her wretchedness.

This scene passed, and another came. It is a familiar one. A young and lovely girl, in the quiet of her chamber, is bending with tearful eyes over the Book of sacred consolation, which she clasps as though it were her last, her *only* friend. She is not beautiful, as the world judges of beauty; but there is an expression of sadness in her countenance, which tells of deep, but patient suffering; and although in the spring-time of life, the season of hope and joy, but few of its flowers have blossomed around her, and she has lingered to see the last one fade and die. Truly, sorrow seems to have marked her for its own. Let us trace her history.

She is the only child of a respected family of one of our New England villages.—She was deprived of a mother's watchful care, long years since; but she has grown up under the guardianship of a beloved father, whose duties as a country clergyman allowed him time to fill, as far as possible, the place of their lost one. But now he too is gone, and she has been obliged to leave the home of her childhood, and come to our distant city, for the purpose of obtaining a livelihood. She has been kindly received; but she is among strangers, and she pines for the sympathies of home. Hers is a spirit that must droop and die, in the uncongenial air of coldness or neglect. Her gentle, unassuming manner, and interesting countenance, have gained her friends among the gentlemen with whom she has met; and, grateful for their kindness, which has fallen upon her spirit like the dews of heaven upon the drooping flowers; she turns with all the confidence of unsuspecting innocence to those who have thus cheered her lonely heart, and for a time beguiled it of its sadness. But she has observed that, by the little circle of her own sex in which she has been placed, she is regarded with suspicion; and when she asks the cause, she is rudely answered by strange insinuations, or congratulated upon the admirable manner with which she assumes the innocent. Her fate is already sealed! Those who should have poured the healing oil of kindness and charity upon that lone one's stricken heart; are armed with barbed arrows that have been dipped in the deadly poison of envy; and now her wan and mournful looks may but faintly tell how fatally true is the aim which they have taken. In few words, her reputation has been injured, her hopes blighted, and all the warm and generous feelings of her heart trampled upon by a systematic course of slander, as base as it has been false, and all this she has received at the hands of her own sex! O could they have known, as each slanderous tale they told, the fearful consummation of their guilt, humanity would have forbidden them utterance!

This is no overwrought picture of the imagination; the history of our own population furnishes many a parallel. Here are gathered from their distant homes many lone and almost friendless strangers, who have come to us with no other protection than the shield of virtue. And shall we attempt to weaken this? or countenance aught which may deprive them of the only blessing, without which life is no longer valuable? No—rather let us extend to them the hand of kindness to cheer and gladden their lonely path, and let us be ever ready to throw the mantle of charity over our sister's faults. I would not that we sanction wrong, or even the shadow of wrong, for charity itself ceases to be a virtue when exercised in concealing vice; yet frail and erring creatures as we ourselves are, surely we should ere this have learned to pity and forgive! Be this our course in future, and we shall redeem ourselves from the fearful imputations which our faults in this respect have merited.—Let us no longer so far forget the higher and holier feelings of our nature, as to yield to the base passions of envy and falsehood, for the unholy purpose of dimming the bright and priceless gem of woman's virtuous reputation.

Viola

(*Author unknown, Series I, No. 4, 1840, pp. 52–53*)

Leisure Hours of the Mill Girls

The leisure hours of the Mill girls—how shall they be spent? As Ann, Bertha, Charlotte, Emily, and others, spent theirs? as *we* spend ours? Let us decide.

No. 4 was to stop a day for repairs. Ann sat at her window until she tired of watching passers-by. She then started up in search of one idle as herself, for a companion in a saunter. She called at the chamber opposite her own. The room was sadly disordered. The bed was not made, although it was past nine o'clock. In making choices of dresses, collars and aprons, *pro tempore*, some half dozen of each had been taken from their places; and there they were, lying about on chairs, trunks and bed, together with mill clothes just taken off. Bertha had not combed her hair; but Charlotte gave hers a hasty dressing before "going out shopping;" and there laid brush, combs and hair on the table. There were a few pictures hanging about the walls, such as "You are the prettiest Rose," "The Kiss," "Man Friday," and a miserable, soiled drawing of a "Cottage Girl." Bertha blushed when Ann entered. She was evidently ashamed of the state of her room, and vexed at Ann's intrusion. Ann understood the reason, when Bertha told her, with a sigh, that she had been "hurrying all the morning to get through the 'Children of the Abbey,' before Charlotte returned."

"Ann, I wish you would talk to her," said she. "Her folks are very poor. I have it on the best authority. Elinda told me that it was confidently reported by girls who came from the same town, that her folks had been known to jump for joy at the sight of a crust of bread. She spends every cent of her wages for dress and confectionary. She has gone out now; and she will come back with lemons, sugar, rich cake, and so on. She had better do as I do—spend her money for books, and her leisure time in reading them. I buy three volumes of novels every month; and when that is not enough, I take some from the circulating library. I think it our duty to improve our minds as much as possible, now the Mill girls are beginning to be thought so much of."

Ann was a bit of a wag. Idle as a breeze, like a breeze she sported with every *trifling* thing that came in her way.

"Pshaw!" said she. "And so we must begin to read silly novels, be very sentimental, talk about tears and flowers, dews and bowers.

There is some poetry for you, Bertha. Don't you think I'd better 'astonish the natives' by writing a poetical rhapsody, nicknamed 'twilight reverie,' or some other silly, inappropriate thing, and sending it to the 'Offering?' Oh, how fine this would be! Then I could purchase a few novels, borrow a few more, take a few more from a circulating library; and then shed tears and grow soft over them—all because we are taking a higher stand in the world, you know, Bertha."

Bertha again blushed. Ann remained some moments silent.

"Did you ever read Pelham?" asked Bertha, by way of breaking the silence.

"No; I read no novels, good, bad or indifferent. I have been thinking, Bertha, that there may be danger of our running away from the reputation we enjoy, as a class. For my part, I sha'n't ape the follies of other classes of females. As Isabel Greenwood says—and you know she is always right about such things—I think we shall lose our independence, originality and individuality of character, if we all take one standard of excellence, and this the customs and opinions of others. This is a jaw-cracking sentence for me. If any body had uttered it but Isabel, I should, perhaps, have laughed at it. As it was, I treasured it up for use, as I do the wise sayings of Franklin, Dudley Leavitt, and Robert Thomas. I, for one, shall not attempt to become so accomplished. I shall do as near right as I can conveniently, not because I have a heavy burden of gentility to support, just because it is quite as easy to do right,

'And then I sleep so sweet at night.'

Good morning, Bertha."

At the door she met Charlotte, on her return, with lemons, nuts and cake.

"I am in search of a companion for a long ramble," said Ann. "Can you recommend a *subject?*"

"I should think Bertha would like to shake herself," said Charlotte. "She has been buried in a novel ever since she was out of bed this morning. It was her turn to do the chamber work this morning; and this is the way she always does, if she can get a novel. She would not mind sitting all day with dirt to her head. It is a shame for her to do so. She had better be wide awake, enjoying life, as I am."

"Nonsense!" exclaimed Ann, in her usual *brusque* manner. "There is not a cent's choice between you, this morning; both are doing wrong, and each is condemning the other without mercy. So far you are both just like me, you see. Good morning."

She walked on to the next chamber. She had enough of the philosopher about her, to reason from appearances and from the occupation of its inmates, that she could succeed no better there. Every thing was in the most perfect order. The bed was shaped, and the sheet hemmed down *just* so. Their lines that hung by the walls were filled "jist." First came starched aprons, then starched capes, then pocket handkerchiefs, folded with the marked corner out, then hose. This room likewise had its paintings, and like those of the other, they were in perfect keeping with the general arrangements of the room and the dress of its occupants. There was an apology for a lady. Her attitude and form were of precisely that uncouth kind which is produced by youthful artificers, who form head, body and feet from one piece of shingle; and wedge in two sticks, at right angles with the body, for arms. Her sleeves increased in dimensions from the shoulders, and the skirt from the belt, but without the semblance of a fold. This, with some others of the same school, and two "profiles," were carefully preserved in frames, and the frames in screens of green barage. Miss Clark was busily engaged in making netting; and Miss Emily in making a dress. Ann made known her wants to them, more from curiosity to hear their reply, than from a hope of success. In measured periods they thanked her—would have been happy to accompany her. "But, really, I must be excused," said Miss Clark. "I have given myself a stint; and I always feel bad if I fall an inch short of my plans."

"Yes; don't you think, Ann?" said Emily; "she has stinted herself to make five yards of netting to-day. And mother says there is ten times as much in the house as we shall ever need. Father says there is twenty times as much; for he knows we shall both be old maids, ha! ha!"

"Yes; and I always tell him that if I am an old maid, I shall need the more. Our folks make twenty or thirty yards of table linen every year. I mean to make fringe for every yard; and have enough laid by for the next ten years, before I leave the Mill."

"Well, Emily," said Ann, "you have no fringe to make. Can't you accompany me?"

"I should be glad to, Ann; but I am over head and ears in work. I have got my work all done up, every thing that I could find to do. Now I am making a dress for Bertha."

"Why, Emily, you are making a slave of yourself, body and mind," said Ann. "Can't you earn enough in the Mill to afford yourself a little time for rest and amusement?"

"La! I don't make but twelve dollars a month, besides my board. I have made a great many dresses evenings; and have stinted myself to finish this to-day. So I believe I can't go, any way. I should be terrible glad to."

"Oh, you are *very* excusable," answered Ann. "But let me ask if you take any time to read."

"No; not much. We can't afford to. Father owns the best farm in Burt; but we always have had to work hard, and always expect to. We generally read a chapter every day. We take turns about it; one of us reads while the other works."

"Yes; but lately we have only taken time to read a short psalm," said Emily, again laughing.

"Well, the Bible says 'Let him that is without sin cast the first stone,' or I might be tempted to remind you that there is such a thing as laboring too much 'for the meat that perisheth.' Good morning, ladies."

Ann heard a loud, merry laugh from the next room, as she reached the door. It was Ellinor Frothingham's; no one could mistake, who had heard it once. It seemed the out-pouring of glee that could no longer be suppressed. Ellinor sat on the floor, just as she had thrown herself on her return from a walk. Her pretty little bonnet was lying on the floor on one side, and on the other, a travelling bag, whose contents she had just poured into her lap. There were apples, pears, melons, a mock-orange, a pumpkin, squash, and a crooked cucumber. Ellinor sprang to her feet when Ann entered, and threw the contents of her lap on the floor with such violence as to set them to rolling all about. Then she laughed and clapped her hands, to see the squash chase the mock-orange under the bed, a great russet running so furiously after a little fellow of the Baldwin family, and finally penning him in a corner. A pear started in the chase; but after taking a few turns, he sat himself down to shake his fat sides and enjoy the scene. Ellinora stepped back a few paces to elude the pursuit of the pumpkin, and then, with well-feigned terror, jumped into a chair. But the drollest personage of the group was the ugly cucumber. There he sat, Forminius-like, watching the mad freaks of his companions.

"Ha! see that cucumber!" exclaimed Ellinora, laughing heartily. "If he had hands, how he would raise them so! If he had eyes and mouth, how he would open them so!" suiting action to her words. "Look, Ann! look, Fanny! See if it does not look like the Clark girls, when one leaves any thing in the shape of dirt on their table or stand!"

Peace was at length restored among the *inanimates*.

"I came to invite you to walk; but I find I am too late," said Ann.

"Yes. Oh, how I wish you had been with us! You would have been so happy!" said Ellinora. "We started out very early, before sunrise— intending to take a brisk walk of a mile or two, and return in season for breakfast. We went over to Dracut, and met such adventures there and by the way, as will supply me with food for laughter, years after I get married and trouble comes. We came along where some oxen were standing yoked, eating their breakfast while their owner was eating his. They were attached to a cart filled with pumpkins. I took some of the smallest, greenest ones, and stuck them fast on the tips of the oxen's horns. I was so interested in observing how the ceremony affected the Messrs. Oxen, that I did not laugh a bit until I had crowned all four of them. I looked up to Fanny, as I finished the work, and there she sat on a great rock, where she had thrown herself when she could no longer stand. Poor girl! tears were streaming down her cheeks. With one hand she was holding her lame side, and with the other filling her mouth with her pocket handkerchief, that the laugh need not run out, I suppose. Well, as soon as I looked at her and at the oxen, I burst into a laugh that might have been heard miles, I fancy. Oh! I shall never forget how reprovingly those oxen looked at me. The poor creatures could not eat with such an unusual weight on their horns, so they pitched their heads higher than usual, and now and then gave them a graceful cant, then stood entirely motionless, as if attempting to conjecture what it all meant.

"Well, that loud and long laugh of mine brought a whole volley of folks to the door—farmer, and farmer's wife, farmer's sons, and farmer's daughters. 'Whoa hish!' exclaimed the farmer, before he reached the door; and 'Whoa hish!' echoed all the farmer's sons. They all stopped as soon as they saw me. I would remind you that I still stood before the oxen, laughing at them. I never saw such comical expressions as those people wore. Did you, Fanny? Even those pictures of mine are not so funny. I thought we should raise the city police; for they had tremendous voices, and I never saw any body laugh so.

"As soon as I could speak, and they could listen to me, I walked up to the farmer. 'I beg your pardon, sir,' said I, 'but I did want to laugh so! Came all the way from Lowell for something new to laugh at.' He was a good, sensible man; and this proves it. He said it was a good thing to have a hearty laugh occasionally—good for the health and spirits. Work would go off easier all day for it, especially with the boys. As he said 'boys,' I could not avoid smiling as I looked at a fine young sprig of a farmer, his oldest son, as he afterwards told us, full twenty-one."

"And now, Miss Ellinora," said Fanny, "I shall avenge myself on you, for certain saucy freaks, perpetrated against my most august commands, by telling Ann, that as you looked at this 'young sprig of a farmer,' he looked at you, and you both blushed. What made you, Nora? I never saw you blush before."

"What made you, Nora?" echoed Ellinora, laughing and blushing slightly. "Well, the farmer's wife invited us to rest and breakfast with them. We began to make excuses, but the farmer added his good natured commands. So we went in; and after a few arrangements, such as placing more plates, &c., a huge pumpkin pie, and some hot potatoes pealed in the cooking, we sat down to a full round table. There were the mealy potatoes, cold boiled dish, warm biscuit and doughnuts, pie, coffee, pickles, sauce, cheese, and just such butter and brown bread as mother makes—bread hot, just taken from the oven. They all appeared so pleasant and kind, that I felt as if in my own home, with my own family around me. Wild as I was, as soon as I began to tell them how it seemed to me, I burst into tears in spite of myself, and was obliged to leave the table. But they all pitied me so much, that I brushed off my tears, went back to my breakfast, and have laughed ever since."

"You have forgotten two very important items," said Fanny, looking archly into Ellinora's face. "This 'fine young sprig of a farmer' happened to recollect that he had business in town to-day; so he took their carriage and brought us home, after Nora and a roguish sister of his had filled her bag as you see. And more and better still, they invited us to spend a day with them soon; and promised to send this 'fine young sprig,' &c., for us on the occasion."

Ellinora was too busily engaged in collecting her fruit to reply. She ran from the room; and in a few moments returned with several young girls, to whom she gave generous supplies of apples, pears and melons. She was about seating herself with a full plate, when a new idea seemed to flash upon her. She laughed and started for the door.

"Ellinora, where now?" asked Fanny.

"To the Clark girls' room, to leave an apple peeling and core on their table, a pear peeling on their stand, and melon, apple and pear seeds all about the floor," answered Ellinora, gaily snapping her fingers, and nodding her head.

"What for? Here, Nora; come back. For what?"

"Why, to see them suffer," said the incorrigible girl. "You know I told you this morning, that sport is to be the order of the day. So no scoldings, my dear."

She left the room, and Fanny turned to one of the ladies who had just entered.

"Where is Alice?" said she. "Did not Ellinora extend an invitation to her?"

"Yes; but she is half dead with the *blues*, to-day. The Brown girls came back last night. They called on Alice this morning, and left letters and presents from home for her. She had a letter from her little brother, ten years old. He must be a fine fellow, judging from that letter, it was so sensible and so witty too! One moment I laughed at some of his lively expressions, and the next cried at his expressions of love for Alice, and regret for her loss. He told her how he cried himself to sleep the night after she left home; and his flowers seemed to have faded, and the stars to have lost their brightness, when he no longer had her by his side to talk to him about them. I find by his letter that Alice is working to keep him at school. That part of it which contained his thanks for her goodness, was blistered with the little fellow's tears. Alice cried like a child when she read it; and I did not wonder at it. But she ought to be happy now. Her mother sent her a fine pair of worsted hose of her own spinning and knitting, and a nice cake of her own making. She wrote, that, trifling as these presents were, she knew they would be acceptable to her daughter, because made by her. When Alice read this, she cried again. Her sister sent her a pretty little fancy basket; and her brother, a bunch of flowers from her mother's garden. They were enclosed in a tight tin box; and were as fresh as when first gathered. Alice sent out for a new vase. She has filled it with her flowers, and will keep them watered with her tears, judging from present appearances.—Alice is a good-hearted girl; and I love her. But she is always talking or thinking of something to make her unhappy. A letter from a friend, containing nothing but good news and assurances of friendship, that ought to make her happy, generally throw her into a crying fit, which ends in a moping fit of melancholy. This destroys her own happiness, and that of all around her."

"You ought to talk to her; she is spoiling herself," said Mary Mason, whose mouth was literally crammed with the last apple of a second plate full.

"I have often urged her to be more cheerful. But she answers me with a helpless, hopeless 'I can't, Jane! you know I can't. I shall never be happy while I live; and I often think that the sooner I go where "the weary are at rest" the better.' I don't know how many times she has given me an answer like this. Then she will sob as if her heart were bursting. She sometimes wears me quite out; and I feel as I did when Ellinora called me, as if released from a prison."

"Would it improve her spirits to walk with me?" asked Ann.

"Perhaps it would, if you can persuade her to go. Do try, dear Ann," answered Jane. "I called at Isabel Greenwood's room as I came along, and asked her to go in and see if she could rouse her up."

Ann heard Isabel's voice in gentle but earnest expostulation, as she reached Alice's room. Isabel paused when Ann entered, kissed her cheek, and resigned her rocking-chair to her. Alice was sobbing too violently to speak. She took her face from her handkerchief, bowed to Ann, and again buried it. Ann invited them to walk with her. Isabel cheerfully acceded to her proposal, and urged Alice to accompany them.

"Don't urge me, Isabel," said Alice. "I am only fit for the solitude of my chamber. I could not add at all to your pleasure. My thoughts would be at my home, and I could not enjoy a walk in the least degree. But, Isabel, I do not want you to leave me so. I know that you think me very foolish to indulge in these useless regrets, as you call them. You will understand me better, if you just consider the situation of my mother's family. My mother a widow, my oldest brother at the West, my oldest sister settled in New York, my youngest brother and sister only with mother, and I a Lowell factory girl! And such I must be—for if I leave the Mill, my brother cannot attend school all of the time; and his heart would almost break to take him from school. And how can I be happy in such a situation? I do not ask for riches; but I would be able to gather my friends all around me. Then I could be happy. Perhaps I am as happy now as you would be in my situation, Isabel."

Isabel's eyes filled, but she answered in her own sweet, calm manner:

"We will compare lots, my dear Alice. I have neither father, mother, sister, or home, in the world. Three years ago I had all of these, and every other blessing that one could ask. The death of my friends, the distressing circumstances attending them, the subsequent loss of our large property, and the critical state of my brother's health at present, are not slight afflictions, nor are they lightly felt."

Isabel's emotions, as she paused to subdue them by a powerful mental effort, proved her assertion. Alice began to dry her tears, and to look as if ashamed of her weakness.

"I, too, am a Lowell factory girl," pursued Isabel. "I, too, am laboring for the completion of a brother's education. If that brother were well, how gladly would I toil! But that disease is upon his vitals which laid father, mother and sister in their graves, in one short year. I can see it in the unnatural and increasing brightness of his eye, and hear it in his hollow cough. He has entered upon his third collegiate year; and is too anxious to graduate next commencement to heed my entreaties, or the warning of his physician."

She again paused. Her whole frame shook with emotion; but not a tear mingled with Ann's, as they fell upon her hand.

"You see, Alice," she at length added, "what reasons I have for regret when I think of the past, and what for fear, when I turn to the future. Still I am happy, almost continually. My lost friends are so many magnets, drawing heaven-ward those affections that would otherwise rivet themselves too strongly to earthly loves. And those dear ones who are yet spared to me, scatter so many flowers in my pathway, that I seldom feel the thorns. I am cheered in my darkest hours by their kindness and affection, animated at all times by a wish to do all in my power to make them happy. If my brother is spared to me, I ask for nothing more. And if he is first called, I trust I shall feel that it is the will of One who is too wise to err, and too good to be unkind."

"You are the most like my mother, Isabel, of any one I ever saw," said Ann. "She is never free from pain, yet she never complains. And if pa, or any of us, just have a cold or headache, she does not rest till 'she makes us well.' You have more trouble than any other girl in the house; but instead of claiming the sympathies of every one on that account, you are always cheering others in their little, half-imaginary trials. Alice, I think you and I ought to be ashamed to shed a tear, until we have some greater cause than mere home-sickness, or low spirits."

"Why, Ann, I can no more avoid low spirits than I can make a world!" exclaimed Alice in a really aggrieved tone. "And I don't want you all to think that I have no trouble. I want sympathy, and I can't live without it. Oh that I was at home this moment!"

"Why, Alice, there is hardly a girl in this house, who has not as much trouble, in some shape, as you have. You never think of pitying them; and pray what gives you such strong claims on their sympathies? Do you walk with us, or do you not?"

Alice shook her head in reply. Isabel whispered a few words in her ear—they might be of reproof, they might be of consolation—then retired with Ann to equip for their walk.

"What a beautiful morning this is!" exclaimed Ann, as they emerged from the house. "*Malgre* some inconveniences, factory girls are as happy as any class of females. I sometimes think it hard to rise so early, and work so many hours, shut up in the house. But when I get out at night, on the sabbath, or at any other time, I am just as happy as a bird, and long to fly and sing with them. And Alice will keep herself shut up all day. Is it not strange that all will not be as happy as they can be? It is so pleasant!"

Isabel returned Ann's smile. "Yes, Ann, it is strange that every one does not prefer happiness. Indeed, it is quite probable that every one does prefer it. But some mistake the modes of acquiring it, through want of judgment. Others are too indolent to employ the means necessary to its attainment; and appear to expect it to flow in to them, without taking any pains to prepare a channel. Others, like our friend Alice, have constitutional infirmities, which entail upon them a deal of suffering, that, to us of different mental organization, appears wholly unnecessary."

"Why, don't you think Alice might be as happy as we are, if she chose? Could she not be as grateful for letters and love-tokens from home? Could she not leave her room, and come out into this pure air, listen to the birds, and catch their spirit? Could she not do all this, Isabel, as well as we?"

"Well, I do not know, Ann. Perhaps not. You know that the minds of different persons are like instruments of different tones. The same touch thrills gaily on one, mournfully on another."

"Yes; and I know, Isabel, that different minds may be compared to the same instruments, *in* and *out* of tune. Now I have heard Alice say that she loved to indulge this melancholy; that she loved to read Byron, Mrs. Hemans and Miss Landon, until her heart was as gloomy as the grave. Is n't this strange—even silly?"

"It is most unfortunate, Ann."

"Isabel, you are the strangest girl! I have heard a great many say that one cannot make you say any thing against any body; and I believe they are correct. And when you reprove one, you do it in such a mild, pretty way, that one only loves you the better for it. Now, I smash on, pell-mell, as if unconscious of a fault in myself. Hence I oftener offend than amend. Let me think.—This morning I have administered reproof in my own blunt way to Bertha for reading novels, to Charlotte for eating confectionary, to the Clark girls for their 'all work and no play,' and to Alice for moping. I have been wondering all along how they can spend their time so foolishly. I see that my own employment would scarcely bear the test of close criticism; for I have been watching motes in others' eyes, while a beam was in my own. Now, Isabel, I must ask a favor. I do not want to be very fine and nice; but I would be gentle and kind-hearted—would do some good in the world. I often make attempts to this end; but always fail, somehow. I know my manner needs correcting; and I want you to reprove me as you would a sister, and assist me with your advice. Will you not, dear Isabel?"

She pressed Isabel's arm closer to her side, and a tear was in her eye as she looked up for an answer to her appeal.

"You know not what you ask, my beloved girl," answered Isabel, in a low and tremulous tone. "You know not the weakness of the staff on which you would lean, or the frailties of the heart to which you would look up for aid. Of myself, dear Ann, I can do nothing. I can only look to God for protection from temptation, and for guidance in the right way. When He keeps me, I am safe; when He withdraws His spirit, I am weak indeed. And can I lead you, Ann? No; you must go to a higher than earthly friend. Pray to Him in every hour of need, and He will be 'more to you than you can ask, or even think.' "

"How often I have wished that I could go to Him as mother does—

just as I would go to a father!" said Ann. "But I dare not. It would be mockery in one who has never experienced religion."

"Make prayer a *means* of this experience, my dear girl. Draw near to God by humble, constant prayer; and He will draw near to you by the influences of His spirit, 'which will make you just what you wish to be, a good, kind-hearted girl. You will learn to love God as a Father, as the Author of your happiness and every good thing. And you will be prepared to meet those trials which must be yours in life as the 'chastisements of a Father's hand, directed by a Father's love.' And when the hour of death comes, dear Ann, how sweet, how soothing will be the deep-felt conviction that you are going *home!* You will have no fears—for your trust will be in One whom you have long loved and served; and you will feel as if about to meet your best and most familiar friend."

Ann answered only by her tears; and for some minutes they walked on in silence. They were now some distance from town. Before them laid farms, farm-houses, groves and scattering trees, from whose branches came the mingled song of a thousand birds. Isabel directed Ann's attention to the beauty of the scene. Ann loved nature; but she had such a dread of sentimentalism, that she seldom expressed herself freely. Now she had no reserves, and Isabel found that she had not mistaken her capacities, in supposing her possessed of faculties, which had only to develope themselves more fully, which had only to become constant incentives to action, to make her all she could wish.

"You did not promise, Isabel," said Ann, with a happy smile as they entered their street, "you did not promise to be my sister; but you will, will you not?"

"Yes, dear Ann; we will be sisters to each other. I think you told me that you have no sister."

"I had none until now; and I have felt as if a part of my affections could not find a resting place, but were weighing down my heart with a burden that did not belong to it. I shall no longer be like a branch of our woodbine when it cannot find a clinging-place, swinging about at the mercy of every breeze; but like that when some kind hand twines it about its frame, firm and trusting. See, Isabel!" exclaimed she, interrupting herself. "There sits poor Alice, just as we left her. I wish she had walked with us—she would have felt so much better. Do you think, Isabel, that religion would make her happy?"

"Most certainly. 'Come unto me, all ye that labor and are heavy laden. Take my yoke upon you; for I am meek and lowly in heart; and ye *shall* find rest to your souls'—is as 'faithful a saying' and as 'worthy of all acceptation' now, as when it was uttered, and when thousands came and 'were healed of *all* manner of diseases.' Yes, Alice may yet be happy," she added musingly, "if she can be induced to read Byron less, and her Bible more; to think less of her own gratification, and more of that of others. And we will be very gentle to her, Ann; but not the less faithful and constant in our efforts to win her to usefulness and happiness."

Ellinora met them at the door, and began describing a frolic that had occupied her during their absence. She threw her arms around Isabel's waist, and entered the sitting-room with her. "Now, Isabel, I know you don't think it right to be so giddy," said she. "I will tell you what I have resolved to do. You shake your head, Isabel, and I do not wonder at all. But this resolution was formed this morning, on my way back from Dracut; and I feel in my 'heart of hearts' 'a sober certainty of waking' energy to keep it unbroken. It is, that I will be another sort of a girl, altogether, henceforth; steady, but not gloomy; less talkative, but not reserved; more studious, but not a bookworm; kind and gentle to others, but not a whit the less independent 'for a' that,' in my opinions and conduct. And, after this day, which I have dedicated to Momus, I want you to be my Mentor. Now I am for another spree of some sort. Nay, Isabel, do not remonstrate. You will make me weep with five tender words."

It needed not so much—for Isabel smiled sadly, kissed her cheek, and Ellinora's tears fell fast and thick as she ran from the room.

Ann went immediately to Alice's room on her return. She apologised to her for reproving her so roughly, described her walk, gave a synopsis of Isabel's advice, and her consequent determinations. By these means she diverted Alice's thoughts from herself, gave her nerves a healthy spring, and when the bell summoned them to dinner, she had recovered much of her happier humor. Ellinora sat beside her at table. She laughingly proposed an exchange, offering a portion of her levity for as much of her gravity. She thought the *equilibrium* would be more perfect. So Alice thought, and she heartily wished that the exchange might be made.

And this exchange seems actually taking place at this time. They are as intimate as sisters. Together they are resolutely struggling against the tide of habit. They meet many discouraging failures; but

Isabel is ever ready to cheer them by her sympathy, and to assist them by her advice.

Ann's faults were not so deeply rooted; perhaps she brought more natural energy to their extermination. Be that as it may, she is now an excellent lady, a fit companion for the peerless Isabel.

The Clark girls do not, as yet, coalesce in their system of improvement. They still prefer making netting and dresses, to the lecture room, the improvement circle, and even to the reading of the "Book of books." So difficult is it to turn from the worship of Plutus!

The delusion of Bertha and Charlotte is partially broken.—Bertha is beginning to understand that much reading does not naturally result in intellectual or moral improvement, unless it be well regulated. Charlotte is learning that "to enjoy is to obey;" and that to pamper her own animal appetites, while her father and mother are suffering for want of the necessaries of life, is not in obedience to Divine command.

And, dear sisters, how is it with each one of *us?* How do *we* spend our leisure hours? Now, "in the stilly hour of night," let us pause, and give our consciences time to render faithful answers.   D.

(Eliza J. Cate, Vol. II, 1842, pp. 65–79)

2
CONTINUING EDUCATION:
"A Glimpse of Something Grand Before Us"

A whiff of the style and tone of the Lyceum lectures, and something of their whirlwind tour through culture, appears in those Offering *essays which suggest classroom assignments. With the "Chapter on the Sciences" (the first of a series) we are reminded of the magazine's origins: the self-improvement circle. This sprightly mock-Socratic dialogue manages, nonetheless, to cover a lot of ground.*

In "Joan of Arc," author "Ella" (Harriet Farley) gives full vent to her ambivalence on the subject of women and power. Surely, she argues, it was circumstance that propelled Joan into such an "unfeminine" role. Had historical conditions been different, the love of one good man would have been chosen over a shamelessly public role—a role which attracted the writer/editor at least as much as it did the Maid of Orleans!

The meditation on "The Western Antiquities" is interesting for the rarity of any writing at this early period on Amerindian petroglyphs. It would be intriguing to know the precise sites which had recently been excavated and the source of the writer's information. Also worth noting is the speculation concerning the ancestors of the American Indian, including then current migration theories.

Poetry was the least happy form of expression for Offering *talents. Most selections, favoring elegaic subjects and form, are frank pastiches of women poets scarcely more gifted than their acolytes. As soon as they set out to "pen verse," the spontaneous, freshly observed detail, the felt experience, were abandoned for the dreariest poetic formulas of the day.*

"Lowell Girls" banknote, engraved by the American Banknote Company ca. 1858. Prints Division, The New York Public Library, Astor, Lenox, and Tilden Foundations.

There is, however, something irresistible about any poem on the funeral of President Harrison, who died of pneumonia four weeks to the day after taking the oath of office in the pouring rain!

Joan of Arc

When, in the perusal of history, I meet with the names of females whom circumstances, or their own inclinations, have brought thus openly before the public eye, I can seldom repress the desire to know more of them. Was it choice, or necessity, which led them to the battle-field, or council hall? Had the woman's heart been crushed within their breasts? or did it struggle with the sterner feelings which had then found entrance there? Were they recreant to their own sex? or were the deeds which claim the historian's notice but the necessary results of the situations in which they had been placed?

These are questions which I often ask, and yet I love not in old and musty records to meet with names which long ere this should have perished with the hearts upon which love had written them; for happier, surely, is woman, when in *one* manly heart she has been "shrined a queen," than when upon some powerful throne she sits with an untrembling form, and an unquailing eye, to receive the homage, and command the services of loyal thousands. I love not to read of woman transformed in all, save outward form, into one of the sterner sex; and when I see, in the memorials of the past, that this has apparently been done, I would fain overleap the barriers of by-gone time, and know how it has been effected. Imagination goes back to the scenes which must have been witnessed then, and perhaps unaided portrays the minuter features of the sketch, of which history has preserved merely the outlines.

But I sometimes read of woman, when I would *not* know more of the places where she has rendered herself conspicuous; when there is something so noble and so bright in the character I have given her, that I fear a better knowledge of trivial incidents might break the spell which leads me to love and admire her; where, perhaps, the picture which my fancy has painted, glows in colors so brilliant, that a sketch by Truth would seem beside it but a sombre shadow.

JOAN OF ARC is one of those heroines of history, who can not fail to

excite an interest in all who love to contemplate the female character. From the gloom of that dark age, when woman was but a play-thing and a slave, she stands in bold relief, its most conspicuous personage. Not, indeed, as a queen, but as more than a queen, even the preserver of her nation's king; not as a conqueror, but as the saviour of her country; not as a man, urged in his proud career by mad ambition's stirring energies, but as a woman, guided in her brilliant course by woman's noblest impulses,—so does she appear in that lofty station which for herself she won.

Though high and dazzling was the eminence to which she rose, yet " 'twas not thus, oh 'twas not thus, her dwelling-place was found." Low in the vale of humble life was the maiden born and bred; and thick as is the veil which time and distance have thrown over every passage of her life, yet that which rests upon her early days is most impenetrable. And much room is there here for the interested inquirer, and Imagination may revel almost unchecked amid the slight revelations of History.

Joan is a heroine—a woman of mighty power—wearing herself the habiliments of man, and guiding armies to battle and to victory; yet never to my eye is "the warrior-maid" aught but *a woman*. The ruling passion, the spirit which nerved her arm, illumed her eye, and buoyed her heart, was woman's faith. Ay, it was *power*—and call it what ye may—say it was enthusiasm, fanaticism, madness—or call it, if ye will, what those *did* name it who burned Joan at the stake,—still it was power, the power of woman's firm, undoubting faith.

I should love to go back into Joan's humble home—that home which the historian has thought so little worthy of his notice; and in imagination I *must* go there, even to the very cradle of her infancy, and know of all those influences which wrought the mind of Joan to that fearful pitch of wild enthusiasm, when she declared herself the inspired agent of the Almighty.

Slowly and gradually was the spirit trained to an act like this; for though, like the volcano's fire, its instantaneous bursting forth was preceded by no prophet-herald of its coming—yet Joan of Arc was the same Joan ere she was maid of Orleans; the same high-souled, pure and imaginative being, the creature of holy impulses, and conscious of superior energies. It must have been so; *a superior mind may burst upon the world, but never upon itself*: there must be a feeling of sympathy with the noble and the gifted, a knowledge of innate though slumber-

ing powers. The neglected eaglet may lie in its mountain nest, long after the pinion is fledged; but it will fix its unquailing eye upon the dazzling sun, and feel a consciousness of strength in the untried wing; but let the mother-bird once call it forth, and far away it will soar into the deep blue heavens, or bathe and revel amidst tempest-clouds—and henceforth the eyrie is but a resting-place.

As the diamond is formed, brilliant and priceless, in the dark bowels of the earth, even so, in the gloom of poverty, obscurity and toil, was formed the mind of Joan of Arc. Circumstances were but the jeweller's cutting, which placed it where it might more readily receive the rays of light, and flash them forth with greater brilliancy.

I have said, that I must in imagination go back to the infancy of Joan, and note the incidents which shed their silent, hallowing influence upon her soul, until she stands forth an inspired being, albeit inspired by naught but her own imagination.

The basis of Joan's character is religious enthusiasm: this is the substratum, the foundation of all that wild and mighty power which made *her*, the peasant girl, the saviour of her country. But the flame must have been early fed; it was not merely an elementary portion of her nature, but it was one which was cherished in infancy, in childhood and in youth, until it became the master-passion of her being.

Joan, the child of the humble and the lowly, was also the daughter of the fervently religious. The light of faith and hope illumes their little cot; and reverence for all that is good and true, and a trust which admits no shade of fear or doubt, is early taught the gentle child. Though "faith in God's own promises" was mingled with superstitious awe of those to whom all were then indebted for a knowledge of the truth; though priestly craft had united the wild and false with the pure light of the gospel; and though Joan's religion was mingled with delusion and error,—still it comprised all that is fervent, and pure, and truthful, in the female heart. The first words her infant lips are taught to utter, are those of prayer—prayer, mayhap, to saints or virgin; but still to her *then*, and in all after time, the aspirations of a spirit which delights in communion with the Invisible.

She grows older, and still amid ignorance, and poverty, and toil, the spirit gains new light and fervour. With a mind alive to every thing that is high and holy, she goes forth into a dark and sinful world, dependent upon her daily toil for daily bread; she lives among the thoughtless and the vile; but like that plant which opens to naught

but light and air, and shrinks from all other contact—so her mind, amid the corruptions of the world, is shut to all that is base and sinful, though open and sensitive to that which is pure and noble.

"Joan," says the historian, "was a tender of stables in a village inn." Such was her outward life; but there was for her *another* life, a life within that life. While the hands perform low, menial service, the soul untramelled is away, and revelling amidst its own creations of beauty and of bliss. She is silent and abstracted; always alone among her fellows—for among them all she sees no kindred spirit; she finds none who can touch the chords within her heart, or respond to their melody, when she would herself sweep its harp-strings.

Joan has no friends; far less does she ever think of earthly lovers; and who would love *her*, the wild and strange Joan! thought, perhaps, the gloomy, dull and silent one: But that soul, whose very essence is fervent zeal and glowing passion, sends forth in secrecy and silence its burning love upon the unconscious things of earth. She talks to the flowers, and the stars, and the changing clouds; and their voiceless answers come back to her soul at morn, and noon, and stilly night. Yes, Joan loves to go forth in the darkness of eve, and sit

"Beneath the radiant stars, still burning as they roll,
    And sending down their prophecies into her fervent soul;"

but better even than this does she love to go into some high cathedral, where the "dim religious light" comes faintly through the painted windows; and when the priests chant vesper hymns, and burning-incense goes upward from the sacred altar—and when the solemn strains and the fragrant vapor dissolve and die away in the distant aisles and lofty dome, she kneels upon the marble floor, and in ecstatic worship sends forth the tribute of a glowing heart.

And when at night she lies down upon her rude pallet, she dreams that she is with those bright and happy beings with whom her fancy has peopled heaven. She is there, among saints and angels, and even permitted high converse with the Mother of Jesus.

Yes, Joan is a dreamer; and she dreams not only in the night but in the day; whether at work or at rest, alone or among her fellow men, there are angel-voices near, and spirit-wings are hovering around her, and visions of all that is pure, and bright, and beautiful, come to the mind of the lowly girl. She finds that she is a favored one; she feels that those about her are not gifted as she has been: she knows

that their thoughts are not as her thoughts; and then the spirit questions, Why is it thus that she should be permitted communings with unearthly ones? Why was this ardent, aspiring mind bestowed upon *her*, one of earth's meanest ones, shackled by bonds of penury, toil, and ignorance of all that the world calls high and gifted? Day after day goes by, night after night wears on, and still these queries will arise, and still they are unanswered.

At length the affairs of busy life, those which to Joan have heretofore been of but little moment, begin to awaken even *her* interest. Hitherto, absorbed in her own bright fancies, she has mingled in the scenes around her, like one who walketh in his sleep. They have been too tame and insipid to arouse her energies, or excite her interest; but now there is a thrilling power in the tidings which daily meet her ears. All hearts are stirred, but none now throb like hers: her country is invaded, her king an exile from his throne; and at length the conquerors, unopposed, are quietly boasting of their triumphs on the very soil they have polluted. And shall it be thus? Shall the victor revel and triumph in her own loved France? Shall her country thus tamely submit to wear the foreign yoke? And Joan says, No! She feels the power to arouse, to quicken, and to guide.

None now may tell whether it was first in fancies of the day, or visions of the night, that the thought came, like some lightning flash, upon her mind, that it was for this that powers unknown to others had been vouchsafed to *her;* and that for this, even new energies should now be given. But the idea once received is not abandoned; she cherishes it, and broods upon it, till it has mingled with every thought of day and night. If doubts at first arise, they are not harbored, and at length they vanish away.

"Her spirit shadowed forth a dream, till it became a creed."

All that she sees and all that she hears—the words to which she eagerly listens by day, and the spirit-whispers which come to her at night,—they all assure her of this, that she is the appointed one. All other thoughts and feelings now crystalize in this grand scheme; and as the cloud grows darker upon her country's sky, her faith grows surer and more bright. Her countrymen have ceased to resist, have almost ceased to hope; but she alone, in her fervent joy, has "looked beyond the present clouds and seen the light beyond." The spoiler shall yet be vanquished, and *she* will do it; her country shall yet be saved, and *she* will save it; her unanointed king shall yet sit on his throne, and "Charles shall be crowned at Rheims." Such is her mission, and she goes forth in her own ardent faith to its accomplishment.

And did those who first admitted the claims of Joan as an inspired leader, themselves believe that she was an agent of the Almighty? None can now tell how much the superstition of their faith, mingling with the commanding influence of a mind firm in its own conviction of supernatural guidance, influenced those haughty ones, as they listened to the counsels, and obeyed the mandates, of the peasant girl. Perhaps they saw that she was their last hope, a frail reed upon which they might lean, yet one that might not break. Her zeal and faith might be an instrument to effect the end which she had declared herself destined to accomplish. Worldly policy and religious credulity might mingle in their admission of her claims; but however this might be, the peasant girl of Arc soon rides at her monarch's side, with helmet on her head, and armor on her frame, the time-hallowed sword girt to her side, and the consecrated banner in her hand; and with the lightning of inspiration in her eye, and words of dauntless courage on her lips, she guides them on to battle and to victory.

Ay, there she is, the low-born maid of Arc! there, with the noble and the brave, amid the clangor of trumpets, the waving of banners, the tramp of the war-horse, and the shouts of warriors; and there she is more at home than in those humble scenes in which she has been wont to bear a part. Now for once she is herself; now may she put forth all her hidden energy, and with a mind which rises at each new demand upon its powers, she is gaining for herself a name even greater than that of queen. And now does the light beam brightly from her eye, and the blood course quickly through her veins—for her task is ended, her mission accomplished, and "Charles is crowned at Rheims."

This is the moment of Joan's glory,—and what is before her now? To stand in courts, a favored and flattered one? to revel in the soft luxuries and enervating pleasures of a princely life? Oh this was not for one like her. To return to obscurity and loneliness, and there to let the over-wrought mind sink back with naught to occupy and support it, till it feeds and drivels on the remembrance of the past,—this is what she would do; but there is for her what is better far, even the glorious death of a martyr.

Little does Joan deem, in her moment of triumph, that this is before her; but when she has seen her mission ended, and her king the anointed ruler of a liberated people, the sacred sword and standard are cast aside; and throwing herself at her monarch's feet, and watering them with tears of joy, she begs permission to return to her humble home. She has now done all for which that power was bestowed; her work has been accomplished, and she claims no longer the special commission of an inspired leader. But Dunois says, No! The English are not yet entirely expelled [from] the kingdom, and the French general would avail himself of that name, and that presence, which have infused new courage into his armies, and struck terror to their enemies. He knows that Joan will no longer be sustained by the belief that she is an agent of heaven; but she will be with them, and that alone must benefit their cause. He would have her again assume the standard, sword and armour; he would have her still retain the title of "Messenger of God," though she believes that her mission goes no farther.

It probably was not the first time, and it certainly was not the last, when woman's holiest feelings have been made the instruments of man's ambition, or agents for the completion of his designs. Joan is now but a woman, poor, weak and yielding woman; and overpowered by their entreaties, she consents to try again her influence. But the power of that faith is gone, the light of inspiration is no more given, and she is attacked, conquered, and delivered to her enemies. They place her in low dungeons, then bring her before tribunals; they wring and torture that noble spirit, and endeavor to obtain from it a confession of imposture, or connivance with the "evil one;" but she still persists in the declaration that her claims to a heavenly guidance were but true.

Once only was she false to herself. Weary and dispirited; deserted by her friends, and tormented by her foes,—she yields to their assertions, and admits that she did deceive her countrymen. Perhaps in that hour of trial and darkness, when all hope of deliverance from without, or from above, had died away,—when she saw herself powerless in the merciless hands of her enemies, the conviction might steal upon her own mind, that she had been self-deceived; that phantasies of the brain had been received as visions from on high,—but though her confession was true in the abstract, yet Joan was surely untrue to herself.

Still it avails her little; she is again remanded to the dungeon, and there awaits her doom.

At length they bring her the panoply of war, the armoured suit in which she went forth at her king's right hand to fight their battle-hosts. Her heart thrills, and her eye flashes, as she looks upon it—for it tells of glorious days. Once more she dons those fatal garments, and they find her arrayed in the habiliments of war. It is enough for those who wished but an excuse to take her life, and the Maid of Orleans is condemned to die.

They led Joan to the martyr-stake. Proudly and nobly went she forth, for it was a fitting death for one like *her*. Once more the spirit may rouse its noblest energies; and with brightened eye, and firm, un-daunted step, she goes where banners wave, and trumpets sound, and martial hosts appear in proud array. And the sons of England weep as they see her, the calm and tearless one, come forth to meet her fate. They bind her to the stake; they light the fire; and upward borne on wreaths of soaring flame, the soul of the martyred Joan ascends to heaven.   Ella

(Harriet Farley, Vol. I, 1841, pp. 193–200)

The Western Antiquities

In the valley of the Mississippi, and the more southern parts of North America, are found antique curiosities and works of art, bear-ing the impress of cultivated intelligence. But of the race, or people, who executed them, time has left no vestige of their existence, save these monuments of their skill and knowledge. Not even a tradition whispers its *guess-work*, who they might be. We only know *they were*.

What proof and evidence do we gather from their remains, which have withstood the test of time, of their origin and probable era of their existence? That they existed centuries ago, is evident from the size which forest trees have attained, which grow upon the mounds and fortifications discovered. That they were civilized, and under-stood the arts, is apparent from the manner of laying out and erecting their fortifications, and from various utensils of gold, copper, and iron, which have occasionally been found in digging below the earth's surface. If I mistake not, I believe even glass has been found, which if so, shows them acquainted with chemical discoveries, which are supposed to have been unknown, until a period much later than the probable time of their existence. That they were not the ancestors of the race which inhabited this country at the time of its discovery by Columbus, appears conclusive from the total ignorance of the Indian tribes of all knowledge of arts and civilization, and the nonexistence of any tradition of their once proud sway. That they were a mighty people, is evident from the extent of territory where these antiquities are scattered. The banks of the Ohio and Mississippi tell they once lived—and even to the shore where the vast Pacific heaves its waves, there are traces of their existence. Who were they? In what period of time did they exist?

In a cave in one of the Western States, there is carved upon the walls a group of people, apparently in the act of devotion; and a rising sun is sculptured above them. From this we should infer, that they were Pagans, worshipping the sun, and the fabulous gods. But what most strikingly arrests the antiquarian's observation, and causes him to repeat the inquiry, "who were they?" is the habiliments of the group. One part of their habit is of the Grecian costume, and the remainder is of the Phœnicians. Were they a colony from Greece? Did they come from that land in the days of its proud glory, bringing with them a knowledge of arts, science, and philosophy? Did they, too, seek a home across the western waters, because they loved liberty in a strange land better than they loved slavery at home? Or what may be as probable, were they the descendants of some band who managed to escape the destruction of ill-fated Troy? the descendants of a people who had called Greece a mother country, but were sacrificed to her vindictive ire, because they were prouder to be Trojans, than the descendants of Grecians? Ay, who were they? Might not America have had its Hector, its Paris, and Helen? its maidens who prayed, and its sons who fought? All this might have been. But their historians and their poets alike have perished. They *have been;* but the history of their existence, their origin, and their destruction, all, all are hidden by the dark chaos of oblivion. Imagination alone, from inanimate landmarks, voiceless walls, and soulless bodies, must weave the record which shall tell of their lives, their aims, origin, and final extinction.

Recently, report says, in Mexico there have been discovered several mummies, embalmed after the manner of the ancient Egyptians. If true, it carries the origin of this fated people still farther back; and we might claim them to be contemporaries with Moses and Joshua. Still, if I form my conclusions correctly from what descriptions I have perused of these Western relics of the past, I should decide that they corresponded better with the ancient Grecians, Phœnicians, or Trojans, than with the Egyptians. I repeat, I may be incorrect in my premises and deductions, but as imagination is their historian, it pleases me better to fill a world with heroes and beauties of Homer's delineations, than with those of "Pharaoh and his host."

Lisette

(*Louisa Currier, Vol. I, 1841, pp. 45–47*)

Chapters on the Sciences

GEOLOGY AND MINERALOGY

Ellinora.　Oh, Isabel, Ann, and all, look here! See what we have found. Alice, Bertha, and I, went out this morning for the ostensible purpose of getting air and exercise, but, in reality, to visit that great ragged ledge yonder—to inspect the cliffs and hills about the river—to collect some minerals for examination this evening; and, seriously, Isabel, we found wonders. You know that brook that falls into the river just above the Falls. Well, we found legible, tangible traces of an earthquake there, in the exact correspondence of the huge and ragged masses of rock on each side of the brook. We met a sensible, loquacious old man near; and he told us that he could remember the time when water enough ran there to carry a mill. Now there is not a drop, except in very wet seasons of the year. I have heard you say, Isabel, that when we find gravel and rounded fragments in under strata, we may infer that they received their round, regular forms by the action of running water, in being transferred from a higher position. We found a shelving declivity of sand; and the sides, far below the surface, exhibited myriads of stones of different sizes, but all rounded and regular, like this. I persist, despite Alice's tame reasonings, in imputing these to diluvian agency. We found large veins running through rock in different directions, sometimes traversing each other; these I attribute to volcanic action, to subterranean fires; and, pray, dear Isabel, do not throw me from my Pegasus, by telling me that I err in this.

Isabel. "Doctors disagree" on this point, as in most others. You are supported in your theory by some of the most learned.

E. "Io triumphe," Alice! What did I say unto thee? *Apropos,* that old gentleman, during our conversation, asked me to tell him just what Geology means. I was completely non-plussed. Please guard me against similar disasters hereafter, by telling me its meaning in good set terms.

I. It comes from the Greek words *ge,* the earth, and *logos,* word, or discourse; and its object, Cleaveland says, is to ascertain the mutual action of the solid, fluid, and aeriform materials of the earth. It investigates the structure, position, and relative situation of the large masses, strata, beds and veins of minerals, which form the external crust of the globe. Its researches extend likewise to the alterations and decompositions effected by air, fire, water, light, and electricity.

E. I thank you. And Mineralogy—

I. Treats of the relations and properties of simple minerals; and assists us in knowing, classing and describing them.

E. Please bring it to our assistance. By mere accident, we found a most beautiful stone this morning. Our old gentleman—

Alice. Let us *dub* him *our hero,* Nora.

E. Ha! well, our hero was driving a cow to pasture—not very chivalric this, for a hero. While we were walking along in company, upon sundry misdemeanors in his charge, he caught up a stone distinguished in nothing, externally, but its rusty aspect, and threw it. It fell in the street before us, and broke. We brought home the fragments; see how splendid they are! There are all the bright colors and beautiful blendings of the rainbow.

Ann. Oh, how pretty! What is the cause of those iris hues?

I. Probably in this case they are merely a tarnish, caused by the action of the air or moisture upon the metallic matter in the mineral. They may not be. The stone, you see, is partially decomposed; and these appearances may be caused by very minute fissures, infinitely too small to be seen by the naked eye, or from a loss of some of the integrant particles, leaving little cavities. From these fissures or cavities light would be reflected in a various manner, producing colored rays by their refraction in passing to the eye. You have all made yourselves familiar with Natural Philosophy; hence this will be easily understood. Similar appearances are sometimes produced by plunging red-hot quartz into cold water.

A.   We found some fine specimens of quartz this morning; we will try the experiment, Nora.

Ann.   Brother has a piece of shell marble, which is extremely beautiful. It is variegated by shells of a mild, pearly lustre, finely irisized. He has also a specimen of the ruin marble, full of figures, which, at certain distances, afford mimic representations of towers, houses, and cities in ruins, with an appropriate back-ground of clouds and sky.

I.   There is a kind of jasper which produces the same beautiful and pleasing illusion.

A.   What is marble, Isabel?

I.   The Latin word *makmor*, marble, is from a Greek word which means *to shine;* and although strictly confined to limestones capable of receiving a high polish, it has been applied by sculptors, ancient and modern, to porphyry, jasper, &c., when in a polished state.

Ann.   I have heard that primitive marbles are very uniform in their color. Whence come the clouds, veins, and spots of different hues and forms, in some of our chimney-pieces?

I.   From an intermixture of oxide of iron, green and yellow serpentine, hornblende, &c.

E.   And whence comes the color of this rose quartz?

I.   One of your specimens is milky quartz, tinged with the oxide of iron. The other is rose quartz; and you were fortunate in finding so beautiful a specimen. It is supposed to receive its color from manganese, one of the chemical elements.

Ann.   Is lava a simple mineral?

I.   No: it is a combination of other minerals; and varies in its aspect and properties according to the nature of its constituents. The word *lava*, is from the Gothic word *lopa*, meaning *to run;* and is applied to the melted matter emitted from the craters of volcanos. Cleaveland mentions a curious fact. On the plains of Iceland, below Hecla, there are *caves* variously formed, and from what is called cavernous lava. The lava produces bubbles of this size; they burst and disclose a cavern within.

A.   How wonderful! And not less so are meteoric stones. Our hero told us of some weighing several pounds, that he saw in Connecticut.

E.   He asked our opinion of their origin, and we could only guess that they came from the moon. He says they are just alike in their external appearance, structure and composition, but that they differ from any other minerals found.

I. Yes: different specimens have been analyzed, and found to contain silex, magnesia, oxide of iron, sulphur, lime, &c. They have been found in all countries, at all ages; and the phenomena accompanying their appearance, are usually the same. They sometimes burst out from a wild cloud, with an explosion like thunder. Their fall is accompanied by a whizzing noise, and is supposed to be at the rate of 300 miles in a minute. They sometimes weigh 50 pounds; and fall into the earth to the depth of 20 inches. They are found to be hot, if examined immediately after their fall; and they emit a strong odor of sulpher. Several years since one appeared in Connecticut in the northern horizon, and passed with great rapidity and an undulating motion to the zenith. Three loud reports were heard, and at each, there were sudden deviations or leaps in the meteor, and masses falling from it were scattered over a surface ten miles in length and three or four in breadth. At the instant of the last report, the stone commenced a rapid descent with a whizzing noise and a curve of light. The largest weighed 37 pounds.

A. Of course nothing is *known* of their origin; but where are they supposed to come from?

I. Some naturalists suppose that they originate in the atmosphere; some, that they are the products of terrestrial volcanos; and yet others, that they fall from comets.

E. "I am sir Oracle." They could not come from the atmosphere, a terrestrial volcano, or a comet; *ergo,* they must be thrown beyond the moon's attraction, within that of the earth. Now this matter is settled, let me ask you about those crystals of yours. You call them all crystals; but they are not all transparent.

I. The term *crystal* was first given to regular forms of rock crystal, or crystallized quartz. But as their regularity was their most distinguished property, all regular solids, whether opaque or transparent, have come to be called *crystals.* So a crystal, in the common acceptation of the term, is a body that by certain laws of affinity, has taken a regular form, with a certain number of plain and polished sides.

E. Please tell us something of this chemical affinity, and something of the process of crystallization. The latter has always been what the Indian calls a *medicine*—a mystery—to me. Perhaps I might solve it, by reading Comstock more thoroughly; but I like verbal descriptions best.

I. I will relate the substance of what Prof. Cleaveland says upon these subjects. He says there are two kinds of affinity, *homogeneous*, and *heterogeneous*. The former, of course, unites particles of the same kind; the latter, those of different kinds. Upon the former, principally, the crystal is dependent for its production. A necessary prerequesite to crystallization is a solution of the mineral substance in some fluid, as water, or caloric. The particles are reduced, by solution, to a state of minute division. They are separated from each other, and left at liberty to move in the solvent with entire freedom. That the crystals may take regular forms, there must be no disturbing force, no external agitation during the process.

A.   Just as in the crystallization of alum in forming baskets.

I.   Yes. Examine these two specimens of crystallized quartz. Of one you see the crystals are perfectly regular, each having five sides; while of the other, some are broken, some have two or three plane faces, and terminate in an uncouth mass of opaque quartz; while all are packed together without any system whatever.

Ann.   Upon what does regularity depend, essentially?

I.   Upon the *regular form of the integrant particles* which go to form the crystal, and upon their *arrangement at the moment of combination*.

E.   The integrant particles, Isabel? Oh, I recollect. Chemistry says,—"We *decompose* a body into its *constituent* parts and *divide* it into its *integrant* parts."

I.   You are correct, Ellinora. Cleaveland says, "a crystal is an assemblage of similar particles; it is formed and increases in size merely by the juxtaposition of these similar, integrant particles. It depends on no interior mechanism, like organic bodies, for its growth; but it is enlarged in its dimensions, by the application of successive layers of particles." He adds, that "both theory and observation induce us to believe that the integrant particles of the same substance, possess the same form and dimensions."

Ann.   Then if these particles always united in the same manner, all crystals formed from the same substance, would present the same outline.

I.   Yes; but they do not; and their difference must be imputed to different dispositions of the integrant particles.

Ann.   In the collection of the Society of Natural History, I saw crystals beautifully colored.

I.   Their coloring comes principally from the metallic oxides; as iron, manganese, &c.

E. See what a pretty piece of granite we found—it is so dark and sparkling!

I. Yes; it contains a great deal of black mica. Granite is composed of quartz, mica, and feldspar. Gneiss, of which I see you have a specimen, is composed of the same minerals as quartz.

Ann. I have seen a piece of amber, with an insect imbedded in it, in a good state of preservation, although the amber was found many feet below the surface of the ground, in the coal mines of Pennsylvania. What is amber? and how came that insect there?

I. As it is generally found with lignite, it is supposed to be a resin from wood, changed by being so long in the earth. The insect must have become entangled, as we have seen them in gums of fruit trees. By an accession of the resinous substance, they are completely covered; and by changes such as have been noticed, buried far below the present surface of the earth.

E. Oh, how I would like to see some of the stupendous animals and vegetables that have been excavated from the depths!

I. Mr. Mantell, in his "Illustrations of the Geology of Sussex," tells us of the "gigantic Megalosaurus, and yet more gigantic Iguanodon, to whom the groves of palms and aborescent ferns would be mere beds of reeds, and who were of such prodigious magnitude, that the *existing* animal creation presents us with no fit objects of comparison. Imagine," he says, "an animal of the lizard tribe, three or four times as large as the largest crocodile, having jaws, with teeth equal in size to the incisors of the rhinoceros, and crested with horns;—such a creature must have been the Iguanodon! Nor were the inhabitants of the waters much less wonderful; witness the Plesiosaurus, which only required wings to be a flying dragon!"

E. Three or four times as large as the crocodile! and a crocodile will enclose an ox in his jaws! it seems utterly incredible; but I know these facts are too well authenticated to be doubted. Oh, what changes have there been!

A. Well might Young say,—

> "What is the world itself? thy world?—a grave!
> Where is the dust that has not been alive?
> The spade, the plough, disturb our ancestors;
> From human mould we reap our daily bread;
> The globe around earth's hollow surface shakes,
> And is the ceiling of her sleeping sons."

And those lines of Beattie—I never saw their full meaning until now.
He says,—

"Art, empire, earth itself, to change are doomed;
    Earthquakes have raised to heaven the humble vale,
And gulfs the mountain's mighty mass entombed,
And where th' Atlantic rolls, wide continents have bloomed."

D.

(Eliza J. Cate, Vol II, 1842, pp. 300–306)

The Funeral of Harrison

In silent grief, in solemn awe,
    They gathered round the coffined dead,
And mutely gazed on what they saw;
    For in that winding sheet, they read
    Their hope of yesterday had fled.

The wreath that lay about him, now—
    Affection's tribute, fondest, last—
How strangely it adorned that brow
    O'er which the spell of death was cast!
    Oh, how unlike the brilliant past!

How wide the contrast, and how sad!
    Who dreamed in grief like this to share,
When heart and lip in smiles were clad?
    When that large boon, a nation's care,
    Was trusted to that sleeper there?

A few short weeks! what have they done?
    Then, he all strength and manliness,
His people's highest, chosen one,
    Exalted in such power to bless!
    Now he is dust and helplessness!

Gaze on your Ruler—well ye may,
    And, statue-like, refuse to weep;—
There is about that shrouded clay
    That bids refreshing tear-drops sleep.
    There is, that lies for grief too deep.

Gaze on him! for he is the first
  Death-offering by your country given!
His body, yielded back to dust—
  His spirit, pure as breath of even,
  Like incense to the court of heaven.

Gaze on! it is your last, last look,
  Your long adieu to him who WAS.
Gaze on! and be your hearts the book
  That links his name and country's laws,
  And both enshrine with freedom's cause.

Now shut the lid, adjust the pall,—
  With gentle hand unwreath his head;
Remove the late Inaugural,
  And holy Book he daily read:—
  Go forth with your illustrious dead.

The prayer hath sounded through these halls;
  Awhile they shall be desolate:
Companion for the crape-hung walls,
  Bring out the vacant chair of state;
  Then go, and follow home the great.

The tolling bells pour out their grief—
  The dirge is sounding far and sad;
And see, upraised in bold relief,
  Yon flag, that erst waved free and glad,
  Now furled, and in deep mourning clad.

With "martial tramp and muffled drum,"
  And death-march solemn, heavy, slow,
They bear him to his narrow home,
  A victim to the last great foe,
  'Mid emblems of the deepest woe.

Walk slowly, ye of ebon brow,
  And mourning badge, and sash of snow;
For precious is your treasure now;
  And eyes that deep affliction know,
  Are fixed upon you in their woe.

'Tis done—the last sad deed is done!
  The people's father lies at rest;—

Sleep on, lamented Harrison!
   They weep above thy cherished dust,
   Who yet shall bear thy holy trust.

Sleep sweetly on! transferred thy care,
   Thy country and her interests,
The burden of thy latest prayer,—
   Sleep where no load of care molests;
   On *these* thy nation's burden rests.

Sleep sweetly, peacefully, our sire;
   Thy children loved thee, Oh, full well!
And when they saw their hope expire,
   Air, earth, and ocean, heard them tell,
   In dirge-like tones, their loud farewell!

                     Adelaide
(Lydia S. Hall, Vol. I, 1841, pp. 84–85)

3

LOOKING BACK:
Nature, Family, and Childhood

The nostalgia so frequently encountered in the Offering *pages is of particular poignancy: the writers had exchanged the unspoiled beauty of the mountains, gorges, and cataracts of the countryside for factory walls, and physical freedom for a constricting lack of exercise, space, and privacy. Some sentiments on the lost glories of nature are, to be sure, borrowed from the literary conventions of the day. But, in fact, the mill girls experienced firsthand a sense of loss. They could see for themselves the encroachment on the town of industrial blight. The splendor of early Lowell, with its forested riverbanks and dramatic waterfalls, was becoming less and less visible as the mills came to line the Merrimack. The "machine in the garden" had come to stay. Remembrance of home became a golden pastoral.*

Nostalgia led some Offering *contributors to see their past and childhood as one long holiday—thus, the fond recollections of sugar-making and quilting, descriptions that beguiled foreign readers, especially, for their rendering of "quaint" American customs.*

"The First Dish of Tea" is a stylishly retold family joke, suggesting a sly Mark Twain tale, as it manages to poke fun at both the rustic ways of countryfolk and the fancy skills needed for sophisticated, acquired tastes. A very different sense of family is revealed in the terrible realism of an uncle's slow death from cancer in "A Sufferer." Finally, "My Grandmother's Fireside" uses the sense of historical and regional roots, the connection to real events in Colonial history, to point up the melan-

133

choly of present reality: death and dispersal have severed the sense of
connectedness and place. Only memories link the survivors.

Home

What a strange and indescribable feeling comes over me, at the
mention of that word,—a sickening sensation, which is almost suf-
focating. You would not wonder, if you knew *all* the associations connected with it. The days of my childhood, those happy, innocent
days, are before me; and I am sporting gaily with those loved ones.
Over the meadows and through the fields we go, plucking here and
there a flower, and trampling the rest under our feet.

Blissful moments! but they will never return. I shall sport with
them no more. Time has sped on, and I am cast upon the waves of a
relentless world; care has stamped its impress upon my brow; but I
cannot forget that I once had a home. Home! It thrills through my
frame like an electric shock. Yes, I once had a home; but now I have
none. The demon of darkness entered our abode of peace; the river of
happiness, which had flowed on in an uninterrupted current, was
dried up. The demon was Intemperance. That bright home of bliss,
that domestic elysium, was turned into an abode of wretchedness.
Oh, Intemperance! thine it has been to blast the hopes of the widow
and orphan—to plant thorns where there should have been roses. But
this is painful; I will pass it over.

I love now to be near the spot where I spent my infantile moments.
It is hard, very hard, to leave it, and the dear ones that are still there.
But I have an object in view, different from what some have. I have
thirsted for knowledge, and have longed to quench my thirst; but I
despair sometimes of ever being able to raise the chalice to my lips, it
has been dashed so many times away. When despair seizes me, then
hope, bright, blessed hope, with his golden wings, comes fluttering
around me, and I am led to think that perhaps I shall yet drink from
the well of knowledge. Oh, I cannot bear to live on this beautiful
earth in ignorance! What! can I sit down, fold my hands, and say, "It
is of no use—fate has decreed it"? No, I shall toil on; and when weary
and sick, shall draw my consolation from the pure fountain of re-

"The Morning Bell" (*Winslow Homer*), *from* Harper's Weekly, *December 13, 1873. Merrimack Valley Textile Museum.*

ligion, which gurgles up at my very feet. This is free. All may drink
from this—the poor as well as the rich.   M. A.

(Mary Anne Spaulding, Vol. II, 1842, p. 320)

Factory Girl's Reverie

'Tis evening. The glorious sun has sunk behind the western horizon. The golden rays, of sunset hues, are fast fading from the western
sky. Gray twilight comes stealing over the landscape. One star after
another sparkles in the firmament. The bird, that warbled its plaintive
song through the long day, has pillowed its head beneath its wing.
The prattle of playful children is hushed. The smith's hammer is no
more heard upon the anvil. The rattle of noisy wheels has ceased. All
nature is at rest.

Evening is the time for thought and reflection. All is lovely without, and why am I not happy? I *cannot* be, for a feeling of sadness
comes stealing over me. I am far, far from that loved spot, where I
spent the evenings of childhood's years. I am here, among strangers—
a factory girl—yes, a *factory girl;* that name which is thought so de-
grading by many, though, in truth, I neither see nor feel its degradation.

But here I am. I toil day after day in the noisy mill. When the bell
calls I must go: and must I always stay here, and spend my days
within these pent-up walls, with this ceaseless din my only music?

O that I were a *child* again, and could wander in my little flower
garden, and cull its choicest blossoms, and while away the hours in
that bower, with cousin Rachel. But alas! that dear cousin has long
since ceased to pluck the flowers, and they now bloom over her grave.
That garden is now cultivated by stranger's hands. I fear they take
but little care of those vines I loved to trail so well; and my bower has
gone to decay. But what is that to me? I shall never spend the sweet
hours there again.

I am sometimes asked, "When are you going home?" "*Home,* that
name ever dear to me." But they would not often ask me, if they only
knew what sadness it creates to say, "*I have no home*"—if they knew
that Death hath taken for his own those dear presiding spirits, and
that strangers now move in their places. Ah! I have

> "No kind-hearted mother to wipe the sad tear,
> No brother or sister my bosom to cheer."

I *will* once more visit the home of my childhood. I will cast one long lingering look at the grave of my parents and brothers, and bid farewell to the spot. I have many friends who would not see me in want. I have uncles, aunts and cousins, who have kindly urged me to share their homes. But I have a little pride yet. I will not be dependent upon friends while I have health and ability to earn bread for myself. I will no more allow this sadness. I will wear a cheerful countenance, and make myself happy by contentment. I will earn all I can, and "lay by something against a *stormy* day." I will do all the good I can, and make those around me happy as far as lies in my power. I see many whose brows are marked with sorrow and gloom; with them I will sympathize, and dispel their gloom if I can. I will while away my leisure hours in reading good books, and trying to acquire what useful knowledge I can. I will ever strive to be contented with my lot, though humble, and not make myself unhappy by repining. I will try to live in reference to that great day of accounts, and ever hope to meet my parents in a land of bliss.

One boon of kind Heaven I ask, though far from that loved spot, that I may be laid beside my mother, " 'neath the dew-drooping willow."   T*******

(Elizabeth E. Turner, Vol. V, 1845, pp. 140–141)

A Weaver's Reverie

NO FICTION

It was a sunny day, and I left for a few moments, the circumscribed spot which is my appointed place of labor, that I might look from an adjoining window upon the bright loveliness of nature. Yes, it was a sunny day; but for many days before, the sky had been veiled in gloomy clouds; and joyous indeed was it to look up into that blue vault, and see it unobscured by its sombre screen; and my heart fluttered, like a prisoned bird, with its painful longings for an unchecked flight amidst the beautiful creation around me.

Why is it, said a friend to me one day, that the factory girls write so much about the beauties of nature?

Oh! why is it, (thought I, when the query afterwards recurred to me,) why is it that visions of thrilling loveliness so often bless the sightless orbs of those whose eyes have once been blessed with the power of vision?

Why is it that the delirious dreams of the famine-stricken, are of tables loaded with the richest viands, or groves, whose pendant boughs droop with their delicious burdens of luscious fruit?

Why is it that haunting tones of sweetest melody come to us in the deep stillness of midnight, when the thousand tongues of man and nature are for a season mute?

Why is it that the desert-traveler looks forward upon the burning, boundless waste, and sees pictured before his aching eyes, some verdant oasis, with its murmuring streams, its gushing founts, and shadowy groves—but as he presses on with faltering step, the bright *mirage* recedes, until he lies down to die of weariness upon the scorching sands, with that isle of loveliness before him?

Oh tell me why is this, and I will tell why the factory girl sits in the hour of meditation, and thinks—not of the crowded, clattering mill, nor of the noisy tenement which is her home, nor of the thronged and busy street which she may sometimes tread,—but of the still and lovely scenes which, in by-gone hours, have sent their pure and elevating influence with a thrilling sweep across the strings of the spirit-harp, and then awakened its sweetest, loftiest notes; and ever as she sits in silence and seclusion, endeavoring to draw from that many-toned instrument a strain which may be meet for another's ear, that music comes to the eager listener like the sound with which the sea-shell echoes the roar of what was once its watery home. All her best and holiest thoughts are linked with those bright pictures which called them forth, and when she would embody them for the instruction of others, she does it by a delineation of those scenes which have quickened and purified her own mind.

It was this love of nature's beauties, and a yearning for the pure, hallowed feelings which those beauties had been wont to call up from their hidden springs in the depths of the soul, to bear away upon their swelling tide the corruption which had gathered, and I feared might settle there,—it was this love, and longing, and fear, which made my heart throb quickly, as I sent forth a momentary glance from the factory window.

I think I said there was a cloudless sky; but it was not so. It was clear, and soft, and its beauteous hue was of "the hyacinth's deep blue"—but there was one bright, solitary cloud, far up in the cerulean vault; and I wished that it might for once be in my power to lie down upon that white, fleecy couch, and there, away and alone, to dream of all things holy, calm, and beautiful. Methought that better feelings, and clearer thoughts than are often wont to visit me, would there take undisturbed possession of my soul.

And might I not be there, and send my unobstructed glance into the depths of ether above me, and forget for a little while that I had ever been a foolish, wayward, guilty child of earth? Could I not then cast aside the burden of error and sin which must ever depress me here, and with the maturity of womanhood, feel also the innocence of infancy? And with that sense of purity and perfection, there would necessarily be mingled a feeling of sweet, uncloying bliss—such as imagination may conceive, but which seldom pervades and sanctifies the earthly heart. Might I not look down from my ærial position, and view this little world, and its hills, valleys, plains, and streamlets, and its thousands of busy inhabitants, and see how puerile and unsatisfactory it would look to one so totally disconnected from it? Yes, there, upon that soft, snowy cloud could I sit, and gaze upon my native earth, and feel how empty and "vain are all things here below."

But not motionless would I stay upon that ærial couch. I would call upon the breezes to waft me away, over the broad, blue ocean, and with nought but the clear, bright ether above me, have nought but a boundless, sparkling, watery expanse below me. Then I would look down upon the vessels pursuing their different courses across the bright waters; and as I watched their toilsome progress, I should feel how blessed a thing it is to be where no impediment of wind or wave might obstruct my onward way.

But when the beams of a mid-day sun had ceased to flash from the foaming sea, I should wish my cloud to bear away to the western sky, and divesting itself of its snowy whiteness, stand there, arrayed in the brilliant hues of the setting sun. Yes, well should I love to be stationed there, and see it catch those parting rays, and, transforming them to dyes of purple and crimson, shine forth in its evening vestment, with a border of brightest gold. Then could I watch the king of day as he sinks into his watery bed, leaving behind a line of crimson light to mark the path which led him to his place of rest.

Yet once, O only once, should I love to have that cloud pass on—

on—on—among the myriads of stars; and leaving them all behind, go far away into the empty void of space beyond. I should love, for once, to be *alone*. Alone! where *could* I be alone? But I would fain be where there is no other, save the INVISIBLE, and there, where not even one distant star should send its feeble rays to tell of a universe beyond, there would I rest upon that soft, light cloud, and with a fathomless depth below me, and a measureless waste above and around me, there would I ———

"Your looms are going without filling," said a loud voice at my elbow; so I ran as fast as possible, and changed my shuttles.

Ella

(*Harriet Farley, Vol. I, 1841, pp. 188–190*)

Sketches of the Past, No. 7

A SUFFERER

A writer celebrated for her powers of pathos, has said, that when she would refine and elevate, she must first soften. The mind must be made plastic by some subduing power, ere it will submit to the mouldings of one who would change it; and whether this theory be correct or not with regard to fiction, it is most certainly true of the influence exerted by the relation of facts.

We may be touched, ay, deeply saddened, by the relation of an affecting story; but yet we say to ourselves, It was not so—this is not true, and wherefore should I weep and sigh, or allow it to disturb my equanimity? But when it *is* true, we cannot dismiss our reflections so easily; and memory will come, with her admonishing tones, and almost compel us to listen to its teachings.

If it is good for us to be afflicted, must it not also be good to learn of others' afflictions?—to know how they have suffered, hoped and trusted?—to learn the lesson, and yet be spared the stripes and smarts of the master? Sorrows and disappointments, received and borne as they should always be, are always salutary. We feel that we have been purified, even when we regret that the refiner should need so fierce a fire; but when we are graciously spared the severest dispensations of Providence, it behooves us to reflect more upon the sad allotments meted out to others; to endeavor, by making their woes our own, to attain also the benefits of their trials.

The story of "the unfortunate man," has excited the sympathy of many of our readers, and I wish now to speak of one who was an acquaintance and townsman of Ezra Baldwin's; promising, however, that mine shall not be all sad stories, if I can learn of the "always happy."

My uncle C. appears to have been one chosen by his Maker, to be an example to all, of how much may be patiently, ay, cheerfully borne and suffered. He inherited from nature that strength of constitution, which enabled him to sustain, for nearly half a century, an existence of incomparable malady. He was always subject to that death-torture, the asthma, and for the last twenty years, it rendered him an invalid, and incapacitated him for labor. But this affliction was but the incipient stage of his distressing experience.

In January, 1838, he was seized with a strange disease in his right arm, which proved to be of a cancerous character, and extended itself to the whole limb, even to the fingers' ends, which became excessively swollen and exquisitely painful. He could obtain no quiet, day nor night; no respite from intense distress. In vain did he throw himself upon his bed at night; it was but a confinement which rendered him more sensitive to his sufferings. In the month of July, convinced that his arm was incurable, and encouraged to hope that the disease had not entered his system, he submitted to its amputation; and it was taken off *at the shoulder joint*.

Reduced, as he long had been, by the asthma, which had often brought him to the brink of the grave, and still more recently weakened by the disease in his arm, this formidable operation nearly cost him his life. After a few days of halting between life and death he revived—afterwards gained a measure of strength, could walk the house, enter his door-yard, and began tremblingly to hope that *what was left of him* might yet enjoy a little of life's sweetness.

It was a few days after the surgical operation that I saw him for the second and last time. The first, (at least since my remembrance,) was when upon a visit to my parents, and rendered a sleepless one by his constitutional malady. He was now hovering upon the confines of a future world, weak, emaciated and agonized—but calm, firm and trustful. It was indeed a privilege to see him then—to watch, tend and learn of him; for though he could speak but little, yet every word had its moral.

There were also some slight circumstances, interesting to an inquiring observer. He could not get rid of his arm. Though amputated, he had still the sensation of its distressing presence. He would sometimes fall into an uneasy slumber, then start and awaken, saying that "the flies" were biting his arm. "Which arm?" would be the question. "The *lame* one," his reply. It was then necessary for his watchers to remind him that it was gone, to excuse themselves from the implied charge of negligence. And this sympathy between the body and its absent member, was not wholly imaginary. When the arm was first severed, it was carried into an adjoining room, placed in a tub of water, and then carefully covered up. After a while his watchful surgeon saw, by his increased distress, that something was wrong; and starting up, he exclaimed that some one was disturbing *that arm*. Upon inquiry, it was ascertained that an intermeddling neighbor *had* been to the tub, and handling the limb. When, unknown to my uncle, it was carried away, and, while *being buried*, he was asked "how that arm felt now?" "*As if it was going lower down*," was his reply; but after that, he gradually lost it.

About a month had passed away, when a tumor appeared under the shoulder of his right side. His surgeon pronounced it the same disease that had destroyed his arm, and *incurable*. This astounding announcement, of course, brought back the dark cloud which was rolling from the brightening prospect he had contemplated. He had sacrificed his arm, but had not saved his life. The malady still remained, and must destroy him. He received the information with composure, and prepared his mind for the issue. His confidence in the perfect rectitude of God's government, remained unshaken. Of Him who made him, he would say, "Though HE slay me, yet will I trust in HIM."

The disease progressed, and again became intensely painful. Another tumor projected from the top of the shoulder, and took the form of "*rose-cancer;*" evolving itself into a large corrosive, running sore. Next, an abscess formed in the back part of the shoulder, working so violently as to push the blade-bone to the distance of inches from its proper place. The discharges from this abscess, when opened, were astonishingly copious. His whole body, with the exception of the remaining arm, became distended, like one bloated with a universal dropsy. For ninety-one days and nights in succession, he laid not down upon his bed, but walked the floor, or when strength failed, was seated in his chair.

Though there was nothing before him in this world, but death and uninterrupted agony until that should come, yet his soul, collecting all its resources, stood firmly up in its strength, calm, patient and unrepining.

On the evening of March 20, several of his friends called to see him. He was unusually communicative, and free from pain—talked with much freedom, and said that *often*, both *before* and *since* the removal of his arm, he had suffered as much, *in the same measure of time*, as during the hour of amputation. When about nine o'clock his visitors retired, he expressed regret that they should leave him, and after they were gone, directed his discourse to his adopted son, (for his three children were so by adoption,) to whom he gave particular directions how to manage the farm for the present year—what portions should be cultivated, and where he should procure his seed-grain, &c. &c.

It was now near ten o'clock, and he directed his son to retire, also desired his wife to seek repose; said he would try to sleep, and did sleep. At two o'clock he called for his wife, who came to him, and found a profuse hemorrhage from the sore—a large artery having corroded. It was now evident that the end had come. With the utmost composure, he called together the members of his family; gave them separately his dying counsel and blessing; expressed his pleasure that he was so near the arms of his Savior, and to that rest which Divine Mercy has prepared for the weary and heavy laden. From loss of blood, he gently fell asleep in death, at seven o'clock, on the morning of March 21, 1839, aged 48 years.

I have spoken of my uncle, as one whose powers were those of endurance—and these were the characteristics most prominently displayed; but had Providence marked out for him another destiny, it would have been acknowledged that he had intellectual and moral endowments, which would have gained for him distinction in life. He paid dearly, as must be obvious, for the pleasure of existence, yet he entertained no thought that his Divine Creator was in debt to him. His hopes of a future and happy immortality, were not grounded on the consideration of *recompense* for things done and suffered by him in this earthly state of being. They rested on the gracious promises of that Gospel which bringeth salvation.

His religion was deep-seated and truly evangelical. It had been a

growing principle from childhood; and was not the result of a momentary and feverish excitement. It was slow in its growth, but stedfast
in its character; and he had not the presumptive confidence to profess
it openly and prematurely. Indeed he erred perhaps in delaying until
nearly forty years of age. Then he came forward, however, a *ripe*
Christian; and, being a gifted and enlightened man, he was soon after
invited to be an officer in the church. His modesty rendered him
reluctant to accept, but, willing ever to be found in the discharge of
duty, he yielded to the wishes of his brethren.

They mourn his departure, and consider it a great loss. Useful,
beloved and esteemed in life, he is remembered and lamented in
death. But though dead he yet speaketh. His story is full of mysterious instruction It tells us how imperfectly we yet understand some of
the principles of God's moral providence. "While all things come alike
unto all; and there is one event to the wise and to the unwise, to the
upright and to the wicked, yet, GOD will cause every man to find according to his ways." HIS work is perfect, and none shall be able to
find fault in HIM.

There are usually some bright spots in the firmament of God's reign
over the world: but there are often clouds and darkness resting upon
it. How needful, then, are the influences of that faith which is "the
substance of things hoped for, and the evidence of things not
seen."   Annette

(*Harriet Farley or Rebecca C. Thompson, Vol. II, 1842, pp. 209–213*)

The Sugar-making Excursion

It was on a beautiful morning in the month of March, (one of those
mornings so exhilarating that they make even age and decrepitude
long for a ramble,) that friend H. called to invite me to visit his sugar-
lot—as he called it—in company with the party which, in the preceding summer, visited Moose Mountain upon the whortleberry excur-
sion. It was with the pleasure generally experienced in revisiting
former scenes, in quest of novelty and to revive impressions and
friendships, that our party set out for this second visit to Moose
Mountain.

A pleasant sleigh-ride of four or five miles brought us safely to the domicile of friend H., who had reached home an hour previously, and was prepared to pilot us to his sugar camp. "Before we go," said he, "you must one and all step within doors, and warm your stomachs with some gingered cider." We complied with his request, and after a little social chat with Mrs. H., who welcomed us with a cordiality not to be surpassed, and expressed many a kind wish that we might spend the day agreeably, we made for the sugar camp, preceded by friend H., who walked by the side of his sleigh, which appeared to be well loaded, and which he steadied with the greatest care at every uneven place in the path.

Arrived at the camp, we found two huge iron kettles suspended on a pole, which was supported by crotched stakes driven in the ground, and each half full of boiling syrup. This was made by boiling down the sap, which was gathered from troughs that were placed under spouts which were driven into rock-maple trees, an incision being first made in the tree with an auger. Friend H. told us that it had taken more than two barrels of sap to make what syrup each kettle contained. A steady fire of oak bark was burning underneath the kettles, and the boys and girls, friend H.'s sons and daughters, were busily engaged in stirring the syrup, replenishing the fire, &c.

Abigail, the eldest daughter, went to her father's sleigh, and taking out a large rundlet, which might contain two or three gallons, poured the contents into a couple of pails. This we perceived was milk, and as she raised one of the pails to empty the contents into the kettles, her father called out, "Ho, Abigail! has thee strained the milk?" "Yes, father," said Abigail.

"Well," said friend H., with a chuckle, "Abigail understands what she is about, as well as her mother would; and I'll warrant Hannah to make better maple sugar than any other woman in New England, or in the whole United States—and you will agree with me in that, after that sugar is turned off and cooled." Abigail turned to her work, emptied her milk into the kettles, and then stirred their contents well together, and put some bark on the fire.

"Come, Jemima," said Henry L., "let us try to assist Abigail a little, and perhaps we shall learn to make sugar ourselves; and who knows but what she will give us a 'gob' to carry home, as a specimen to show our friends; and besides, it is possible that we may have to make sugar ourselves at some time or other; and even if we do not, it will never do us any harm to know how the thing is done." Abigail furnished us each with a large brass scummer, and instructed us to take off the scum as it arose, and put it into the pails; and Henry called two others of our party to come and hold the pails.

"But tell me, Abigail," said Henry, with a roguish leer, "was that milk really intended for whitening the sugar?"

"Yes," said Abigail, with all the simplicity of a Quakeress, "for thee must know that the milk will all rise in a scum, and with it every particle of dirt or dust which may have found its way into the kettles."

Abigail made a second visit to her father's sleigh, accompanied by her little brother, and brought from thence a large tin baker, and placed it before the fire. Her brother brought a peck measure two-thirds full of potatoes, which Abigail put into the baker, and leaving them to their fate, returned to the sleigh, and with her brother's assistance carried several parcels, neatly done up in white napkins, into a little log hut of some fifteen feet square, with a shed roof made of slabs. We began to fancy that we were to have an Irish lunch. Henry took a sly peep into the hut when we first arrived, and he declared that there was nothing inside, save some squared logs, which were placed back against the walls, and which he supposed were intended for seats. But he was mistaken in thinking that seats were every convenience which the building contained,—as will presently be shown.

Abigail and her brother had been absent something like half an hour, and friend H. had in the mean time busied himself in gathering sap, and putting it in some barrels hard by. The kettles were clear from scum, and their contents were bubbling like soap. The fire was burning cheerfully, the company all chatting merrily, and a peep into the baker told that the potatoes were cooked.

Abigail and her brother came and taking up the baker carried it inside the building, but soon returned, and placed it again before the fire. Then she called to her father, who came and invited us to go and take dinner.

We obeyed the summons; but how were we surprised, when we saw how neatly arranged was every thing. The walls of the building were ceiled around with boards, and side tables fastened to them, which could be raised or let down at pleasure, being but pieces of boards fastened with leather hinges and a prop underneath. The tables were covered with napkins, white as the driven snow, and loaded with cold ham, neat's tongue, pickles, bread, apple-sauce, preserves, dough-nuts, butter, cheese, and *potatoes*—without which a yankee dinner is never complete. For beverage, there was chocolate, which was made over a fire in the building—there being a rock chimney in one corner. "Now, neighbors," said friend H., "if you will but seat yourselves on these squared logs, and put up with these rude accommodations, you will do me a favor. We might have had our dinner at the house, but I thought that it would be a novelty, and afford more amusement to have it in this little hut, which I built to shelter us from what stormy weather we might have in the season of making sugar."

We arranged ourselves around the room, and right merry were we, for friend H.'s lively chat did not suffer us to be otherwise. He recapitulated to us the manner of his life while a bachelor; the many bear-fights which he had had; told us how many bears he had killed; how a she-bear denned in his rock-dwelling the first winter after he commenced clearing his land—he having returned home to his father's to attend school; how, when he returned in the spring, he killed her two cubs, and afterwards the old bear, and made his Hannah a present of their skins to make a muff and tippet; also his courtship, marriage, &c.

In the midst of dinner, Abigail came in with some hot mince pies, which had been heating in the baker before the fire out of doors, and which said much in praise of Mrs. H.'s cookery.

We had finished eating, and were chatting as merrily as might be, when one of the little boys called from without, "Father, the sugar has grained." We immediately went out, and found one of the boys stirring some sugar in a bowl, to cool it. The fire was raked from beneath the kettles, and Abigail and her eldest brother were stirring their contents with all haste. Friend H. put a pole within the bail of one of the kettles, and raised it up, which enabled two of the company to take the other down, and having placed it in the snow, they assisted friend H. to take down the other; and while we lent a helping hand to stir and cool the sugar, friend H.'s children ate their dinners, cleared away the tables, put what fragments were left into their father's sleigh, together with the dinner dishes, tin baker, rundlet, and the pails of scum, which were to be carried home for the swine. A firkin was also put into the sleigh; and after the sugar was sufficiently cool, it was put into the firkin, and covered up with great care.

After this we spent a short time promenading around the rock-maple grove, if leafless trees can be called a grove. A large sap-trough, which was very neatly made, struck my fancy, and friend H. said he would make me a present of it for a cradle. This afforded a subject for mirth. Friend H. said that we must not ridicule the idea of having sap-troughs for cradles; for that was touching quality, as his eldest child had been rocked many an hour in a sap-trough, beneath the shade of a tree, while his wife sat beside it knitting, and he was hard by, hoeing corn.

Soon we were on our way to friend H.'s house, which we all reached in safety; and where we spent an agreeable evening, eating maple sugar, apples, beech-nuts, &c. We also had tea about eight o'clock, which was accompanied by every desirable luxury—after which we started for home.

As we were about taking leave, Abigail made each of us a present of a cake of sugar, which was cooled in a tin heart.—"Heigh ho!" said Henry L., "how lucky! We have had an agreeable visit, a bountiful feast—have learned how to make sugar, and have all got sweethearts!"

We went home, blessing our stars and the hospitality of our Quaker friends.

I cannot close without telling the reader, that the sugar which was that day made, was nearly as white as loaf-sugar, and tasted much better.   Jemima

(Betsey Chamberlain, Vol. I, 1841, pp. 225–229)

The First Dish of Tea

Tea holds a conspicuous place in the history of our country; but it is no part of my business to offer comments, or to make any remarks upon the spirit of olden time, which prompted those patriotic defenders of their country's rights to destroy so much tea, to express their indignation at the oppression of their fellow citizens. I only intend to inform the readers of the Lowell Offering, that the first dish of tea which was ever made in Portsmouth, N. H., was made by Abigail Van Dame, my great-great-grandmother.

Abigail was early in life left an orphan, and the care of her tender years devolved upon her aunt Townsend, to whose store fate had never added any of the smiling blessings of Providence; and as a thing in course, Abigail became not only the adopted, but also the well-beloved, child of her uncle and aunt Townsend. They gave her every advantage for an education which the town of Portsmouth afforded; and at the age of seventeen, she was acknowledged to be the most accomplished young lady in Portsmouth.

Many were the worshipers who bowed at the shrine of beauty and learning, at the domicil of Alphonzo Townsend; but his lovely niece was unmoved by their petitions, much to the perplexity of her aunt, who often charged Abigail with carrying an obdurate heart in her bosom. In vain did Mrs. Townsend urge her niece to accept the offers of a young student of law; and equally vain were her efforts to gain a clue to the cause of the refusal, until, by the return of an East India merchantman, Mr. Townsend received a small package for his niece, and a letter from Capt. Lowd, asking his consent to their union, which he wished might take place the following year, when he should return to Portsmouth.

Abigail's package contained a Chinese silk hat, the crown of which was full of Bohea tea. A letter informed her that the contents of the hat was the ingredient which, boiled in water, made what was called the 'Chinese soup.'

Abigail, anxious to ascertain the flavor of a beverage of which she had heard much, put the brass skillet over the coals, poured in two quarts of water, and added thereto a pint basin full of tea and a gill of molasses, and let it simmer an hour. She then strained it through a linen cloth, and in some pewter basins set it around the supper table, in lieu of bean-porridge, which was the favorite supper of the epicures of the olden time.

Uncle, aunt and Abigail seated themselves around the little table, and after crumbling some brown bread into their basins, commenced eating the Chinese soup. The first spoonful set their faces awry, but the second was past endurance; and Mrs. Townsend screamed with fright, for she imagined that she had tasted poison. The doctor was sent for, who administered a powerful emetic; and the careful aunt persuaded her niece to consign her hat and its contents to the vault of an out building.

When Capt. Lowd returned to Portsmouth, he brought with him a chest of tea, a China tea-set, and a copper tea-kettle, and instructed Abigail in the art of tea-making and tea-drinking, to the great annoyance of her aunt Townsend, who could never believe that Chinese soup was half so good as bean-porridge.

The *first dish of tea* afforded a fund of amusement for Captain Lowd and lady; and I hope that the narrative will be acceptable to modern tea-drinkers.   Tabitha.

(Betsey Chamberlain, Vol. II, 1842, pp. 143–144)

The Patchwork Quilt

There it is! in the inner sanctum of my "old-maid's hall"—as cosy a little room as any lady need wish to see attached to her *boudoir*, and gloomy only from the name attached to it—for there is *much in a name;* and the merriest peal of laughter, if echoed from an "old-maid's hall," seems like the knell of girlhood's hopes.

Yes, there is the PATCHWORK QUILT! looking to the uninterested observer like a miscellaneous collection of odd bits and ends of calico, but to me it is a precious reliquary of past treasures; a storehouse of valuables, almost destitute of intrinsic worth; a herbarium of withered flowers; a bound volume of hieroglyphics, each of which is a key to some painful or pleasant remembrance, a symbol of—but, ah, I am poetizing and spiritualizing over my "patchwork quilt." Gentle friends! it contains a piece of each of my childhood's calico gowns, and of my mother's and sisters'; and that is not all. I must tell you, and then you will not wonder that I have chosen for this entertainment my *patchwork quilt*.

It is one of my earliest recollections, and that of the memorable period when I emerged from babyhood to childhood—the commencement of this patchwork quilt. I was learning to sew! O, the exultations, the aspirations, the hopes, the fears, the mortifications, the perseverance—in short, all moral emotions and valuable qualities and powers, were brought out in this grand achievement—the union of some little shreds of calico. And can I ever forget the long-suffering, patience and forbearance of my kind mother?—her smiles and words of encouragement and sympathy; her generosity in the donation of calico bits; her marvellous ingenuity in joining together pieces of all shapes, so that they would result in a perfect square! Parents, never purchase for your children mathematical puzzles—you can teach them and amuse them by making patchwork.

Nor must I forget the beautiful brass thimble that my father gave me, with the assurance that if I never would lose it he would one day give me one of silver! Nor the present of the kind old lady who expressed her gratification over my small stitches by a red broadcloth strawberry, which was introduced to me as an emery-bag. An emery-bag! its office and functions were all to be learned! How much there was that I did not know. But when I had so far learned to sew that five minutes' interval of rest and triumph did not occur between every two stitches, the strenuous application, by which I drove the perspiration from every pore of the hand, soon taught me the value of the emery-bag. O what a heroine was I in driving the stitches! What a martyr under the pricks and inflictions of the needle, which often sent the blood from my fingers but could not force a tear from my eyes! These were the first lessons in heroism and fortitude. How much, too, I learned of the world's generosity in rewarding the efforts of the industrious and enterprising. How many pieces in that quilt were presented because I "could sew," and *did sew*, and was such an adept in sewing. What predictions that I should be a noted sempstress; that I should soon be able to make shirts for my father, sheets for my mother, and nobody knows what not for little brothers and sisters. What legends were told me of little girls who had learned patchwork at three years of age, and could put a shirt together at six. What magical words were *gusset, felling, buttonhole-stitch*, and so forth, each a Sesame, opening into an arcana of workmanship—through and beyond which I could see embroidery, hem-stitch, open-work, tambour, and a host of magical beauties. What predictions that I could some day earn my living by my needle—predictions, alas! that have most signally failed.

Here, also, are the remembrances of another memorable period—the days when the child emerged into girlhood!—when the mind expanded beyond the influence of calico patchwork, and it was laid aside for more important occupations. O what a change was there! Once there could have been nothing more important—now the patchwork was almost beneath my notice. But there was another change. Muslin and lace, with cloths of more common texture, had long occupied my attention when my thoughts and efforts were returned to my patchwork quilt. Well do I remember the boy who waited upon me home from singing-school "six times running." I do not mean that he *waited "running,"* but that he escorted me home six times in succession. What girl would not, under such circumstances, have resumed her patchwork quilt? But how stealthily it was done. Hitherto the patchwork joys had been enhanced by the sympathy, praises and assistance of others; but now they were cherished "in secrecy and silence." But the patchwork quilt bears witness to one of the first lessons upon the vanity of youthful hopes—the mutability of earthly wishes; and—and—any body might accompany me home six hundred times now, and such attentions would never be succeeded by a renewal of those patchwork hopes. Well do I remember the blushes of painful consciousness with which I met my sister's eye, when she broke into my sanctuary, and discovered my employment. By these alone might my secret have been discovered.

But how many passages of my life seem to be epitomized in this patchwork quilt. Here is the piece intended for the centre; a *star* as I called it; the rays of which are remnants of that bright copperplate cushion which graced my mother's easy chair. And here is a piece of that radiant cotton gingham dress which was purchased to wear to the dancing school. I have not forgotten the almost supernatural exertions by which I attempted to finish it in due season for the first night; nor how my mantua-maker, with pious horror, endeavored as strenuously to disappoint me; but spite of her it was finished, and she was guiltless—finished, all but the neck-binding, and I covered that with my little embroidered cape.

Here is a piece of the first dress I ever saw, cut with what were called "mutton-leg" sleeves. It was my sister's, and what a marvellous fine fashion we all thought that was. Here, too, is a remnant of the first "bishop sleeve" my mother wore; and here is a fragment of the first gown that was ever cut for me with a bodice waist. Was there ever so graceful beautiful pointed a fashion for ladies' waists before? Never, in my estimation. By this fragment I remember the gown with wings on the shoulders, in which I supposed myself to look truly angelic; and, oh, down in this corner a piece of that in which I first felt myself a woman—that is, when I first discarded pantalettes.

Here is a fragment of the beautiful gingham of which I had so scanty a pattern, and thus taxed my dress-maker's wits; and here a piece of that of which mother and all my sisters had one with me. Wonderful coincidence of taste, and opportunity to gratify it! Here is a piece of that mourning dress in which I thought my mother looked so graceful; and here one of that which should have been warranted "not to wash," or to wash all white. Here is a fragment of the pink apron which I ornamented so tastefully with "tape trimming;" and here a piece of that which was pointed all around. Here is a token of kindness in the shape of a square of the old brocade-looking calico, presented by a venerable friend; and here a piece given by the naughty little girl with whom I broke friendship, and then wished to take it out of its place, an act of vengeance opposed by my then forbearing mother—on this occasion I thought too forbearing. Here is a fragment of the first dress which baby brother wore when he left off long clothes; and here are relics of the long clothes themselves. Here a piece of that pink gingham frock, which for him was so splendidly decked with pearl buttons; and here a piece of that for which he was so unthankful, for he thought he was big enough to wear something more substantial than calico frocks. Here is a piece of that calico which so admirably imitated vesting, and my mother—economical from necessity—bought it to make "waistcoats" for the boys. Here are pieces of that I thought so bright and beautiful to set off my quilt with, and bought strips of it by the cent's worth—strips more in accordance with the good dealer's benevolence than her usual price for the calico. Here is a piece of the first dress which was ever earned by my own exertions! What a feeling of exultation, of self-dependence, of *self-reliance*, was created by this effort. What expansion of mind!— what awakening of dormant powers! Wellington was not prouder, when he gained the field of Waterloo, than I was with that gown. The belle, who purchases her dresses with the purse her father has always filled, knows not of the triumphant beatings of my heart upon this occasion. And I might now select the richest silk without that honest heart-felt joy. To do for myself—to earn my own living—to meet my daily expenses by my own daily toil, is now a task quite deprived of its novelty, and Time has robbed it of some of its pleasure. And here are patterns presented by kind friends, and illustrative of their tastes; but enough for you.

Then was another era in the history of my quilt. My sister—three years younger than myself—was in want of patchwork, while mine lay undisturbed, with no prospect of being ever called from its repository. Yes, she was to be married; and I not spoken for! She was to be taken, and I left. I gave her the patchwork. It seemed like a transference of girlish hopes and aspirations, or rather a finale to them all. Girlhood had gone, and I was a woman. I felt this more than I had ever felt it before, for my baby sister was to be a wife. We arranged it into a quilt. Those were pleasant hours in which I sympathized so strongly in all her hopes that I made them mine. Then came the quilting; a party not soon to be forgotten, with its jokes and merriment. Here is the memento of a mischievous brother, who was determined to assist, otherwise than by his legitimate occupation of rolling up the quilt as it was finished, snapping the chalk-line, passing thread, wax and scissors, and shaking hands across the quilt for all girls with short arms. He must take the thread and needle. Well, we gave him white thread, and appointed him to a very dark piece of calico, so that we might pick it out the easier; but there! to spite us, he did it so nicely that it still remains, a memento of his skill with the needle—there in that corner of the patchwork quilt.

And why did the young bride exchange her snowy counterpane for the patchwork quilt? These dark stains at the top of it will tell—stains left by the night medicines, taken in silence and darkness, as though to let another know of her pains and remedies would make her sickness more real. As though Disease would stay his hand if met so quietly, and repulsed so gently. The patchwork quilt rose and fell with the heavings of her breast as she sighed in the still night over the departing joys of youth, of health, of newly wedded life. Through the bridal chamber rang the knell-like cough, which told us all that we must prepare for her an early grave. The patchwork quilt shrouded her wasted form as she sweetly resigned herself to the arms of Death, and fell with the last low sigh which breathed forth her gentle spirit. Then settled upon the lovely form, now stiffening, cold and lifeless.

And back to me, with all its memories of childhood, youth, and maturer years; its associations of joy, and sorrow; of smiles and tears; of life and death, has returned to me THE PATCHWORK QUILT.

Annette

(*Harriet Farley or Rebecca C. Thompson, Vol. V, 1845, pp. 201–203*)

My Grandmother's Fireside

At the mention of that beloved fireside, the magic power of memory conveys me back to childhood, and I live over the past. I behold

my aged grandmother sitting in her easy chair, knitting; and a group
of happy children gathered around her, listening to some traditional
tale she is relating, or to the narrative of events which have taken
place during her life.—Before commencing her story, her favorite
grandchild is seated by her side, looking up into her face, in all the
trust and innocence of infancy; while she, in endearing fondness,
gently parts the dark curls on his brow. The rest are seated around
the blazing fire, eagerly waiting for the story.—Incidents of the Revo-
lution interested us most, and especially the one so beautifully described by Whittier, as the "Spectre Warrior." My grandmother related it in the following manner:

"Your grandfather heard the alarm, and had gone to meet the foe.
Feeling lonely and sad, I took my children, and went home to my
mother. As I was lighting a candle for the night, I heard a horse gal-
loping towards the house; a loud rap quickly followed, and upon
going to the door, I beheld a man on a large grey horse. 'Are there
any men here?' demanded the stranger. 'Only two old men,' was my
reply. 'Then you will be all dead before morning; for the English are
landing on the coast at many places, destroying property, and killing
the inhabitants in their march.' While he was talking, his high mettled
horse was champing the bit of his foam-covered bridle, and prancing
about like the trained charger upon the field of battle, impatient for
the carnage to commence. As the rider finished his commission, he
struck his spurs deep in the sides of his restless beast, and rode off as
furiously as he came. Sleep was a stranger to many an eye that night;
for he called at every house, giving the same alarming intelligence.

"All night I sat by my sick mother and sleeping children, in fearful
expectation every hour would bring the tramp of soldiers, and the
torch and sword. But morning came, and brought no foe. Your grandfather soon returned, and assured us that the English had retreated
to Boston. From that time until the close of the war, he was wholly
absorbed in the interests of his country. Long months he would be
absent, and the whole care of our farm and family devolved upon
me."

After finishing her story, my grandmother would draw a deep sigh,
bend forward, lean her head upon her hand, and appear to be com-
muning with the past. But she was soon aroused from her reverie, by
some one of her auditors desiring to know who the stranger was on

the grey horse. As she raised her head, there was a mysterious expression upon her countenance, and her answer was, "Child, we never knew. My sister B., who lived several miles distant, saw the same grey horse and furious rider, at the same hour of twilight, and he spoke the very same words that I heard him speak. Every body saw him, but none could tell whence he came, nor whither he went.—A long war was now before us; and many and great were the privations we endured in the contest for freedom. The poor soldiers were not half clothed or fed; and to add to their wretchedness, they knew their families were suffering at home."

As we listened to the long catalogue of miseries they endured, our young hearts thrilled with emotions of gratitude and veneration for those noble patriots, who had so freely shed their blood in the struggle for liberty, and transmitted so rich a legacy to their descendants.

My grandmother is at rest; but her grandchildren love and revere her memory; and never will her instructions be forgotten, while one heart shall beat that gathered around her fireside.

Where, O where is now that happy band? All are scattered. One has made her home beside a western lake; and more luxuriant fields will meet her eye, and softer breezes fan her brow, and kind friends will press around her,—yet will her thoughts come back to those who watched her infancy and childhood, and the joyous ones that met around that fireside. One has sought classic halls; and as he sits beside his midnight lamp, his mind will wander from his book, and "home, sweet home," and loved ones there, will take its place. One roams the forest and the prairie, and at night rests his head with strangers, and sometimes in the red man's hut; but the long legendary tale he heard around that dear familiar fireside, flits at times across his memory, and the bitter tear starts for those he never more may greet.

All have sought new homes, and some are with the dead. One fell the victim of consumption. Day after day, he faded like the withering flower, and at last calmly sank to his rest. And he, that favorite one, O where is he? Gone, forever gone! We saw him growing up to manhood, all that our love could wish him; but suddenly we saw him robed for the grave, and placed within its narrow limits. In agony of soul we wept and mourned, and never more can our stricken hearts know the joyousness of former days.

Strangers now crowd around that fireside.—Not again shall gather there that happy group; yet do the living hope again to meet each other and the departed, where parting is no more, and where death is unknown.   S. W. S.

(Sarah Shedd(?), Series I, No. 3, 1840, p. 43)

"*New England Factory Life—Bell Time*" (*Winslow Homer*), *from* Harper's
Weekly, *Vol. XII, July 25, 1868. Depicts the Washington Mills, Lawrence,
Massachusetts. Merrimack Valley Textile Museum.*

4
CHOICE AND CONFLICT: The Cost of Independence

Nostalgia can be unreliable, as "The Spirit of Discontent" demon-strates. Ellen, the dissatisfied mill girl, had not come to Lowell directly from the farm; she had most recently been a milliner's assistant, where, her friend and confidante reminds her, she not only worked all day, but all evening, too (like Margaret, the seamstress blinded by overwork, in Mrs. Gaskell's Mary Barton, *written seven years later). In refusing to be a "white slave," Ellen echoes a favorite analogy of Boston reformers. Charles Sumner's phrase "Lords of the lash and the loom" was a con-stant theme of articles in the influential journal* The Boston Quar-terly Review. *Convinced by her friend's arguments and ready to con-cede the superiority of the mills over other work, Ellen and the writer reflect the attitude which so enraged Sarah Bagley and her radical sis-ters in the Lowell Female Labor Reform Association; the fact that other labor open to women was worse than the mills did not excuse Corpora-tion irresponsibility and greed.*

The painful choice—saving or spending—is vividly illustrated, with variations on a theme, in "Evening Before Pay-Day." It is not difficult to appreciate how decisions of this kind became crises of conscience. Habits of thrift and self-denial were not only rigid tenets of the girls' religious upbringing but often the key to their families' survival as well. Now, far from the world of homespun and homegrown necessities, they were wage earners, waiting for the "beautiful paymaster" with his "jingling coppers." Lured by the luxuries of Merrimack Street, the mill girls did not find it hard to advance arguments in favor of spending. Here, one needed finery to appear in church; even the sermon to strengthen the soul against temptation was not free! When a pew cost one week's salary per year, churchgoing, too, had to be weighed against other needs.

The stoicism, sacrifice, and loss tersely expressed by "Susan Miller" suggests another bleak regional tale, Mary Wilkins Freeman's A New England Nun. *For Susan Miller, in this complex story, love fulfilled is equated with acceptance of the servant role; the reward of freely chosen unselfishness, on the other hand, is the life of an old maid.*

The Spirit of Discontent

"I will not stay in Lowell any longer; I am determined to give my notice this very day," said Ellen Collins, as the earliest bell was tolling to remind us of the hour for labor.

"Why, what is the matter, Ellen? It seems to me you have dreamed out a new idea! Where do you think of going? and what for?"

"I am going home, where I shall not be obliged to rise so early in the morning, nor be dragged about by the ringing of a bell, nor confined in a close noisy room from morning till night. I will not stay here; I am determined to go home in a fortnight."

Such was our brief morning's conversation.

In the evening, as I sat alone, reading, my companions having gone out to public lectures or social meetings, Ellen entered. I saw that she still wore the same gloomy expression of countenance, which had been manifested in the morning; and I was disposed to remove from her mind the evil influence, by a plain common-sense conversation.

"And so, Ellen," said I, "you think it unpleasant to rise so early in the morning, and be confined in the noisy mill so many hours during the day. And I think so, too. All this, and much more, is very annoying, no doubt. But we must not forget that there are advantages, as well as disadvantages, in this employment, as in every other. If we expect to find all sun-shine and flowers in any station in life, we shall most surely be disappointed. We are very busily engaged during the day; but then we have the evening to ourselves, with no one to dictate to or control us. I have frequently heard you say, that you would not be confined to house-hold duties, and that you disliked the millinery business altogether, because you could not have your evenings, for leisure. You know that in Lowell we have schools, lectures, and meetings of every description, for moral and intellectual improvement."

"All that is very true," replied Ellen, "but if we were to attend every public institution, and every evening school which offers itself for our improvement, we might spend every farthing of our earnings, and even more. Then if sickness should overtake us, what are the probable consequences? Here we are, far from kindred and home; and if we have an empty purse, we shall be destitute of *friends* also."

"I do not think so, Ellen. I believe there is no place where there are so many advantages within the reach of the laboring class of people, as exist here; where there is so much equality, so few aristocratic distinctions, and such good fellowship, as may be found in this community. A person has only to be honest, industrious, and moral, to secure the respect of the virtuous and good, though he may not be worth a dollar; while on the other hand, an immoral person, though he should possess wealth, is not respected."

"As to the morality of the place," returned Ellen, "I have no fault to find. I object to the constant hurry of every thing. We cannot have time to eat, drink or sleep; we have only thirty minutes, or at most three quarters of an hour, allowed us, to go from our work, partake of our food, and return to the noisy clatter of machinery. Up before day, at the clang of the bell—and out of the mill by the clang of the bell—into the mill, and at work, in obedience to that ding-dong of a bell—just as though we were so many living machines. I will give my notice to-morrow: go, I will—I won't stay here and be a white slave."

"Ellen," said I, "do you remember what is said of the bee, that it gathers honey even in a poisonous flower? May we not, in like manner, if our hearts are rightly attuned, find many pleasures connected with our employment? Why is it, then, that you so obstinately look altogether on the dark side of a factory life? I think you thought differently while you were at home, on a visit, last summer—for you were glad to come back to the mill, in less than four weeks. Tell me, now—why were you so glad to return to the ringing of the bell, the clatter of the machinery, the early rising, the half-hour dinner, and so on?"

I saw that my discontented friend was not in a humour to give me an answer—and I therefore went on with my talk.

"You are fully aware, Ellen, that a country life does not exclude people from labor—to say nothing of the inferior privileges of attending public worship—that people have often to go a distance to meeting of any kind—that books cannot be so easily obtained as they can here—that you cannot always have just such society as you wish—that you"—

She interrupted me, by saying, "We have no bell, with its everlasting ding-dong."

"What difference does it make," said I, "whether you shall be awaked by a bell, or the noisy bustle of a farm-house? For, you know, farmers are generally up as early in the morning as we are obliged to rise."

"But then," said Ellen, "country people have none of the clattering of machinery constantly dinning in their ears."

"True," I replied, "but they have what is worse—and that is, a dull, lifeless silence all around them. The hens may cackle sometimes, and the geese gabble, and the pigs squeal"——

Ellen's hearty laugh interrupted my description—and presently we proceeded very pleasantly, to compare a country life with a factory life in Lowell. Her scowl of discontent had departed, and she was prepared to consider the subject candidly. We agreed, that since we must work for a living, the mill, all things considered, is the most pleasant, and best calculated to promote our welfare; that we will work diligently during the hours of labor; improve our leisure to the best advantage, in the cultivation of the mind,—hoping thereby not only to increase our own pleasure, but also to add to the happiness of those around us.   Almira

(Author unknown, Vol. I, 1841, pp. 111–114)

Evening Before Pay-Day

CHAPTER I

"To-morrow is pay-day; are you not glad, Rosina, and Lucy? *Dorcas* is, I know; for she always loves to see the money. Don't I speak truth *now*, Miss Dorcas Tilton?"

"I wish you would stop your clack, Miss Noisy Impudence; for I never heard you speak anything that was worth an answer. Let me alone, for I have not yet been able to obtain a moment's time to read my tract."

" 'My tract'—how came it 'my tract,' Miss Stingy Old-maid?—for I can call names as fast as you," was the reply of Elizabeth Walters. "Not because you bought it, or paid for it, or gave a thank'ee to those who did; but because you lay your clutches upon every thing you can get without down-right stealing."

"Well," replied Dorcas, "I do not think I have clutched anything now which was much coveted by any one else."

"You are right, Dorcas," said Rosina Alden, lifting her mild blue eyes for the first time towards the speakers; "the tracts left here by the monthly distributors are thrown about, and trampled under foot, even by those who most approve the sentiments which they contain. I have not seen any one take them up to read but yourself."

"She likes them," interrupted the vivacious Elizabeth, "because she gets them for nothing. They come to her as cheap as the light of the sun, or the dews of heaven; and thus they are rendered quite as valuable in her eyes."

"And that very cheapness, that freedom from exertion and expense by which they are obtained, is, I believe, the reason why they are generally so little valued," added Rosina. "People are apt to think things worthless which come to them so easily. They believe them cheap, if they are offered cheap. Now I think, without saying one word against those tracts, that they would be more valued, more perused, and exert far more influence, if they were only to be obtained by payment for them. If they do good now, it is to the publishers only; for I do not think the community in general is influenced by them in the slightest degree. If Dorcas feels more interested in them because she procures them gratuitously, it is because she is an exception to the general rule."

"I like sometimes," said Dorcas, "to see the voice of instruction, of warning, of encouragement, and reproof, coming to the thoughtless, ignorant, poor, and sinful, as it did from him who said to those whom he sent to inculcate its truths, Freely ye have received, *freely give*. The gospel is an expensive luxury now, and those only who can afford to pay their four, or six, or more, dollars a year, can hear its truths from the successors of him who lifted his voice upon the lonely mountain, and opened his lips for counsel at the table of the despised publican, or under the humble roof of the Magdalen."

"Do not speak harshly, Dorcas," was Rosina's reply; "times have indeed changed, since the Saviour went about with not a shelter for his head, dispensing the bread of life to all who would but reach forth their hands and take it; but circumstances have also changed since then. It is true, we must lay down our money for almost every thing we have; but money is much more easily obtained than it was then. It is true, we cannot procure a year's seat in one of our most expensive churches for less than your present week's wages; and if you really wish for the benefits of regular gospel instruction, you must make for it as much of an exertion as was made by the woman who went on her toilsome errand to the deep well of Samaria, little aware that she was there to receive the waters of eternal life. Do not say that it was by no effort, no self-denial, that the gospel was received by those who followed the great Teacher to the lonely sea-side, or even to the desert, where, weary and famished, they remained day after day, beneath the heat of a burning sun, and were relieved from hunger but by a miracle. And who so poor now, or so utterly helpless, that they cannot easily obtain the record of those words which fell so freely upon the ears of the listening multitudes of Judea? If there *are* such, there are societies which will cheerfully relieve their wants, if application be made. And these tracts, which come to us with scarcely the trouble of stretching forth our hands for their reception, are doubtless meant for good."

"Well, Rosina," exclaimed Elizabeth, "if you hold out a little longer, I think Dorcas will have no reason to complain but that she gets *her* preaching cheap enough; but as I, for one, am entirely willing to pay for mine, you may be excused for the present; and those who wish to hear a theological discussion, can go and listen to the very able expounders of the Baptist and Universalist faiths who are just now holding forth in the other chamber. As Dorcas hears no preaching but that which comes *as cheap as the light of the sun*, she will probably like to go; and do not be offended with me, Rosina, if I tell you plainly, that you are not the one to rebuke her. What sacrifice have you made? How much have you spent? When have you ever given any thing for the support of the gospel?"

A tear started to Rosina's eye, and the colour deepened upon her cheek. Her lip quivered, but she remained silent.

"Well," said Lucy to Elizabeth, "all this difficulty is the effect of the very simple question you asked; and I will answer for one, that I am glad to-morrow is pay-day. Pray, what shall you get that is new, Elizabeth?"

"Oh, I shall get one of those beautiful new damask silk shawls which are now so fashionable. How splendid it will look! Let me see: this is a five week's payment, and I have earned about two dollars per week; and so have you, and Rosina; and Dorcas has earned a great deal more, for she has extra work. Pray, what new thing shall *you* get, Dorcas?" added she, laughing.

"She will get a new bank book, I suppose," replied Lucy. "She has already deposited in her own name five hundred dollars, and now she has got a book in the name of her little niece, and I do not know but she will soon procure another. She almost worships them, and Sundays she stays here reckoning up her interest, while we are at meeting."

"I think it is far better," retorted Dorcas, "to stay at home, than to go to meeting, as Elizabeth does, to show her fine clothes. I do not make a mockery of public worship to God."

"There, Lizzy, you must take that, for you deserve it," said Lucy to her friend. "You know you *do* spend almost all your money in dress."

"Well," said Elizabeth, "I shall sow all my wild oats now, and when I am an old maid I will be as steady, though *not quite* so stingy, as Dorcas. I will get a bank book, and trot down Merrimac street as often as she does, and every body will say, 'What a remarkable change in Elizabeth Walters! She used to spend all her wages as fast as they were paid her, but now she puts them in the bank. She will be quite a fortune for some one, and I have no doubt she will get married for what she *has*, if not for what she *is*.' But I cannot begin now, and I do not see how *you* can, Rosina."

"I have not begun," replied Rosina, in a low, sorrowful tone.

"Why, yes, you have; you are as miserly now as Dorcas herself; and I cannot bear to think of what you may become. Now tell me if you will not get a new gown and bonnet, and go to meeting."

"I cannot," replied Rosina, decidedly.

"Well do, if you have any mercy on us, buy a new gown to wear into the Mill, for your old one is so shabby. When calico is nine-pence a yard, I do think it is mean to wear such an old thing as that; besides, I should not wonder if it should soon drop off your back."

"Will it not last me one month more?" and Rosina began to mend the tattered dress with a very wistful countenance.

"Why, I somewhat doubt it; but at all events, you must have another pair of shoes."

"These are but just beginning to let in the water," said Rosina; "I think they must last me till another pay-day."

"Well, if you have a fever or consumption, Dorcas may take care of you, for *I* will not; but what," continued the chattering Elizabeth, "shall you buy that is new, Lucy?"

"Oh, a pretty new, though cheap, bonnet, and I shall also pay my quarter's pew-rent, and a year's subscription to the Lowell Offering; and that is all that I shall spend. You have laughed much about old maids; but it was an old maid who took care of me when I first came to Lowell, and she taught me to lay aside half of every month's wages. It is a rule from which I have never deviated, and thus I have quite a pretty sum at interest, and have never been in want of any thing."

"Well," said Elizabeth, "will you go out to-night with me, and we will look at the bonnets, and also the damask silk shawls. I wish to know the prices. How I wish to-day had been pay-day, and then I need not have gone out with an empty purse."

"Well, Lizzy, *you* know that 'to-morrow is pay-day,' do you not?"

"Oh yes, and the beautiful pay-master will come in, rattling his coppers so nicely."

"Beautiful!" exclaimed Lucy; "do you call our pay-master *beautiful?*"

"Why, I do not know that he would look beautiful, if he was coming to cut my head off; but really, that money-box makes him look delightfully."

"Well, Lizzy, it *does* make a great difference in his appearance, I know; but if we are going out to-night, we must be in a hurry."

"If you go by the Post Office, do ask if there is a letter for me," said Rosina.

"Oh, I hate to go near the Post Office in the evening; the girls act as wild as so many Carribee Indians. Sometimes I have to stand there an hour on the ends of my toes, stretching my neck, and sticking out my eyes; and when I think I have been pommeled and jostled long enough, I begin to 'set up on my own hook,' and I push away the heads that have been at the list as if they were committing it all to

memory, and I send my elbows right and left in the most approved
style, till I find myself 'master of the field.' "

"Oh, Lizzy! you know better; how can you do so?"

"Why, Lucy, pray tell me what *you* do?"

"I go away, if there is a crowd; or if I feel very anxious to know
whether there is a letter for me, the worst that I do is to try 'sliding
and gliding.' I dodge between folks, or slip through them, till I get
waited upon. But I know that we all act worse there than any where
else, and if the post-master speaks a good word for the factory girls, I
think it must come against his conscience, unless he has seen them
somewhere else than in the office."

"Well, well, we must hasten along," said Elizabeth, "and stingy as
Rosina is, I suppose she will be willing to pay for a letter; so I will
buy her one, if I can get it. Good evening, ladies," continued she,
tying her bonnet; and she hurried after Lucy, who was already down
the stairs, leaving Dorcas to read her tract at leisure, and Rosina to
patch her old calico gown, with none to torment her.

CHAPTER II

"Two letters!" exclaimed Elizabeth, as she burst into the chamber,
holding them up, as little Goody in the story-book held up her 'two
shoes,' "two letters! one for *you*, Rosina, and the other is for *me*. Only
look at it! It is from a cousin of mine, who has never lived out of sight
of the Green Mountains. I do believe, notwithstanding all that is said
about the ignorance of the factory girls, that the letters which *go out* of
Lowell, look as well as those which *come into it*. See here: up in the left
hand corner, the direction commences, 'Miss'; one step lower is 'Elizabeth'; then down another step, 'Walters.' Another step brings us
down to 'Lowell'; one more is the 'City'; and down in the right hand
corner, is 'Massachusetts' at full length. Quite a regular stair-case, if
the steps had been all of an equal width. Miss Elizabeth Walters,
Lowell City, Massachusetts, anticipates much edification from the perusal thereof," said she, as she broke the seal.

"Oh, I must tell you an anecdote," said Lucy. "While we were
waiting there, I saw one girl push her face into the little aperture, and
ask if there was a paper for her; and the clerk asked her if it was a
transient paper. 'A what?' said she. 'A transient paper,' he repeated.

'Why, I don't know what paper it is,' was the reply; 'sometimes our folks send me one, and sometimes another.'"

Dorcas and Elizabeth laughed, and the latter exclaimed, "Girls, I am not so selfish as to be unwilling that you should share my felicity. Should you not like to see my letter?" and she held it up before them. "It is quite a contrast to our Rosina's delicate Italian penmanship, although she is a factory girl."

Dear Cousin: I write this to let you know that I am well, and hope you are enjoying the same great blessing. Father and Mother are well too. Uncle Joshua is sick with the information of the brain. We think he will die, but he says that he shall live his days out. We have not had a letter from you since you went to Lowell. I send this by Mary Twining, an old friend of mine. She works upon the Appletown Corporation. She will put this in the Post Office, because we do not know where you work. I hope you will go and see her. We have had a nice time making maple sugar this spring. I wish you had been with us. When you are married, you must come with your husband. Write to me soon, and if you don't have a chance to send it by private conveyance, drop it into the Post Office. I shall get it, for the mail-stage passes through the village twice a week.

> I want to see you more I think
> Than I can write with pen and ink;
> But when I shall, I cannot tell—
> At present I must wish you well.
>
> Your loving cousin,
> Judith Walters.

"Well," said Elizabeth, drawing a long breath, "I do not think my *loving cousin* will ever die of the 'information of the brain'; but if it should get there, I do not know what might happen.—But, Rosina, from whom is *your* letter?"

"My mother," said Rosina; and she seated herself at the little light-stand, with a sheet of paper, pen, and ink-stand.

"Why, you do not intend to answer it to-night."

"I must commence it to-night," replied Rosina, "and finish it to-morrow night, and carry it to the Post Office. I cannot write a whole letter in one evening."

"Why, what is the matter?" said Dorcas.

"My twin-sister is very sick," replied Rosina; and the tears she could no longer restrain gushed freely forth. The girls, who had before been in high spirits over cousin Judy's letter, were subdued in an instant. Oh how quick is the influence of sympathy for grief! Not another word was spoken. The letter was put away in silence, and the girls glided noiselessly around the room, as they prepared to retire to rest.

Shall we take a peep at Rosina's letter? It may remove some false impressions respecting her character, and many are probably suffering injustice from erroneous opinions, when, if all could be known, the very conduct which has exposed them to censure would excite approbation. Her widowed mother's letter was the following:

My Dear Child: Many thanks for your last letter, and many more for the present it contained. It was very acceptable, for it reached me when I had not even a cent in the world. I fear you deprive yourself of necessaries to send me so much. But all you can easily spare will be gladly received. I have as much employment at tailoring as I can find time to do, and sometimes I sit up all night, when I cannot accomplish my self-allotted task during the day.

I have delayed my reply to your letter, because I wished to know what the doctors really thought of your sister Marcia. They consulted to-day, and tell me *there is no hope.* The suspense is now over, but I thought I was better prepared for the worst than I am. She wished me to tell her what the doctors said. At length I yielded to her importunities. "Oh mother," said she, with a sweet smile, "I am so glad they have told you, for I have known it for a long time. You must write to Rosina to come and see me before I die." Do as you think best, my dear, about coming; you know how glad we should be to see you. But if you cannot come, do not grieve too much about it. Marcia must soon die, and you, I hope, will live many years; but the existence which you commenced together here, I feel assured will be continued in a happier world. The interruption which will now take place will be short, in comparison with the life itself which shall have no end. And yet it is hard to think that one so young, so good and lovely, is so soon to lie in the silent grave. While the blue skies of heaven are daily growing more softly beautiful, and the green things of earth are hourly putting forth a brighter verdure, she, too, like the lovely creatures of nature, is constantly acquiring some new charm, to fit her for that world which she will so soon inhabit. Death is coming, with his severest tortures, but she arrays her person in bright loveliness at his approach, and her spirit is robed in graces which well may fit her for that angel-band, which she is so soon to join.

I am now writing by her bed-side. She is sleeping soundly now, but there is a heavy dew upon the cheek, brow and neck of the tranquil sleeper. A rose—it is one of *your* roses, Rosina—is clasped in her transparent hand; and one rosy petal has somehow dropped upon her temple. It breaks the line which the blue vein has so distinctly traced on the clear white brow. I will take it away, and enclose it in the letter. When you see it, perhaps it will bring more vividly to memory the days when you and Marcia frolicked together among the wild rose-bushes.—Those which you transplanted to the front of the house, have grown astonishingly. Marcia took care of them as long as she could go out of doors; for she wished to do something to show her gratitude to you. Now that she can go among them no longer, she watches them through the window, and the little boys bring her every morning the most beautiful blossoms. She enjoys their beauty and fragrance as she does every thing which is reserved for her enjoyment. There is but one thought which casts a shade upon that tranquil spirit, and it is that she is such a helpless burden upon us. The last time that she received a compensation for some slight article which she had exerted herself to complete, she took the money and sent Willy for some salt. "Now, mother," said she, with the arch smile which so often illuminated her countenance in the days of health, "Now, mother, you cannot say that I do not earn my salt."

But I must soon close, for in a short time she will awaken, and suffer for hours from her agonizing cough. No one need tell me now, that a consumption makes an easy path to the grave. I watched too long by your father's bed-side, and have witnessed too minutely all of Marcia's sufferings, to be persuaded of this.

But she breathes less softly now, and I must hasten. I have said little of the other members of the family, for I knew you would like to hear particularly about her. The little boys are well—they are obedient to me, and kind to their sister. Answer as soon as you receive this, for Marcia's sake; unless you come and visit us.

And now, hoping that this will find you in good health, as, by the blessing of God, it leaves me, (a good, though an old-fashioned manner of closing a letter,) I remain as ever,

Your affectionate Mother.

Rosina's reply was as follows:

Dear Mother: I have just received your long-expected letter, and have seated myself to commence an answer, for I cannot go home.

I do wish very much to see you all, especially dear Marcia, once more; but it is not best. I know you think so, or you would have urged my return. I think I shall feel more contented here, earning comforts for my sick sister and necessaries for you, than I should be there, and unable to relieve a want. "To-morrow is pay-day," and my earnings, amounting to ten dollars, I shall enclose in this letter. Do not think I am suffering for any thing, for I get along very well. But I am obliged to be extremely prudent, and the girls here call me miserly. Oh mother! it is hard to be so misunderstood; but I cannot tell *them* all.

But your kind letters are indeed a solace to me, for they assure me that the mother whom I have always loved and reverenced, approves of my conduct. I shall feel happier to-morrow night, when I enclose that bill to you, than my room-mates can be in the far different disposal of theirs.

What a blessing it is that we can send money to our friends; and indeed what a blessing that we can send them a letter. Last evening you was penning the lines which I have just perused, in my far-distant home; and not twenty-four hours have elapsed since the rose-leaf before me was resting on the brow of my sister; but it is now ten o'clock, and I must bid you good night, reserving for to-morrow evening the remainder of my epistle, which I shall address to Marcia.

It was long before Rosina slept that night; and when she did, she was troubled at first by fearful dreams. But at length it seemed to her that she was approaching the quiet home of her childhood. She did not remember where she had been, but had a vague impression that it was in some scene of anxiety, sorrow and fatigue; and she was longing to reach that little cot, where it appeared so still and happy. She thought the sky was very clear above it, and the yellow sunshine lay softly on the hills and fields around it. She saw her rose-bushes blooming around it, like a little wilderness of blossoms; and while she was admiring their increased size and beauty, the door was opened, and a body, arrayed in the snowy robes of the grave, was carried beneath the rose-bushes. They bent to a slight breeze which swept above them, and a shower of snowy petals fell upon the marble face and shrouded form. It was as if nature had paid this last tribute of gratitude to one who had been one of her truest and loveliest votaries.

Rosina started forward that she might remove the fragrant covering, and imprint one last kiss upon the fair cold brow; but a hand was laid upon her, and a well-known voice repeated her name. And then she started, for she heard the bell ring loudly; and she opened her eyes as Dorcas again cried out, "Rosina, the second bell is ringing." Elizabeth and Lucy were already dressed, and they exclaimed at the same moment, "Remember, Rosina, that *to-day is pay-day.*"   Lucinda

(Harriet Farley, Vol. I, 1841, pp. 239–249)

Susan Miller

CHAPTER I

"Mother, it is all over now," said Susan Miller, as she descended from the chamber where her father had just died of *delirium tremens.*

Mrs. Miller had for several hours walked the house, with that ceaseless step which tells of fearful mental agony; and when she had heard from her husband's room some louder shriek or groan, she had knelt by the chair or bed which was nearest, and prayed that the troubled spirit might pass away. But a faintness came over her, when a long interval of stillness told that her prayer was answered; and she leaned upon the railing of the stairway for support, as she looked up to see the first one who should come to her from the bed of death.

Susan was the first to think of her mother; and when she saw her sink, pale, breathless and stupified upon a stair, she sat down in silence, and supported her head upon her own bosom. Then for the first time was she aroused to the consciousness, that she was to be looked upon as a stay and support; and she resolved to bring from the hidden recesses of her heart, a strength, courage and firmness, which should make her to her heart-broken mother, and younger brothers and sisters, what *he* had not been for many years, who was now a stiffening corpse.

At length she ventured to whisper words of solace and sympathy, and succeeded in infusing into her mother's mind a feeling of resignation to the stroke they had received. She persuaded her to retire to her bed, and seek that slumber which had been for several days denied them; and then she endeavored to calm the terror-stricken little ones, who were screaming because their father was no more. The neighbors came in and proffered every assistance; but when Susan retired that night to her own chamber, she felt that she must look to HIM for aid, who alone could sustain through the tasks that awaited her.

Preparations were made for the funeral; and though every one knew that Mr. Miller had left his farm deeply mortgaged, yet the store-keeper cheerfully trusted them for articles of mourning, and the dress-maker worked day and night, while she expected never to receive a remuneration. The minister came to comfort the widow and her children. He spoke of the former virtues of him who had been wont to seek the house of God on each returning Sabbath, and who had brought his eldest children to the font of baptism, and been then regarded as an example of honesty and sterling worth; and when he adverted to the one failing which had brought him to his grave in the very prime of manhood, he also remarked, that he was now in the hands of a merciful God.

The remains of the husband and father were at length removed from the home which he had once rendered happy, but upon which he had afterwards brought poverty and distress, and laid in that narrow house which he never more might leave, till the last trumpet should call him forth; and when the family were left to that deep silence and gloom which always succeeded a death and burial, they began to think of the trials which were yet to come.

Mrs. Miller had been for several years aware that ruin was coming upon them. She had at first warned, reasoned and expostulated; but she was naturally of a gentle, and almost timid disposition; and when she found that she awakened passions which were daily growing more violent and ungovernable, she resolved to await in silence a crisis which sooner or later would change their destiny. Whether she was to follow her degenerate husband to his grave, or accompany him to some low hovel, she knew not; she shrunk from the future, but faithfully discharged all present duties, and endeavored, by a strict economy, to retain at least an appearance of comfort in her household.

To Susan, her eldest child, she had confided all her fears and sorrows; and they had watched, toiled, and sympathized together. But when the blow came at last, when he who had caused all their sorrow and anxiety was taken away by a dreadful and disgraceful death, the long-enduring wife and mother was almost paralyzed by the shock.

But Susan was young; she had health, strength and spirits to bear her up, and upon her devolved the care of the family, and the plan for its future support. Her resolution was soon formed; and without saying a word to any individual, she went to Deacon Rand, who was her father's principal creditor.

It was a beautiful afternoon in the month of May, when Susan left the house in which her life had hitherto been spent—determined to know before she returned to it, whether she might ever again look upon it as her home. It was nearly a mile to the Deacon's, and not a single house upon the way. The two lines of turf in the road, upon which the bright green grass was springing, shewed that it was but seldom travelled; and the birds warbled in the trees, as though they feared no disturbance. The fragrance of the lowly flowers, the budding shrubs, and the blossoming fruit-trees, filled the air; and she stood for a moment to listen to the streamlet which she crossed upon a rude bridge of stones. She remembered how she had loved to look at it in summer, as it murmured along among the low willows, and alderbushes; and how she had watched it in the early spring, when its swollen waters forced their way through the drifts of snow which had frozen over it, and wrought for itself an arched roof, from which the little icicles depended in diamond points, and rows of beaded pearls. She looked also at the meadow, where the grass was already so long and green; and she sighed to think that she must leave all that was so dear to her, and go where a ramble among fields, meadows and orchards, would be henceforth a pleasure denied to her.

CHAPTER II

When she arrived at the spacious farm-house, which was the residence of the Deacon, she was rejoiced to find him at home and alone. He laid aside his newspaper, as she entered; and kindly taking her hand, inquired after her own health, and that of her friends. "And now, Deacon," said she, when she had answered all his questions; "I wish to know whether you intend to turn us all out of doors, as you have a perfect right to do—or suffer us still to remain, with a slight hope that we may sometime pay you the debt for which our farm is mortgaged."

"You have asked me a very plain question," was the Deacon's reply, "and one which I can easily answer. You see that I have here a house, large enough and good enough for the President himself; and plenty of every thing in it, and around it; and how in the name of common sense, and charity, and religion, could I turn a widow and her fatherless children out of their house and home! Folks have called me mean, and stingy, and close-fisted; and though in my dealings with a rich man I take good care that he shall not over-reach me, yet I never stood for a cent with a poor man in my life. But you spake about sometime paying me; pray, how do you hope to do it?"

"I am going to Lowell," said Susan quietly, "to work in the Factory,—the girls have high wages there now; and in a year or two, Lydia and Eliza can come, too; and if we all have our health, and mother and James get along well with the farm and the little ones, I hope, I do think, that we can pay it all up in the course of seven or eight years."

"That is a long time for you to go and work so hard, and shut yourself up so close, at your time of life," said the Deacon, "and on many other accounts I do not approve of it."

"I know how prejudiced the people here are against factory girls," said Susan, "but I should like to know what real good *reason* you have for disapproving of my resolution. You cannot think there is any thing really wrong in my determination to labor, as steadily and as profitably as I can, for myself and the family."

"Why, the way that I look at things, is this," replied the Deacon. "Whatever is not right, is certainly wrong; and I do not think it right for a young girl like you, to put herself in the way of all sorts of temptation. You have no idea of the wickedness and corruption which exist in that town of Lowell. Why, they say that more than half of the girls have been in the House of Correction, or the County Jail, or some other vile place; and that the other half are not much better; and I should not think you would wish to go and work, and eat, and sleep, with such a low, mean, ignorant, wicked, set of creatures."

"I know such things are said of them, Deacon, but I do not think they are true. I have never seen but one factory girl, and that was my cousin Esther, who visited us last summer. I do not believe there is a better girl in the world than she is; and I cannot think she would be so contented and cheerful among such a set of wretches as some folks think factory girls must be. There may be wicked girls there; but among so many, there must be some who are good; and when I go there, I shall try to keep out of the way of bad company, and I do not doubt that cousin Esther can introduce me to girls who are as good as any with whom I have associated. If she cannot, I will have no companion but her, and spend the little leisure I shall have, in solitude; for I am determined to go."

"But supposing, Susan, that all the girls there were as good, and sensible, and pleasant as yourself—yet there are many other things to be considered. You have not thought how hard it will seem to be boxed up fourteen hours in a day, among a parcel of clattering looms, or whirling spindles, whose constant din is of itself enough to drive a girl out of her wits; and then you will have no fresh air to breathe, and as likely as not come home in a year or two with a consumption, and wishing you had staid where you would have had less money, and better health. I have also heard that the boarding women do not give the girls food which is fit to eat, nor half enough of the mean stuff they do allow them; and it is contrary to all reason, to suppose that folks can work, and have their health, without victuals to eat."

"I have thought of all these things, Deacon, but they do not move me. I know the noise of the Mills must be unpleasant at first; but I shall get used to that; and as to my health, I know that I have as good a constitution to begin with, as any girl could wish, and no predisposition to consumption, nor any of those diseases which a factory life might otherwise bring upon me. I do not expect all the comforts which are common to country farmers; but I am not afraid of starving—for cousin Esther said, that she had an excellent boarding place, and plenty to eat and drink, and that which was good enough for any body. But if they do not give us good meat, I will eat vegetables alone; and when we have bad butter, I will eat my bread without it."

"Well," said the Deacon, "if your health is preserved, you may lose some of your limbs. I have heard a great many stories about girls who had their hands torn off by the machinery, or mangled so that they could never use them again; and a hand is not a thing to be despised, nor easily dispensed with. And then, how should you like to be ordered about, and scolded at, by a cross overseer?"

"I know there is danger," replied Susan, "among so much machinery; but those who meet with accidents are but a very small number, in proportion to the whole; and if I am careful, I need not fear any injury. I do not believe the stories we hear about bad overseers,—for such men would not be placed over so many girls; and if I have a cross one, I will give him no reason to find fault; and if he finds fault without reason, I will leave him, and work for some one else. You know that I must do something, and I have made up my mind what it shall be."

"You are a good child, Susan," and the Deacon looked very kind when he told her so, "and you are a courageous, noble-minded girl. I am not afraid that *you* will learn to steal, and lie, and swear, and neglect your Bible, and the meeting-house; but lest any thing unpleasant should happen, I will make you this offer: I will let your mother live upon the farm, and pay me what little she can, till your brother James is old enough to take it at the halves; and if you will come here, and help my wife about the house and dairy, I will give you four and sixpence a week, and you shall be treated as a daughter—perhaps you may one day be one."

The Deacon looked rather sly at her, and Susan blushed; for Henry Rand, the Deacon's youngest son, had been her play-mate in childhood, her friend at school, and her constant attendant at all the parties, and evening meetings. Her young friends all spoke of him as her lover, and even the old people had talked of it as a very fitting match, as Susan, besides good sense, good humor, and some beauty, had the health, strength and activity, which are always reckoned among the qualifications for a farmer's wife.

Susan knew of this; but of late, domestic trouble had kept her at home, and she knew not what his present feelings were. Still she felt that they must not influence her plans and resolutions. Delicacy forbade that she should come and be an inmate of his father's house, and her very affection for him had prompted the desire that she should be as independent as possible of all favors from him, or his father; and also the earnest desire that they might one day clear themselves of debt. So she thanked the Deacon for his offer, but declined accepting it, and arose to take leave.

"I shall think a great deal about you, when you are gone," said the Deacon, "and will pray for you, too. I never used to think about the sailors, till my wife's brother visited us, who had led for many years a sea-faring life; and now I always pray for those who are exposed to the dangers of the great deep. And I will also pray for the poor factory girls, who work so hard, and suffer so much."

"Pray for me, Deacon," replied Susan in a faltering voice, "that I may have strength to keep a good resolution."

She left the house with a sad heart; for the very success of her hopes and wishes, had brought more vividly to mind the feeling that she was really to go and leave for many years her friends and home.

She was almost glad that she had not seen Henry; and while she was wondering what he would say and think, when told that she was going to Lowell, she heard approaching footsteps, and looking up, saw him coming towards her. The thought—no, the idea, for it had not time to form into a definite thought—flashed across her mind, that she must now rouse all her firmness, and not let Henry's persuasions shake her resolution to leave them all, and go to the factory.

But the very indifference with which he heard of her intention, was of itself sufficient to arouse her energy. He appeared surprised, but otherwise wholly unconcerned, though he expressed a hope that she would be happy and prosperous, and that her health would not suffer from the change of occupation.

If he had told her that he loved her—if he had entreated her not to leave them, or to go with the promise of returning to be his future companion through life—she could have resisted it; for this she had resolved to do; and the happiness attending an act of self-sacrifice would have been her reward.

She had before known sorrow, and she had borne it patiently and cheerfully; and she knew that the life which was before her would have been rendered happier by the thought, that there was one who was deeply interested for her happiness, and who sympathized in all her trials.

When she parted from Henry it was with a sense of loneliness, of utter desolation, such as she had never before experienced. She had never before thought that he was dear to her, and that she had wished to carry in her far-off place of abode, the reflection that she was dear to him. She felt disappointed and mortified, but she blamed not him, neither did she blame herself; she did not know that any one had been to blame. Her young affections had gone forth as naturally and as involuntarily as the vapours rise to meet the sun. But the sun which had called them forth, had now gone down, and they were returning in cold drops to the heart-springs from which they had risen; and Susan resolved that they should henceforth form a secret fount, whence every other feeling should derive new strength and vigor. She was now more firmly resolved that her future life should be wholly devoted to her kindred, and thought not of herself but as connected with them.

CHAPTER III

It was with pain that Mrs. Miller heard of Susan's plan; but she did not oppose her. She felt that it must be so,—that she must part with her for her own good, and the benefit of the family; and Susan hastily made preparations for her departure.

She arranged every thing in and about the house for her mother's convenience; and the evening before she left, she spent in instructing Lydia how to take her place, as far as possible; and told her to be always cheerful with mother, and patient with the younger ones, and to write a long letter every two months, (for she could not afford to hear oftener,) and to be sure and not forget her for a single day.

Then she went to her own room; and when she had re-examined her trunk, band-box and basket, to see that all was right, and laid her riding dress over the great arm-chair, she sat down by the window to meditate upon her change of life.

She thought, as she looked upon the spacious, convenient chamber in which she was sitting, how hard it would be to have no place to which she could retire and be alone; and how difficult it would be to keep her things in order in the fourth part of a small apartment; and how possible it was that she might have unpleasant room-mates; and how probable that every day would call into exercise all her kindness and forbearance. And then she wondered if it would be possible for her to work so long, and save so much, as to render it possible that she might one day return to that chamber and call it her own. Sometimes she wished she had not undertaken it, that she had not let the Deacon know that she hoped to be able to pay him; she feared that she had taken a burden upon herself which she could not bear, and sighed to think, that her lot should be so different from that of most young girls.

She thought of the days when she was a little child; when she played with Henry at the brook, or picked berries with him on the hill; when her mother was always happy, and her father always kind; and she wished that the time could roll back, and she could again be a careless little girl.

She felt, as we sometimes do, when we shut our eyes, and try to sleep, and get back into some pleasant dream, from which we have been too suddenly awakened. But the dream of youth was over, and before her was the sad, waking reality, of a life of toil, separation and sorrow.

When she left home the next morning, it was the first time she had ever parted from her friends. The day was delightful, and the scenery beautiful,—a stage-ride was of itself a novelty to her, and her companions pleasant and sociable; but she felt very sad, and when she retired at night to sleep in a hotel, she burst into tears.

Those who see the factory girls in Lowell, little think of the sighs and heart-aches which must attend a young girl's entrance upon a life of toil and privation, among strangers.

To Susan, the first entrance into a factory boarding-house, seemed something dreadful. The rooms looked strange and comfortless, and the women cold and heartless; and when she sat down to the supper table, where, among more than twenty girls, all but one were strangers, she could not eat a mouthful. She went with Esther to their sleeping apartment, and after arranging her clothes and baggage, she went to bed, but not to sleep.

The next morning she went into the Mill; and at first, the sight of so many bands, and wheels, and springs, in constant motion, was very frightful. She felt afraid to touch the loom, and she was almost sure that she could never learn to weave; the harness puzzled, and the reed perplexed her; the shuttle flew out, and made a new bump upon her head; and the first time she tried to spring the lathe, she broke out a quarter of the treads. It seemed as if the girls all stared at her, and the overseers watched every motion, and the day appeared as long as a month had been at home. But at last it was night; and O, how glad was Susan to be released! She felt weary and wretched, and retired to rest without taking a mouthful of refreshment. There was a dull pain in her head, and a sharp pain in her ankles; every bone was aching, and there was in her ears a strange noise, as of crickets, frogs, and jews-harps, all mingling together; and she felt gloomy and sick at heart. "But it won't seem so always," said she to herself; and with this truly philosophical reflection, she turned her head upon a hard pillow, and went to sleep.

Susan was right; it did not seem so always. Every succeeding day seemed shorter and pleasanter than the last; and when she was accustomed to the work, and had become interested in it, the hours seemed shorter, and the days, weeks and months flew more swiftly by, than they had ever done before. She was healthy, active and ambitious, and was soon able to earn even as much as her cousin, who had been a weaver several years.

Wages were then much higher than they are now; and Susan had the pleasure of devoting the avails of her labor to a noble and cherished purpose. There was a definite aim before her, and she never lost sight of the object for which she left her home, and was happy in the prospect of fulfilling that design. And it needed all this hope of success, and all her strength of resolution, to enable her to bear up against the wearing influences of a life of unvarying toil. Though the days seemed shorter than at first, yet there was a tiresome monotony about them. Every morning the bells pealed forth the same clangor, and every night brought the same feeling of fatigue. But Susan felt, as all factory girls feel, that she could bear it for a while. There are few who look upon factory labor as a pursuit for life. It is but a temporary vocation; and most of the girls resolve to quit the Mill when some favorite design is accomplished. Money is their object—not for itself, but for what it can perform; and pay-days are the landmarks which cheer all hearts, by assuring them of their progress to the wished-for goal.

Susan was always very happy when she enclosed the quarterly sum to Deacon Rand, although it was hardly won, and earned by the deprivation of many little comforts, and pretty articles of dress, which her companions could procure. But the thought of home, and the future happy days which she might enjoy in it, was the talisman which ever cheered and strengthened her.

She also formed strong friendships among her factory companions, and became attached to her pastor, and their place of worship. After the first two years, she had also the pleasure of her sister's society; and in a year or two more, another came. She did not wish them to come while very young. She thought it better that their bodies should be strengthened, and their minds educated in their country home; and she also wished, that in their early girlhood, they should enjoy the same pleasures which had once made her own life a very happy one.

And she was happy now; happy in the success of her noble exertions, the affection and gratitude of her relatives, the esteem of her acquaintances, and the approbation of conscience. Only once was she really disquieted. It was when her sister wrote that Henry Rand was married to one of their old school-mates. For a moment, the colour fled from her cheek, and a quick pang went through her heart. It was

but for a moment; and then she sat down, and wrote to the newly
married couple a letter, which touched their hearts by its simple, fervent wishes for their happiness, and assurances of sincere friendship.

Susan had occasionally visited home, and she longed to go, never to
leave it; but she conquered the desire, and remained in Lowell more
than a year after the last dollar had been forwarded to Deacon Rand.
And then, O how happy was she when she entered her chamber the
first evening after her arrival, and viewed its newly painted wainscot-
ing, and brightly colored paper hangings, and the new furniture with
which she had decorated it; and she smiled as she thought of the
sadness which had filled her heart the evening before she first went to
Lowell.

She now always thinks of Lowell with pleasure; for Lydia is married here, and she intends to visit her occasionally, and even sometimes thinks of returning for a little while to the Mills. Her brother
James has married, and resides in one half of the house, which he has
recently repaired; and Eliza, though still in the factory, is engaged to a
wealthy young farmer.

Susan is with her mother and younger brothers and sisters. People
begin to think she will be an old maid, and she thinks herself that it
will be so. The old Deacon still calls her a good child, and prays every
night and morning for the factory girls.   F. G. A.

(*Author unknown, Vol. I, 1841, pp. 161–171*)

5
CASTE AND CLASS:
Mill Job or Marriage

A *radical minister turned editor, Orestes A. Brownson (1803–1876)
was the one real revolutionary in his crowd of benevolent Brook
Farmers. Brownson's journal,* The Boston Quarterly Review, *regularly attacked the rich, advocating an end to wage slavery and the
redistribution of wealth among labor. "Your enemy is the employer,"
Brownson thundered.*

*But in enumerating the evils of the factory system, this "friend of the
Laboring Classes" included the moral degradation of the factory girl,
thus exposing the deepest anxiety of the class he was busy defending—the
loss of respectability. And there could be no doubt for writer or reader
of* The Lowell Offering *as to the price of this moral and social
"downward mobility": stigmatized by her working environment, the
mill girl became an unmarriageable outcast.*

"Gold Watches" illustrates another painful confrontation with assigned class identity. Dress must now be considered an unreliable indication of class, Mrs. Sarah Hale, editor of Godey's Lady's Book, *had
written, since "even factory girls" now wore gold watches in imitation
of their betters. The* Offering *rebuttal manages to make ironic sport of
such genteel snobbery—"O the times! O the manners!"—while using
the occasion for a moral lesson: perhaps the victims of such ugly attitudes are themselves too prone to attach undue importance to finery.*

"Ann and Myself," with equally neat irony, contrasts the middle-class status of the "school-ma'am" with the better paid, but socially

demeaned, position of the mill girl. The price of continued friendship is concealment of the real nature of Ann's work. The heroine, by rejecting this evasion, has refused, at the same time, assent to the implied shame of labor.

Gold Watches

It is now more than two years since an article appeared in the Lady's Book, in the form of a tale, though it partakes more of the character of an essay. It was written by Mrs. Hale, and exhibits her usual judgment and talent. Her object evidently was, to correct the many erroneous impressions which exist in society with regard to the folly of extravagance in dress, and all outward show. I was much pleased with all of it, with the exception of a single sentence. Speaking of the impossibility of considering dress a mark of distinction, she observed,—(addressing herself, I presume, to the *ladies* of New England,)—"How stands the difference now? Many of the factory girls wear gold watches, and an imitation, at least, of all the ornaments which grace the daughters of our most opulent citizens."

O the times! O the manners! Alas! how very sadly the world has changed! The time was when the *lady* could be distinguished from the *no-lady* by her dress, as far as the eye could reach; but now, you might stand in the same room, and, judging by their outward appearance, you could not tell "which was which." Even gold watches are now no *sure* indication—for they have been worn by the lowest, even by "many of the factory girls." No *lady* need carry one now, for any other than the simple purpose of easily ascertaining the time of day, or night, if she so please!

But seriously: why is the idea so prevalent that dress appears more objectionable in the factory girl than in any other female? Extravagance should be objected to in any one; but the exercise of taste in dress, should not be denied to *them*, more than to other young females.

A gentleman may receive a thousand dollars per annum, and have half a dozen daughters, who all think they should dress in a style superior to that of the factory girl, who receives one or two hundred dollars per year. And when they find this is impossible, they say, "O

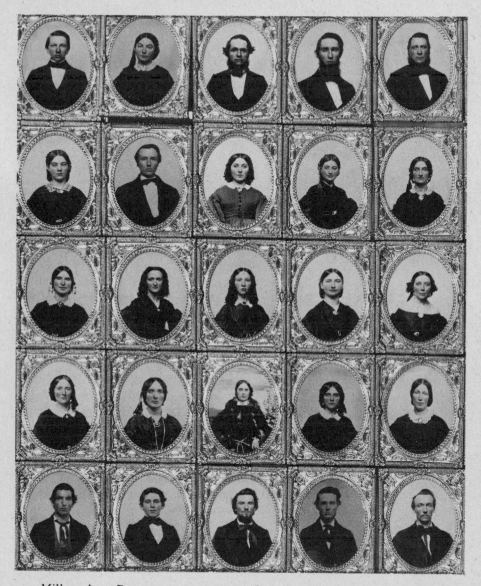

Mill workers. Daguerreotypes ca. 1844, framed together at the time the portraits were made. A group of young men and women in their Sunday best from the Amoskeag Manufacturing Company, Manchester, New Hampshire. Manchester Historic Association.

dear! how the factory girls do rig up! We cannot get anything but they will imitate us." What a dreadful evil! But it is a part of my belief that out of evil good may eventually come; and if the impossibility of making dress a mark of distinction, induces the conviction that *ladies* must attain some higher distinctive trait, this deplorable evil must result in a great benefit.

Those who do not labor for their living, have more time for the improvement of their minds, for the cultivation of conversational powers, and graceful manners; but if, with these advantages, they still need richer dress to distinguish them from *us*, the fault must be their own, and they should at least learn to honor merit and acknowledge talent wherever they see it.

I pity the girl who cannot take pleasure in wearing the new and beautiful bonnet which her father has presented her, because, forsooth, she sees that some factory girl has, with her hard-won earnings, procured one just like it. I said I pitied the girl; but I fear there is too much of contempt and indignation in the feeling which swells my heart, to render it worthy of the gentle name of pity. Yet such things are said by Lowell girls, whose fathers are as dependent on the factories as any female operatives in the city, and who, if deprived of them, would perhaps be obliged to labor themselves.

And now I will address myself to my sister operatives in New England factories. Good advice should be taken, from whatever quarter it may come, whether from friend or foe; and part of the advice which Mrs. Hale has given to the readers of the Lady's Book, may be of advantage to us. Is there not among us, as a class, too much of this striving for distinction in dress? Is it not the only aim and object of too many of us, to wear something a little better than others can obtain? Do we not sometimes see the girl who has half a dozen silk gowns, toss her head, as if she felt six times better than her neighbor who has none? Oh, how they will sometimes walk, "mincing as they go," as if the ground was hardly good enough for them. And many of them can put on an air of haughty contempt, which would do honor (or disgrace) to the proudest lady in the court of Victoria. And all this, because their Florence bonnet is finer, and their shawl much more costly, than is usually worn! I have often been reminded of the words of the Scottish bard—

> "O wad some power the giftie gie us,
> To see oursels as·ithers see us,—

It wad frae mony a blunder free us,
    An' foolish notion;
Sic airs in dress and gait wad lea'e us,
    An' e'en devotion."

I have often thought that *we* should have more common sense about such things, than those who have been brought up in higher circles. We cannot expect all girls to overcome educational prejudices. The mind which can do that, is of a higher order than is common. But we have not this to do. We see things more as they really are, and not through the false medium which misleads the aristocracy. Oh, how foolish is the feeling which prompts some among us to neglect or ridicule the poorly-clad girl, who has just come from her country home, to seek among strangers a toilsome subsistence! Too often the first things she learns are, that she must assume an air of self-confidence or impudence, and buy fine clothes as fast as she can earn them; or she must hang her head with a feeling of inferiority, and submit to the insolence of the vain and worthless. I do not say that this is often the case, but *too often*—for it is sometimes so—and even once is too often.

We all have many opportunities for the exercise of the kindly affections, and more than most females. We should look upon one another something as a band of orphans should do. We are fatherless and motherless: we are alone, and surrounded by temptation. Let us caution each other; let us watch over and endeavor to improve each other; and both at our boarding-houses and in the mill, let us strive to promote each other's comfort and happiness. Above all, let us endeavor to improve ourselves by making good use of the advantages we here possess. I say, let us all strive to do this; and if we succeed, it will finally be acknowledged that Factory Girls shine forth in ornaments more valuable than *Gold Watches*.   A Factory Girl

(Author unknown, Vol. II, 1842, pp. 377–379)

Factory Girls

"SHE HAS WORKED IN A FACTORY, *is sufficient to damn to infamy the most worthy and virtuous girl.*"

So says Mr. Orestes A. Brownson; and either this horrible assertion is true, or Mr. Brownson is a slanderer. I assert that it is *not* true, and Mr. B. may consider himself called upon to prove his words, if he can.

This gentleman has read of an Israelitish boy who, with nothing but a stone and sling, once entered into a contest with a Philistine giant, arrayed in brass, whose spear was like a weaver's beam; and he may now see what will probably appear to him quite as marvellous; and that is, that a *factory girl* is not afraid to oppose herself to the *Editor of the Boston Quarterly Review*. True, he has upon his side fame, learning, and great talent; but I have what is better than either of these, or all combined, and that is *truth*. Mr. Brownson has not said that this thing should be so; or that he is glad it is so; or that he deeply regrets such a state of affairs; but he has said it *is* so; and *I* affirm that it is *not*.

And whom has Mr. Brownson slandered? A class of girls who in this city alone are numbered by thousands, and who collect in many of our smaller towns by hundreds; girls who generally come from quiet country homes, where their minds and manners have been formed under the eyes of the worthy sons of the Pilgrims, and their virtuous partners, and who return again to become the wives of the free intelligent yeomanry of New England, and the mothers of quite a proportion of our future republicans. Think, for a moment, how many of the next generation are to spring from mothers doomed to infamy! "Ah," it may be replied, "Mr. Brownson acknowledges that you may still be worthy and virtuous." Then we must be a set of worthy and virtuous idiots, for no virtuous girl of common sense would choose for an occupation one that would consign her to infamy.

Mr. Brownson has also slandered the community; and far over the Atlantic the story will be told, that in New England, the land to which the Puritans fled for refuge from social as well as religious oppression—the land where the first blood was shed in defence of the opinion that all are born free and equal—the land which has adopted the theory that morals and intellect are alone to be the criterions of superiority—that *there*, worthy and virtuous girls are consigned to infamy, if they work in a factory!

That there has been prejudice against us, we know; but it is wearing away, and has never been so deep nor universal as Mr. B's statement will lead many to believe. Even now it may be that "the mushroom aristocracy," and "would-be-fashionables" of Boston, turn up their eyes in horror at the sound of those vulgar words, *factory girls;* but *they* form but a small part of the community, and theirs are not the opinions which Mr. Brownson intended to represent.

Whence has arisen the degree of prejudice which has existed against factory girls, I cannot tell; but we often hear the condition of the factory population of England, and the station which the operatives hold in society there, referred to as descriptive of *our* condition. As well might it be said, as say the *nobility* of England, that *labor itself* is disgraceful, and that all who work should be consigned to contempt, if not to infamy. And again: it has been asserted that to put ourselves under the influence and restraints of corporate bodies, is contrary to the spirit of our institutions, and to that love of independence which we ought to cherish. There is a spirit of independence which is averse to social life itself; and I would advise all who wish to cherish it, to go far beyond the Rocky Mountains, and hold communion with none but the untamed Indian, and the wild beast of the forest. We are under restraints, but they are voluntarily assumed; and we are at liberty to withdraw from them, whenever they become galling or irksome. Neither have I ever discovered that any restraints were imposed upon us, but those which were necessary for the peace and comfort of the whole, and for the promotion of the design for which we are collected, namely, to get money, as much of it and as fast as we can; and it is because our toil is so unremitting, that the wages of factory girls are higher than those of females engaged in most other occupations. It is these wages which, in spite of toil, restraint, discomfort, and prejudice, have drawn so many worthy, virtuous, intelligent, and well-educated girls to Lowell, and other factories; and it is the wages which are in a great degree to decide the characters of the factory girls as a class. It was observed (I have been told) by one of the Lowell overseers to his superintendent, that he could get girls enough who would work for one dollar per week. I very much doubt whether it would be possible; but supposing it true, they would not be such girls as will come and work for two, three and four dollars per week. Mr. Brownson may rail as much as he pleases against the real injustice of capitalists against operatives, and we will bid him *God speed*, if he will but keep truth and common sense upon his side. Still, the avails of factory labor are now greater than those of many domestics, seamstresses, and school-teachers; and strange would it be, if in money-loving New England, one of the most lucrative female employments should be rejected because it is toilsome, or because some people are prejudiced against it. Yankee girls have too much *independence* for *that*.

But it may be remarked, "You certainly cannot mean to intimate, that all factory girls are virtuous, intelligent," &c. No, I do not; and Lowell would be a stranger place than it has ever been represented, if among eight thousand girls there were none of the ignorant and depraved. Calumniators have asserted, that *all* were vile, because they knew *some* to be so; and the sins of *a few* have been visited upon *the many*. While the mass of the worthy and virtuous have been unnoticed, in the even tenor of their way, the evil deeds of a few individuals have been trumpeted abroad, and they have been regarded as specimens of factory girls. It has been said, that factory girls are not thought as much of any where else as they are in Lowell. If this be true, I am very glad of it; it is quite to our credit to be more respected where we are best known. Still, I presume, there are girls here who are a disgrace to the city, to their sex, and to humanity. But *they* do not fix the tone of public sentiment, and their morals are not the standard. There is an old adage, that "Birds of a feather flock together;" and a Captain Marryatt could probably find many females here who do not appear like "woman as she should be"—but men of a better sort have found females here of whom they have made companions, not for an evening or a day, but for life. The erroneous idea, wherever it exists, must be done away, that there is in factories but one sort of girls, and *that* the baser and degraded sort. There are among us *all sorts* of girls. I believe that there are few occupations which can exhibit so many gradations of piety and intelligence; but the majority may at least lay claim to as much of the former as females in other stations of life. The more intelligent among them would scorn to sit night after night to view the gestures of a Fanny Elssler. The Improvement Circles, the Lyceum and Institute, the social religious meetings, the Circulating and other libraries, can bear testimony that the little time they have is spent in a better manner. Our well filled churches and lecture halls, and the high character of our clergymen and lecturers, will testify that the state of morals and intelligence is not low.

Mr. Brownson, I suppose, would not judge of our moral characters by our church-going tendencies; but as many do, a word on this subject may not be amiss. That there are many in Lowell who do not regularly attend any meeting, is as true as the correspondent of the Boston Times once represented it; but for this there are various reasons. There are many who come here for but a short time, and who are willing for a while to forego every usual privilege, that they may carry back to their homes the greatest possible sum they can save. There are widows earning money for the maintenance and education of their children; there are daughters providing for their aged and destitute parents; and there are widows, single women, and girls, endeavoring to obtain the wherewithal to furnish some other home than a factory boarding-house. Pew rent, and the dress which custom has wrongly rendered essential, are expenses which they cannot afford, and they spend their Sabbaths in rest, reading, and meditation. There may also be many other motives to prevent a regular attendance at church, besides a disinclination to gratify and cultivate the moral sentiments.

There have also been nice calculations made, as to the small proportion which the amount of money deposited in the Savings Bank bears to that earned in the city; but this is not all that is saved. Some is deposited in Banks at other places, and some is put into the hands of personal friends. Still, much that is earned is immediately, though not foolishly, spent. Much that none but the parties concerned will ever know of, goes to procure comforts and necessaries for some lowly home, and a great deal is spent for public benevolent purposes. The fifteen hundred dollars which were collected in one day for Missionary purposes by a single denomination in our city, though it may speak of what Mrs. Gilman calls the "too great tendency to overflow in female benevolence," certainly does not tell of hearts sullied by vice, or souls steeped in infamy. And it is pleasing to view the interest which so many of the factory girls take in the social and religious institutions of this place, who do not call Lowell aught but a temporary home. Many of them stay here longer than they otherwise would, because these institutions have become so dear to them, and the letters which they send here after they do leave, show that the interest was too strong to be easily eradicated. I have known those who left homes of comfort and competence, that they might here enjoy religious privileges which country towns would not afford them. And the Lowell Offering may prove to all who will read it, that there are girls here whose education and intellect place them above the necessity of pursuing an avocation which will inevitably connect them with the ignorant and vicious.

And now, if Mr. Brownson is *a man*, he will endeavor to retrieve the injury he has done; he will resolve that "the dark shall be light, and the wrong made right," and the assertion he has publicly made will be as publicly retracted. If he still doubts upon the subject, let him come among us: let him make himself as well acquainted with us as our pastors and superintendents are; and though he will find error, ignorance, and folly among us, (and where would he find them not?) yet he would not see worthy and virtuous girls consigned to infamy, because they work in a factory.   A Factory Girl

(Author unknown, Series I, No. 2, 1840, pp. 17–19)

Ann and Myself

NO FICTION

Ann W. and myself were friends from childhood, nor did our friendship decline in maturer years; it grew with our growth, and strengthened with our strength. We were partakers of each other's joys and sorrow. We were nearly of the same age, though of quite different temperaments. I will not say that I was of a more amiable disposition than was Ann. Suffice it to say, there was a marked contrast. We attended school together, and were always in the same class; and though our advantages for an education were very limited—having only six months schooling in a year—at the age of fifteen, we were qualified for the responsible station of "country school ma'ams."

We were shortly employed as such: Our avocation served to increase our own importance, especially in our own estimation; for a "school ma'am" in a country village, is of no little consequence, I can assure you. She is generally the "beau ideal;"—and the favored one who succeeds, by his proffered acts of gallantry, in winning her favor, applauds himself as having achieved some mighty conquest.

Before I proceed farther with my story, I will furnish my readers with a little history of my situation, when I began "to teach the young idea how to shoot." My place of destination was about fifteen miles from my native village, in the north-western part of New Hampshire. The day previously to the one that was to raise me to such an eminence, my employer might have been seen riding up to the door, leading another steed by his side—for the road was so rough and unfrequented, that "horse-back" was the only safe mode of travelling.

I had selected such articles of apparel as were indispensable for my convenience,—and tying them in a 'kerchief, they were suspended from the horn of the saddle on which I rode. My heart sickened at first at the idea of going among strangers; but being of quite a romantic turn, and desirous of rendering myself more conspicuous in the world's estimation, the honors that awaited me in my new station quelled all my forebodings. I arrived at Mr. H's about six o'clock, P. M., and was received very kindly by Mrs. H. and her daughter. In a few moments, I was summoned to tea; and the neatly-spread table bespoke the hospitalities of the inmates of the house.

The following morning, I was escorted by Mr. H.'s daughter (who, by the way, was to be one of my pupils,) to the school-house, about three quarters of a mile from the house where I was to board. I summoned all my dignity, and with an air of self-importance hastened towards my task, with a palpitating heart. But with all my feigned seriousness, I could hardly suppress a smile as I overtook many of my pupils, one after another, each accosting me with "Good morning, school ma'am."

When I arrived in sight of the school-house, I saw a large group of children assembled around the door, anxiously looking for my approach. As soon as I drew near, they all modestly courtesied, and following me immediately into the house, seated themselves, and gazed intently at me. I felt somewhat embarrassed at first, for many of my scholars were my seniors. However, I mustered fortitude sufficient to make a few remarks, and proceeded to the best of my ability.

My school consisted of about forty scholars—most of whom were peaceable and docile. I was employed for three months, at the rate of one dollar per week, and succeeded in gaining the good will of my scholars, and the approbation of my employer.

In the mean time, my friend Ann was employed in the same task, though much nearer home—which separated us for a season, though we often sympathized together by writing.

After having completed my task and returned home, I received a letter from some friends then living in a manufacturing village in New Hampshire, with an invitation to spend a few weeks in visiting them. The proposal was gladly accepted, although I had no favorable opinion of factory places, and more especially of factory girls. Notwithstanding my fastidious notions and educational prejudices, I ventured to accept, remembering that I was a "school ma'am." But what was my surprise, when I arrived at my uncle's, to find that one of my cousins was employed in the factory! I had not seen cousin C. for three years, during which time she had become much altered. From the giddy flirt of thirteen, she seemed to have sprung into years of mature judgment, and was intelligent and agreeable. She left her employment the day after my arrival, and accompanied me about the village; and at length, invited me to visit the factory. My pride revolted at the thought of going to a place I had held in such contempt. However, I consented, because I fancied they would know I was a "school-ma'am."

My cousin took me through several rooms, and introduced me to many neat and beautiful-looking young ladies, with whom I was highly pleased, though not a little chagrined to find they so much surpassed their visiter. Notwithstanding all my self-esteem, my views of factory girls were vastly different when I returned home from what they were when I went out.

Sabbath day I attended meeting, and to my surprise saw many young ladies there whom I recognized as factory girls! for, to tell the truth, I hardly expected to find them civilized. In fact, I became so much changed in opinion, that I concluded to adopt the appalling name of factory girl myself, with all its consequences. My cousin generously offered to procure me a place in the same room in which she was employed; and one week from the time I left home, in all the pomp of a "school-ma'am," I was known as a "factory girl!"

I found my task much less perplexing as a factory girl than as a school teacher, and my pay was much more satisfactory. My only trouble now was, how I should contrive to get my friend Ann with me—for she had been educated with the same prejudices against factories as myself. But I resolved to make an effort. I accordingly wrote, informing her of my adventure in the factory, and earnestly desiring her to come and do likewise; and in one week after the reception of my letter, Ann was with me. She was immediately employed in the same room, and we were once more happily in each other's companionship.

One year elapsed before we visited our homes. During that time, our friends had become more reconciled to our employment—for instead of three months in a year, as teachers, we then had constant employment, which furnished us the means of advancing our education, which we otherwise could not have done. Besides, we had acquired much information from observation, extensive reading, Lyceums, and other means of increasing our little fund of knowledge.

I shall never forget our first visit to our own village—for we were the first who had ever adopted the avocation of factory girl. We were prepared for a cool reception from our former associates—nor were we in the least disappointed. They at first stood aloof from us with a look of mingled envy and contempt. We submitted to this with as good a grace as possible, well remembering that we had once entertained the same uncharitable opinions. But this by degrees wore away, for they found we had not become uncivilized, as they expected; and ere the time arrived for our return, many who had looked upon us with scornful eyes, solicited us to aid them in obtaining situations in the factory.

Ann and I remained three years in the same manufacturing village, in uninterrupted friendship. But as the journey of human life is not all sun-shine, our felicity was soon destined to be eclipsed. Ann received a letter from a sister, informing her of ill-health, and requesting her to come immediately to the family residence in Maine. The intelligence was painful to Ann, but doubly so to me—for while I sympathized sincerely with her in affliction, my heart could not bear the thought of an uncertain separation. But I nerved myself sufficiently to assist her in making necessary arrangements for her journey; and in tears we parted, mutually agreeing to maintain a punctual correspondence.

Six long months glided by, and Ann returned not, though her sister had been completely restored to health. I began to suspect there was some attractive planet in Maine, which kept Ann away from me so long; nor was I in error, for my next letter brought an invitation to attend her wedding. This was really more painful than the separation. The idea of a rival was more than I could endure; yet I could not reproach her for I had reason to believe her affianced husband was worthy her choice. But I was not willing to have her affections bestowed upon another. I resolved therefore to give her up for lost.

After many solicitations from Ann and her husband, I was prevailed on to visit them, though much against my inclination. She had then been married two years, and was blessed with a kind husband and a competency of this world's goods. She received me with all her former affection, and I anticipated much pleasure from my visit; but it vanished, when she whispered to me, "You must be 'school-ma'am' while you are here, for factory girls are nothing thought of in this place." By this title, I passed off pretty well among the aristocrats of the place, and was often compelled to hear my avocation slandered and my associates misrepresented, without the privilege of saying one word in their vindication. I could not long endure such bondage, and resolved to return where I could enjoy a dearly-loved freedom. I have never visited Ann since, though I have been often entreated so to do; and I am confident when I visit her again, I shall not be the dupe of false opinions.   Matilda

(Author unknown, Vol. I, 1841, pp. 74–78)

6
CHANGES:
Reform, Regret, and a
Vision of the Future

The two editorials "Plan for Mutual Relief" and "Editor's Valedictory," written by the Reverend Abel C. Thomas, have been included as evidence that the Offering *began life committed to improving factory conditions. The "Plan for Mutual Relief" is far more critical in implication than its mild tone would indicate. The Corporation hospital, an elegant Greek Revival house which had been designed by the first Lowell agent-engineer-and-architect, Kirk Boott, was the pride of the Boston Associates, constantly offered as an example of their unprecedented philanthropy. In fact, as Thomas points out, there was nothing philanthropic about it; if an operative did not have the weekly fee at hand, it was subsequently docked from her salary. In his valedictory, the words "privations, evils, and decay" used to describe factory life are not the words of a Corporation mouthpiece, and there is no reason to assume that he encouraged suppression of criticism in his successors. Harriet Farley's editorial on the "Report of the Labor Committee of the Legislature" (which decided that any Ten Hour Law would endanger free trade) adds still another abuse to those enumerated by the petitioners: she notes that the desire of some girls to work longer hours and earn more money—frequently cited in defense of the "freedom to work"—was only dog-eat-dog competitiveness ruthlessly flogged by Corporation agents. With "Two Suicides," Farley seems to confront the fact that paternalism was dead; the words of the "lady philanthropist" are a fitting epitaph.*

Woman at the loom. Daguerreotype (late 1840s–early 1850s). The isolated setting may indicate that the photograph was taken in the machine shop of a mill. Merrimack Valley Textile Museum.

The utopian vision of "A New Society" is as remarkable for the specificity of its hopes (the eight-hour day, which did not become law until 1938) as for its articulation of that social justice for which women, and indeed all the powerless, still wait.

Plan for Mutual Relief

The expenses incident to sickness among the Lowell operatives, frequently make sad inroads on the savings of the sufferers; and in many cases, restoration to health is accompanied by the prospect of long months of toil, to liquidate debts contracted for boarding, nursing, physician's attention, and the like.

The several Corporations have jointly purchased and fitted up an elegant Hospital, in which the total expense is $4 for men, and $3 for females, weekly. The Superintendents constitute a Committee of Management; and their reputation is a sufficient guaranty that matters will be rightly conducted.

But $3 weekly for a few months would greatly diminish, if not wholly absorb the savings of many of the operatives. The expenses incident to sickness in a boarding-house are generally much larger than the Hospital charges; and in many cases, the sick prefer being taken care of in their usual abode, even at the greater cost.

The evil referred to may in part be remedied, by adopting a plan for mutual relief. The following outlines are suggested: the details may afterwards be considered.

1. The operatives shall allow a certain sum to be deducted from their wages monthly—say 12½ cts for males, and 10 cts for females—to constitute a Fund for Mutual Relief.

2. In cases of sickness, (certified by a physician, or a committee of overseers,) females shall receive $3 per week, and males $4—not as a gratuity, but as a RIGHT.

3. A joint committee of three operatives from each of the Corporations, shall constitute a Board of Control—one of whose duties shall be to see that the weekly sum above noted is regularly paid, so long as it shall be justly due.

4. The Treasurer shall be chosen by the Board of Control, and he shall give ample security for the faithful discharge of his trust.

The annual sum that would be raised on this plan, would probably be as follows:

Say 6000 females at $1 20 per annum, $7,200
    3000 males at $1 50 per annum, $4,500
                                                                                 —————

52 weeks, at $225 per week, $11,700

If 45 females and 22 males were constantly on the sick list, this sum would pay the demands stipulated in item 2d of the foregoing outline.

Several objections may be urged. First of all, Would the operatives accede to the proposed deduction from their monthly wages? We answer, A few would probably demur—but we cannot think that any considerable number would object to so small a premium for insurance against the expenses of sickness. It is a little more than three-fourths of a cent on a dollar.

In the second place, Would the Superintendents encourage the plan? Of this there cannot be a doubt. It would cost them a little trouble to make the monthly deductions aforesaid; but they would be abundantly compensated by the pleasure enjoyed in promoting the object herein recommended.—Eds.

(Abel C. Thomas, Series I, No. 2, 1840, p. 48)

Editor's Valedictory

It has been the object of the editor to encourage the cultivation of talent, and thus open and enlarge the sources of enjoyment in the midst of a toilsome life. In this way he has done something toward modifying the privations and other evils incident to employment in the Mills; and it must be acknowledged, that even if no other good be effected, something is gained by retarding the progress of decay.

We hoped ere this to have seen a spacious room, with a Library, &c., established on each Corporation, for the accommodation of the female operatives in the evenings. The example, we trust, will shortly be set by the Merrimack. And why should not bathing-rooms be fitted up in the basement of each Mill? The expense would not be felt by the Company, and the means of health and comfort thus provided, would be gratefully acknowledged. We suggest, in addition, a better ventilation of the boarding-houses. Diminution of the hours of mill-labor, and the entire abrogation of premiums to Overseers, should also be included in the list of improvements.

There is another matter, some time since presented to the operatives, and now repeated, namely, the payment of a small sum monthly, say 8 or 10 cents, to constitute a fund for the relief of the sick. The amount might be deducted by the pay-master, as agent of the Superintendent. The details of the plan could readily be agreed upon. Two cents each week would surely be well spent as insurance against the expenses of sickness, to be fixed at about three dollars weekly—to be received, not as *charity*, but as a lawful demand.

(*Abel C. Thomas, Vol. II, 1842, p. 380*)

Editorial: The Ten-Hour Movement

REPORT OF THE COMMITTEE OF THE MASSACHUSETTS LEGISLATURE UPON THE HOURS OF LABOR. We have just received a copy of this document, and will improve the short space allowed us here to make a few remarks upon it, though we should like to say a great deal.

It appears that the petitioners to the Legislature for a reduction of labor hours are but a very small proportion of the whole number of laborers; and yet we are surprised that they effected nothing. Their aim was to introduce the "Ten-Hour System." This could not have been expected in the present state of things; but might not an arrangement have been made which would have shown some respect to the petitioners, and a regard for the ease and comfort of the operatives.

It seems to have been generally conceded, that the time allotted to meals is very short—where the operatives have tolerable appetites: and this is usually the case with persons who *work so regularly* and indefatigably. Why not have compromised then with the petitioners, and allowed them one hour for dinner through the year, and three-quarters of an hour for breakfast? The dinner *hour* is given in some manufacturing places, therefore the plea with regard to competition is not unanswerable. We believe also that LOWELL is expected to take the lead in all improvements of this nature, and, should she amend her present system, it is more probable that she would be imitated than successfully contended against.

The testimony of the petitioners is full; and, with the addition of that of a few others, appears complete. But a wrong impression might be received from some of their statements. As, for instance, in the remarks of the first witness—"There is always a large number of girls at the gate, wishing to get in before the bell rings." This is frequently spoken of as evidence of a general desire to work even more hours than at present. It is not generally known how much the feeling of emulation is appealed to among the operatives. The desire to be "the smartest girl in the room," or among the smartest, and to get off so many "*sets*" or "*pieces*" often stimulates to exertions which no love of money would ever prompt. One girl goes to the mill, and waits until the gate is opened, that she may rush in first, and have her machine oiled and cleaned, and ready to start the moment the works are put in motion; not so much because she wishes for the few additional cents, which she will thus obtain, as because she is ambitious to have her name at the head of the list. The rest follow her—either in hopes of successful competition, or of ranking next in order. It is more on account of these girls that the meal hours should be prolonged, than of those who are behind them in time and "*honors*." And yet a word or two should be spoken in their behalf. They feel that they are unable to work all these hours, and "work upon the stretch," as they say. They are older, or weaker, or more heavily moulded, or unwilling, if not unable. Therefore they are not favorites with their overseer. They are not so "profitable servants," and the kind look and word, or obliging act, is not so often bestowed upon them. This is one instance where the testimony is liable to misconstruction, and had we space, we might find many more.

The LEGISLATURE seem to have doubted the propriety of their commencing action upon this subject. Where should it commence? How is it to be done? When, where, and by whom? All, connected with manufacturing establishments, feel confident that, "as surely as there is benevolence and justice in the heart of man," this wrong will be righted. But objections are brought against every movement. Of late the efforts of the dissatisfied operatives have been of a quiet nature. This petition to the Legislature is both proper and dignified. Picknicks, if *conducted with propriety*, would be unobjectionable, as demonstrations of public sentiment. Conventions, as affording opportunity for a free expression of opinion, should also be favored; notwithstanding there may be much bombast and rhodomontade, with a little injustice and demagoguism.

No effort originating among a promiscuous number of laborers, and conducted wholly by them, can be expected to be free from every imputation. So far we should be gratified that the dissatisfied and "despised" have conducted so quietly and well.   H. F.

(Harriet Farley, Vol. V, 1845, p. 96)

Editorial: Two Suicides

One more unfortunate,
     Weary of breath,
Rashly importunate,
     Gone to her death!

Take her up tenderly,
     Lift her with care;
Fashion'd so slenderly,
     Young and so fair!

Touch her not scornfully;
Think of her mournfully,
Gently and humanly;

. . . . . .

Perishing gloomily,
Spurned by contumely,
Cold inhumanity,
Burning insanity,
     Into her rest.

Hood's Magazine.

Within a few weeks the papers of the day have announced the deaths of two young female operatives, by their own hands—one in Lowell, the other in an adjacent manufacturing town. With the simple announcement these papers have left the affair to their readers—appending to one, however, the remark that the unfortunate had neither friends nor home; to the other the assertion, that reports injurious to her fair fame had been circulated—reports which, after her death, were ascertained to be false. And how have the community received this intelligence? Apparently with much indifference; but where we hear an expression of opinion it is one of horror. The human being who has dared, herself, to wrench away the barrier which separated her from the Giver of her life, and who will judge her for this rash act, is spoken of as a reckless contemner of His laws, both natural and revealed. People are shocked that any human being should dare imbrue her hands in blood, and rush, all stained and gory, before her God. But He, who placed us here, and commanded that we should stay until he willed to call us hence, has enforced His law by one written on our own hearts—a horror of death inwrought into our nature, so that we violate our own sensibilities by disobeying His will; unless, indeed, our feelings have become so distorted and perverted that they are untrue to their original action. So possible is a discord in this "harp of thousand strings," and so improbable is a violation of its harmony while perfectly attuned, that many have supposed this last discordant note, which rings from the ruined lyre, a proof that its perfect unison had been previously destroyed, though unobserved by all around.

We may easily conceive of the feelings of those who give away their lives in some noble cause—we can imagine how the higher feelings of the soul bear it away from all subordinate doubts and fears, and the greatest boon we can ever give is laid upon the altar, a holy sacrifice. We can in some degree enter into the feelings of the martyrs of old, and can perhaps imperfectly apprehend the philosophy of a Cato or a Cleopatra; but when one, in the very prime of womanhood, with no philosophy to support her, and no great misfortune to impel her to the deed, yields up her life, we feel that the soul itself must have become distorted and diseased.

When we reflect upon the shudder which the thought of death occasions in our season of health and prosperity—when we find that it requires all our strength of soul to look upon it, and prepare our minds for its always possible approach—when, in a healthy and natural state of feeling, it needs all the consolation and hopes of religion to reconcile us to this last event, then we may think how heavy has been the weight which has pressed upon some poor spirit till, crushed and mutilated, it has writhed from beneath its influence, into the dark abyss of despair. How heavily must life weigh upon her who flees to death for refuge!—who waits not for the grim tyrant, but rushes impetuously into his loathsome embrace! There must have been a fearful change in the nature of her, whose natural reluctance to pain is so wholly overcome that no bodily agony is dreaded if but the prison bars of this clay tenement be loosened—and, when the innate delicacy of her nature is so far forgotten that the body, itself, is yielded up to the cold eye, and unshrinking hand, of the dissector—for this must always follow. Let us contemplate all this, and feel assured that, though reason may have been left, though it may even have been actively manifest in the preparations for this dreadful *finale,* that something was gone even more essential to vitality than reason itself—that "the life of life was o'er"—that the something, which gives zest to being, was taken away—that the *vitativeness* of the phrenologist no longer acted and harmonized with the other faculties of the brain.

In the first instance, were the causes mental or physical which led to the deed? We believe in this, and indeed in all cases, that both operated upon the individual. There was action and reaction, and it is impossible that the mind should be so deeply affected without injury to the body: as, on the contrary, oppression of any part of the physical system must depress and weaken the mind. We will not make a long sermon, for we have a short text. "She had no parents or home." She was alone in the world—she had no kindred to support and cheer her in life's toilsome journey, and no place of refuge to which she might retreat, when weary and faint with the tedious pilgrimage. She was alone; and none came forward to cheer her with their companionship—she had no home, and saw no prospect of one. Life, before her, was a dreary waste, and her path more rugged than any other. It was uncheered. There was not the voice of sympathy to sustain her, nor the necessity of acting for others to arouse her energies. When her spirits drooped there were none to revive them—then they sank still lower, and there was nothing to sustain them. Mere acquaintance seldom strive to remove the dark cloud which may rest upon another's brow. Perhaps they think it habitual, and that nothing may remove it—perhaps that, if it is not so, they have not the power to drive it away. They are so distrustful that they strive not to lighten that which they might possibly remove. Perhaps their own hearts are saddened, and they flee rather to the gay hearted, that they may be infected by their joyousness. They shrink from the sad one lest sympathy should reveal that which in their own hearts had better be concealed.

Mere acquaintance strove not to comfort her, and "she had no parents or home." O, how soothingly might a mother's voice have fallen upon her ear!—her words, like healing balm, might have sunk into her heart, and her kind glance have been the charm to drive away the demon. But, *she had no home*. She rose at early dawn, and toiled till night. Day after day brought the same wearisome round of duties; and, as she looked forward, she saw no prospect of a brighter future. It would take long years to procure an independence by her slight savings, and mayhap, with her sinking energies, she hardly gained a maintenance. Her spirits were gone, but life remained; and vitality seemed fixed upon her as a curse. The physical laws of her nature had not been violated, and nature still resisted the spirit's call for death. Perhaps it was frenzy, perhaps despondency, but—the rest is a short item in the common newspaper.

The other had friends and home—at least, we learn nothing to the contrary. She probably had a father, mother, sister, or brother.

> "And there was a nearer one
> Still, and a dearer one
> Yet, than all other."

She, too, had toiled daily and hourly, but not hopelessly. There was one near whose smile was her joy, and whose voice was her strength. She had turned from all others to devote herself more entirely to him. All other affections were absorbed in this. She was affianced to him, and, in anticipation of the time when they twain should become one, her soul had made his its stay. But, when Calumny had sent its blasting simoon over this fair prospect, how changed the scene! That which was so bright is, O how dark! How susceptible must have been that heart which the consciousness of innocence could not sustain! How keen must have been those sufferings which could only find relief in the sleep of the grave?

And here may it not be well to add one word against the sin of detraction?—of rashly and wantonly speaking ill where there is no proof of error—of lightly repeating the gossip of the day, which may or may not be true—of carelessly passing opinions upon those of whom no close acquaintance justifies us in passing this judgment. People may talk of *village* gossip; but in no place is an evil report more quickly circulated, and apparently believed, than in a factory. One fiendish-minded girl can start a calumny which will soon ruin the good name of another, unless she be unusually fortunate in friends, or circumstances are peculiarly favorable; or her whole past life has been as remarkable for the wisdom of the serpent as the harmlessness of the dove. But enough!—this evil is already curing itelf, and "it is only a factory story" is considered as an intimation to inquire further.

But we return from our digression to the theme which suggested it. Morbid dejection, and wounded sensibility, have, in these instances, produced that insanity which prompted suicide. Is it not an appropriate question to ask here whether, or not, there was any thing in their mode of life which tended to this dreadful result?

We have been accused of representing unfairly the relative advantages and disadvantages of factory life. We are thought to give the former too great prominence, and the latter too little, in the pictures we have drawn. Are we guilty?

We should be willing to resign our own individual contributions to the harshest critic, and say to him, *Judge ye!* And, with regard to the articles of our contributors, we have never published any thing which our own experience had convinced us was unfair. But, if in our sketches, there is too much light, and too little shade, let our excuse be found in the circumstances which have brought us before the public. We have not thought it necessary to state, or rather to constantly reiterate that our life was a toilsome one—for we supposed that would be universally understood, after we had stated how many hours in a day we tended our machines. We have not thought a constant repetition of the fact necessary, that our life was one of confinement; when it was known that we work in one spot of one room. We have not thought it necessary to enlarge upon the fact that there was ignorance and folly among a large population of young females, away from their homes, and indiscriminately collected from all quarters. These facts have always been so generally understood that the worth, happiness and intelligence, which really exists, have been undervalued. But, are the operatives here as happy as females in the prime of life, in the constant intercourse of society, in the enjoyment of all necessaries, and many comforts—with money at their own command; and the means of gratifying their peculiar tastes in dress, &c.—are they as happy as they would be, with all this, in some other situations? We sometimes fear they are not.

And was there any thing, we ask again, in the situation of these young women which influenced them to this melancholy act? In factory labor it is sometimes an advantage, but also sometimes the contrary, that the mind is thrown back upon itself—it is forced to depend upon its own resources, for a large proportion of the time of the operative. Excepting by sight, the females hold but little companionship with each other. This is why the young girls rush so furiously together when they are set at liberty. This is why the sedate young woman, who loves contemplation, and enjoys her own thoughts better than any other society, prefers this to any other employment. But, when a young woman is naturally of a morbid tone of mind, or when afflictions have created such a state, that employment which forces the thoughts back upon an unceasing reminiscence of its own misery, is not the right one. This is not the life suited to a misanthrope, or an unfortunate, although they, in their dejection, might think otherwise. However much of a materialist, and little of a sentimentalist, we may appear, we still believe that fresh bracing air, frequent bathings, and carefully prepared food, may do much in reconciling us to the sorrows and disappointments of life. The beneficial influence of social intercourse, and varied employment, has never been questioned.

Last summer a young woman of this city, who was weary of her monotonous life, but saw no hope of redemption, opened her heart to a benevolent lady, who was visiting us upon a philanthropic mission. "And now," said she, as she concluded her tale of grievances, "what shall I do?" She could do nothing but dig, and was ashamed to beg. The lady was appalled by a misery for which there was no relief. There was no need of pecuniary aid, or she might have appealed to the benevolent. She could give her kind and soothing words, but these would have no permanent power to reconcile her to her lot. "I can tell you of nothing," she replied, "but *to throw yourself into the canal.*"

There is something better than this—and we are glad that so noble a spirit is manifested by our operatives, for there *is* something noble in their general cheerfulness and contentment. "They also serve who only stand and wait." They serve, even more acceptably, who labor patiently and wait.   H.F.

(*Harriet Farley, Vol. IV, 1844, pp. 212–215*)

A New Society

"Dreams are but interludes which fancy makes;
When monarch reason sleeps, this mimic wakes:

Compounds a medley of disjointed things,
A court of cobblers, and a mob of kings.
Light fumes are merry, grosser fumes are sad;
Both are the reasonable soul run mad:—
And many forms and things in sleep we see,
That neither were, nor are—but haply yet may be."

It was Saturday night. The toils of the week were at an end; and, seated at the table with my book, I was feasting upon the treasures of knowledge which it contained. One by one my companions had left me, until I was alone. How long I continued to read I know not; but I had closed my book, and sat ruminating upon the many changes and events which are continually taking place in this transitory world of ours. My reverie was disturbed by the opening of the door, and a little boy entered the room, who, handing me a paper, retired without speaking. I unfolded the paper, and the first article which caught my eye was headed, "Annual Meeting of the Society for the promotion of Industry, Virtue and Knowledge." It read as follows: "At the annual meeting of this society, the following resolutions were unanimously adopted:

"1. *Resolved*, That every father of a family who neglects to give his daughters the same advantages for an education which he gives his sons, shall be expelled from this society, and be considered a heathen."

"2. *Resolved*, That no member of this society shall exact more than eight hours of labour, out of every twenty-four, of any person in his or her employment."

"3. *Resolved*, That, as the laborer is worthy of his hire, the price for labor shall be sufficient to enable the working-people to pay a proper attention to scientific and literary pursuits."

"4. *Resolved*, That the wages of females shall be equal to the wages of males, that they may be enabled to maintain proper independence of character, and virtuous deportment."

"5. *Resolved*, That no young gentleman of this society shall be allowed to be of age, or to transact business for himself, until he shall have a good knowledge of the English language, understand bookkeeping, both by single and double entry, and be capable of transacting all town business."

"6. *Resolved*, That no young lady belonging to this society shall be considered marriageable, who does not understand how to manage the affairs of the kitchen, and who does not, each month, write at least enough to fill one page of imperial octavo."

"7. *Resolved.* That we will not patronize the writings of any person who does not spend at least three hours in each day, when health will permit, either in manual labor, or in some employment which will be a public benefit, and which shall not appertain to literary pursuits."

"8. *Resolved,* That each member of this society shall spend three hours in each day in the cultivation of the mental faculties, or forfeit membership, extraordinaries excepted."

"9. *Resolved,* That industry, virtue and knowledge, (not wealth and titles,) shall be the standard of respectability for this society."

I stopped at the ninth resolution, to ponder upon what I had read; and I thought it was remarkably strange that I had not before heard of this society. There was a gentle tap at the door and a gentleman entered the room, with a modest request for subscribers to a new periodical which was about to be issued from the press. I showed him what I had been reading. He glanced his eyes upon it, and exclaimed, "Oh happy America! Thrice happy land of Freedom! Thy example shall yet free all nations from the galling chains of mental bondage; and teach to earth's remotest ends, in what true happiness consists!"

By reading the remainder of the article, I learned that the society, and its auxiliaries, already numbered more than two thirds of the population of the United States, and was rapidly increasing; but the date puzzled me extremely; it was April 1, 1860.

The agent for the new periodical reminded me of his business; I ran up stairs to ascertain if any of our girls would become subscribers; but before reaching the chambers, I stumbled, and awoke.

Tabitha

(Betsey Chamberlain, Vol. I, 1841, pp. 191–192)

Afterword

Although there were only approximately seventy *Offering* contributors—a tiny proportion of the mill women—the interest, both generating and sustaining, in such activity was obviously far greater.

Offering writers were responsible for twenty-eight published volumes. Lucy Larcom logged in with eight books; Harriet Hanson Robinson and Eliza J. Cate, the next most prolific, with five published works each.

The beleaguered editor, Harriet Farley, remained in Lowell to try again. When her adversary, the *Voice of Industry*, folded in 1847, Farley was encouraged to return with *The New England Offering* in 1848. It was not a success, dying two years later, unmourned by labor or capital. Farley married an inventor in 1854 and moved to New York, where she wrote and lectured energetically until her death in 1907. Her coeditor, Harriott Curtis (who had, in fact, resigned from the *Offering* a year before its end), worked for a short time on the *Vox Populi*, a Lowell newspaper of moderately liberal hue. She spent the remainder of her long life in a vocation all too typical of New England spinsters: the care of convalescent or dying relatives.

Martha or Margaret Foley ("M.F.F.") left mill work and the Saturday afternoon art classes she taught in Lowell to become a cameo cutter and sculptor in Boston. Among her sitters were

Longfellow, Charles Sumner, and Julia Ward Howe. Like the other women sculptors of Henry James's "white marmorean flock," Foley spent the last years of her life in Rome. Her marble *Fountain*, a group of female figures, was purchased for the Hall of Agriculture at the Philadelphia Centennial Exhibition in 1876.

Eliza Jane Cate wrote five books after she left the mills, beginning with *The Rights and Duties of Mill Girls*, first serialized in *The New England Offering*.

Lydia S. Hall, who, for the *Guinness Book of World Records*, may be said to have beaten out Farley, Curtis, and Mrs. Green of Fall River to be the first—if most briefly tenured—editor of a factory girls' magazine, had the most checkered career. Leaving Lowell in 1848, she was variously missionary to the Choctaw Indians, keeper of a Temperance Inn in Kansas, and clerk in the U.S. Treasury Department, where, it is reported, she served "briefly" as Acting Secretary, the most prestigious—and short-lived—of her jobs.

Sarah Shedd had worked in the mills to help educate a brother for the ministry. This accomplished, she returned to Washington, New Hampshire, to teach school. She left her life savings of $2,500 to establish the Shedd Free Library in her native town. Carroll D. Wright, the first U.S. Commissioner of Labor, who was her pupil, later attributed his interest in labor to the example of his teacher as mill worker. Lura Currier joined Shedd as library benefactor, establishing the first free public library in Haverhill, New Hampshire.

Lucy Larcom left Lowell in 1847 to teach school in Illinois and later returned east to teach at Wheaton Female Seminary. Finding it impossible to support herself by writing, she served as editor of the journal *Our Young Folks* and the publication with which it merged, the well-known *St. Nicholas* magazine.

Harriet Hanson Robinson married a journalist-biographer, had four children, and wrote *Loom and Spindle*, the best book of reminiscences about the early days of the mills. Most of what we know of the other *Offering* writers stems from Robinson's

Two women weavers, probably New England. Tintype, ca. 1865–1870. Merrimack Valley Textile Museum.

unofficial role as "alumnae Secretary." She was an officer of the National Women's Suffrage Association and a founder of the General Federation of Women's Clubs. Nor was her example lost on her daughter Harriette Shattuck, who became the second woman admitted to the bar in New England.

Clementine Averill pioneered in two senses: settling in the then Florida wilderness, near Tampa, she struggled to start a cooperative industrial home for retired workers—a solution for housing the elderly still described as "innovative."

Sarah Bagley wrote for the *Voice of Industry* in 1845–46 and served variously as editor of the Female Department, interim editor-in-chief, and finally, roving correspondent reporting on New England prisons and insane asylums, while also managing to organize branches of the Female Labor Reform Association in other mill towns. A delegate to the New England Workingmen's Association and to the first National Industrial Congress, held in Boston in 1846, Bagley in the same year became the first woman telegraph operator and superintendent of the new Boston-Lowell telegraph service. By the end of 1846 Sarah Bagley had disappeared from masthead and boards of all her organizations. The total silence surrounding the end of this extraordinary woman is all the more bizarre given the propensity of labor to eulogize its leaders.

The information we possess about some *Offering* writers, as against the unknown destinies of hundreds of thousands of mill women, does not provide the kind of random sample demanded by sociologists to justify any hypotheses. It seems safe to assume, however, that many mill girls—like many non-mill girls—"disappeared" into domesticity. The disappearance of the former, however, had another dimension. As several *Offering* stories illustrate, "upward mobility" in marriage often buried a past in the mills. It is equally impossible to know how many former mill women followed Harriet Hanson Robinson and Elizabeth Emerson Turner into the Woman's Rights Movement, or how many went into teaching, library professions, journalism, or small business ventures. But if social scientists will allow us to speculate, it is worth pondering the influence and example provided over a period of twenty-five years by the 20,000 estimated annual "graduates" of the mills: women who had left home as frightened farm girls and who became wage earners, "dependent on no one."

After the plaudits of contemporaries had died down, the *Lowell Offering* seemed of no historical interest; not even the publication and success of memoirs by Lucy Larcom and Harriet Robinson at the turn of the century occasioned renewed interest in the mill girls or their writings. Perhaps the most important factor explaining this neglect was the peculiarly American desire to ignore the unpleasant. Lowell and the other textile centers of Lawrence, Methuen, Fall River, and Chicopee had become grim slums of deteriorating mills and tenements. Greek, French-Canadian, and Polish workers had followed the Irish in providing ever-cheaper labor to maintain dividends for ever more remote stockholders. Beginning in the 1850s with Irish dominance of the mill population, the ratio of women to men dropped steadily; with this change, the Corporation boardinghouse disappeared. In Lowell, workers and their families were herded into ethnic ghettoes, whose statistics of infant mortality, tuberculosis, and smallpox were not the stuff of local boosterism. To compare twentieth-century Lowell with its beginnings a century earlier was, as one historian mourned, "to sit down beside the waters of the Merrimack and weep." And to avoid weeping, most historians chose to ignore the disparity between the industrial dream and the present reality—until the 1930s. Before that period, the disparaging term "muckrakers" had been used for those historians and journalists who persisted in exposing the ugly realities of "industrial democracy." Then, in the thirties, the Depression dealt the precarious health of New England mills a mortal blow. One by one they closed, throwing millions out of work; some shut up shop forever while others moved south to a corporate utopia of cheap land and cheaper nonunion labor. But the thirties also produced social scientists who identified with the cause of labor.

A new generation of historians discovered the *Offering* but, in keeping with the prevailing political measure of the times, gave it low marks in class consciousness. Displaying a notable lack of curiosity about the mill girls' background—religious, social, and geographical—one writer could lament, "We of today, who like realism and rebellion, regret the lack of proletarian quality in the contributions." Why, in other words, couldn't the *Offering* writers sound more like Rosa Luxemburg or Emma Goldman? Still more implacable, Dr. Bertha Monica Stearns dismissed the magazine with epithets like "pathetic" and "naïve." Not even the militant Sarah Bagley escaped her disapproval: during Bagley's editorial stint, the *Voice of Industry* had become "soft" on the Ten Hour Movement. Bagley's influence had "feminized" it, producing too many articles reflecting only "the social and personal concerns of women." Hannah Josephson's *The Golden Threads: New England's Mill Girls and Magnates* (1949) was the first full-length study of both protagonists in the early drama of industrialization. Compassionate as well as fair-minded, *The Golden Threads* rescued the mill girls from revisionism. A specialist in French literature and New Deal politics, Mrs. Josephson, who died in 1976, brought wide erudition and stylistic elegance to her work on Lowell.

Feminist studies have provided the impulse for much resurgent interest in the women of Lowell. But, whatever the focus, most recent work on this subject is happily characterized by diversity of method and approach, combined with an encouraging freedom from ideological bias. Perhaps historians themselves are the best example of progress.

*   *   *   *

There are mills still standing throughout the Merrimack Valley. In Lowell, only the Boott Mill, built in 1835, survived urban renewal in the 1950s; but in Lawrence, Methuen, and

Manchester long red-brick buildings with blind broken windows still line the banks of the rapidly flowing river. Everywhere in the region, memories have outlasted the mills. For, in defiance of statistics on America's mobility, the children and grandchildren of later mill workers are still there. Some are now the official keepers of a collective memory; the conservators, librarians, and archivists of Lowell and Manchester have Irish, Polish, Greek, and French-Canadian surnames. But there are other historians, too.

"There's nothing I don't know about Lowell. I grew up there, and my grandmother worked in the mills," says Frank Jarek, who drives a limousine that goes from Manchester to Boston's Logan Airport. He remembers his Polish immigrant grandmother's stories about the mills for a particular reason: "They were horror stories . . . she worked fourteen hours a day for fourteen cents an hour for six years. . . . But my grandfather and some friends of his saved their money," he said proudly, "so when he married my grandmother, she didn't have to work in the mills anymore."

She didn't have to work in the mills anymore—a badge of pride, still. And with good reason. The recollections of a grandmother in the mills, of a mother working in a factory when times were bad—neither memory nor experience encourages the association of work with opportunity.

The end of the Lowell dream was the beginning of the scarring divisions that separate us still: work and class: hands and head, blue collar and white, ethnics and minorities. Its end ushered in other conflicts in the experience and perceptions of women: work as possibility or prison, a right worth fighting for, or a condition demanding rescue.

The *Lowell Offering* is our most valuable record of a moment caught between reality and myth, seized by the women who lived it. The fierce aspirations of their valedictory shame our failed promises.

Notes

p. 13 "he supervised the 're-invention' ": Nathan Appleton, *Introduction of the Power Loom and Origin of Lowell*, pp. 15–16.

p. 16 " 'a fund of labor' " Ibid., p. 16.

p. 16 Mill girls' wages compared with teachers' salaries: Elfrieda B. McCauley, "The New England Mill Girls: Feminine Influence in the Development of Public Libraries in New England, 1820–1860," p. 30.

p. 16 Women as wage earners: Ibid., pp. 9ff.

p. 17 " 'Daughters are now . . . a blessing' ": Patrick Tracy Jackson, *Report on the Production and Manufacture of Cotton* (Boston, 1832). Quoted by McCauley, op. cit., p. 9.

p. 17 "One would swear": Charles Dickens, *American Notes*, p. 76.

p. 18 "I am living on no one": Ann Swett Appleton, "Sister Ann" Letters, January 8, 1847, quoted by permission of the Manchester (New Hampshire) Historic Association.

p. 22 "the first planned industrial community": John Coolidge, *Mill and Mansion*.

p. 24 "a day without meat": Anthony Trollope, *North America*, p. 248.

p. 24 "for dinner, meat and potatoes": Letter of Clementine Averill, a Lowell mill girl, to Senator Clemens, quoted by Harriet H. Robinson in *Loom and Spindle*, p. 193.

p. 26 "sleep six or eight in a room": Harriet Martineau, *Society in America*, p. 357.

p. 26 "Quite a lady": Ann Appleton, "Sister Ann" Letters, ibid.

p. 26 "the behavior of her own child": Robinson, op. cit., p. 85.

p. 26 "closely knit community of female workers": Thomas L. Dublin, "Women, Work and Protest in the Early Lowell Mills: 'The Oppressing Hand of Avarice Would Enslave Us,' " *Labor History* 16, 1975, No. 1, p. 107.

p. 28 "air was polluted": Caroline F. Ware, *The Early New England Cotton Manufacture*, p. 252.

p. 28 "Some come with the seeds of disease": Henry A. Miles, *Lowell As It Was and As It Is*, pp. 124–25.

p. 29 "Sabbath School libraries": McCauley, op. cit., p. 116.

p. 31 "Lowell's circulating libraries": Ibid., p. 136.

p. 31 "drew them and kept them there": Robinson, op. cit., p. 91.

p. 31 "the express purpose of getting books": Ibid., p. 43.

p. 32 "pasting up pages from books": Lucy Larcom, "Among Mill Girls: A Reminiscence," *Atlantic Monthly*, Vol. XLVIII, No. 289, November, 1881, p. 602.

p. 32 "No one objects": Lucy Larcom, *An Idyll of Work*, p. 129.

p. 32 "make better use of 'precious privileges' ": Elizabeth Woolson, "Correspondence, 1827–1856." Letters to Eliza Woolson, then working in the Lowell mills, from her family and friends.

p. 32 "the Lowell Lyceum": Quoted in Robinson, op. cit., p. 74.

p. 33 "the Brook Farm Community": Larcom, "Among Mill Girls," p. 607.

p. 33 "the first women's literary clubs": Allan MacDonald, "Lowell: A Commercial Utopia," *New England Quarterly*, Vol. 10, 1937, p. 48.

p. 34 "the new Offering": The only comparable factory magazine was the Fall River *Wampanoag and Operatives' Journal*, edited by former mill girl Frances Whipple Green. Its brief life was ended by the Fall River fire of 1842.

p. 34 "the girls should edit the magazine": *Lowell Offering*, Vol. II, p. 47.

p. 35 "comparison of . . . the mill girls [with] nuns": Michel Chevalier, *Society, Manners and Politics in the United States*, p. 113.

p. 36 "Low expectations of labor": John Greenleaf Whittier, *Prose Works*, II, p. 380.

p. 38 "signatures from the Lowell mills": Thomas L. Dublin, op. cit., p. 113.

p. 38 "corporation subsidy": *Voice of Industry*, August 14, 1845.

p. 39 "the fatal error of neutrality": Ibid., January 2, 1846.

p. 40 "scant allusion to fine clothes": Dickens, op. cit., p. 80.

p. 43 "city way of speaking": Robinson, op. cit., pp. 65ff.

p. 43 "The new arrival would be 'sponsored' ": Dublin, op. cit., p. 101.

p. 44 "very little interaction with men": Ibid., p. 106.

p. 214 "Sarah Bagley had disappeared": A forthcoming biography of Sarah Bagley by Helena Wright promises to dispel some of the mystery.

p. 215 "To compare twentieth-century Lowell": MacDonald, op. cit., p. 37.

p. 216 "the lack of proletarian quality": Ibid., p. 51.

p. 216 " 'pathetic' and 'naïve' ": Bertha Monica Stearns, "Early Factory Magazines in New England," *Journal of Economic and Business History*, Vol. 2, No. 4, August, 1930, p. 699.

Selected Bibliography

Abbott, Edith. *Women in Industry: A Study in American Economic History*. New York: D. Appleton and Co., 1913.

Appleton, Ann Swett. "Sister Ann" Letters, 1847–1850. Edited by her grandniece, Priscilla Ordway, 1953. Typescript. Manchester Historic Association.

Appleton, Nathan. *Introduction of the Power Loom and Origin of Lowell*. Lowell: B. H. Penhallow, 1858.

Bartlett, Elisha. *A Vindication of the Character and Condition of the Females Employed in the Lowell Mills against the Charges Contained in the Boston Quarterly Review*. Lowell: Powers and Bagley, 1841.

Baxandall, Rosalyn; Gordon, Linda; and Reverby, Susan. *America's Working Women*. New York: Random House and Vintage Books, 1976.

Beecher, Catherine E. *The Evils Suffered by American Women and Children: the Causes and the Remedy. Also: An Address to the Protestant Clergy of the United States*. New York: Harper and Brothers, 1846.

Chevalier, Michel. *Society, Manners and Politics in the United States: Being a Series of Letters on North America*. Translated from the 3rd Paris edition. Boston: Weeks, Jordan and Company, 1839.

Coolidge, John. *Mill and Mansion*. New York: Columbia University Press, 1942.

Cowley, Charles. *A Handbook of Business in Lowell with a History of the City*. Lowell: E. D. Green, 1856.

Dickens, Charles. *American Notes for General Circulation*. Boston: Ticknor and Fields, 1867.

Dublin, Thomas L. "Women at Work: The Transformation of Work and Community in Lowell, Massachusetts. 1826–1860." Ph.D. dissertation, Columbia University, 1975.

———. "Women, Work and Protest in the Early Lowell Mills," *Labor History* 16 (1975), No. 1.

Horwitz, Richard P. "Architecture and Culture: the Meaning of the Lowell Boardinghouse." *American Quarterly* XXV, No. 1, March 1973.

Josephson, Hannah. *The Golden Threads: New England's Mill Girls and Magnates* New York: Duell, Sloan and Pearce, 1949.

Kenngott, George F. *The Record of a City: a Social Survey of Lowell.* New York: The Macmillan Company, 1912.

Larcom, Lucy. *An Idyll of Work.* Boston: James R. Osgood and Company, 1875.

———. "Among Mill Girls: a Reminiscence," *Atlantic Monthly,* Vol. XLVIII, No. 289, November 1881.

———. *A New England Girlhood.* Boston: Houghton Mifflin and Company, 1889.

Macdonald, Allan. "Lowell: A Commercial Utopia." *New England Quarterly.* Norwood: Vol. 10, 1937.

McCauley, Elfrieda B. *The New England Mill Girls: Feminine Influence in the Development of Public Libraries in New England 1820–1860.* Unpublished dissertation, Columbia University, 1971.

Martineau, Harriet. *Society in America.* New York: Saunders and Otley, 1837.

Miles, Henry A. *Lowell As It Was and As It Is.* Lowell: Powers and Bagley, 1845.

Mind Among the Spindles: A Selection from the Lowell Offering. London: Charles Knight, 1844.

Robinson, Harriet H. *Loom and Spindle: Or Life Among the Early Mill Girls.* New York: Thomas Y. Crowell, 1898.

Scoresby, William. *American Factories and their Female Operatives.* London: Longman, Brown, Green and Longman, 1845.

Stearns, Bertha Monica. "Early Factory Magazines in New England." *Journal of Economic and Business History,* Vol. II, No. 4, August 1930.

Stern, Madeleine B. *We, the Women: Career Firsts of Nineteenth Century America.* New York: Schulte Publishing Company, 1963.